# Environmentalism of the Rich

# Environmentalism of the Rich

Peter Dauvergne

The MIT Press
Cambridge, Massachusetts
London, England

This book was set in Stone Serif and Stone Sans by Toppan Best-set Premedia Limited. Printed and bound in the United States of America.

Library of Congress Cataloging-in-Publication Data

Names: Dauvergne, Peter, author.
Title: Environmentalism of the rich / Peter Dauvergne.
Description: Cambridge, MA : The MIT Press, 2016. | Includes bibliographical references and index.
Identifiers: LCCN 2016010268 | ISBN 9780262034951 (hardcover : alk. paper)
Subjects: LCSH: Environmentalism–Economic aspects. | Environmental degradation–Economic aspects. | Consumption (Economics)–Environmental aspects.
Classification: LCC HC79.E5 D3463 2016 | DDC 333.72–dc23 LC record available at https://lccn.loc.gov/2016010268

10 9 8 7 6 5 4 3 2 1

In memory of Pablo (1599–1607),
with remorse
for kidnapping
and christening you Pablo

# Contents

# Acknowledgments

Looking back I can now see this book began to take form in the summer of 1972. That was when my family moved from Montreal to Hackett's Cove, a fishing village on the South Shore of Nova Scotia, Canada. It was an enchanting place for a boy of seven. In front of my house, crabs scurried over a rocky shore of periwinkles and mussels; in the marsh behind, frogs croaked like an orchestra. Some of my fondest memories of this time are of deep-sea fishing with my father and Kenny Green, a local fisherman.

Decades have drifted by since I was last in Hackett's Cove, or the neighboring village of Indian Harbour where my family would later move. Cod was the backbone of these village economies. I remember the marine biologists and conservationists who would wander through to decry overfishing. Even more vividly I recall how angry locals were that foreign trawlers were raking the sea of life. Yet few foresaw how swiftly Atlantic cod stocks would collapse in the early 1990s, or how severely the closure of the cod fishery would wound these communities.

My time in Nova Scotia left me with a deep respect for nature as well as admiration for people who live off the land and sea: to this day foundations of my understanding of environmentalism. My childhood also left me with a nagging anxiety about the ability of adults to control the world around us. Why, I have never stopped wondering, did those in charge not avert this tragedy? How did they not hear the cries of alarm of so many? How could reasonable people consume away 99 percent of a species once so plentiful?

To this day the adults in charge are still failing to prevent the world around us from descending into an ever-greater environmental crisis. The collapse of Atlantic cod stocks is just one sign. More than three-quarters of the world's commercial fish species are now in or near biological crisis. And we're equally failing to rein in agricultural pollution, biodiversity loss, chemical contamination, climate change, deforestation, desertification, freshwater loss, ocean acidification, plastic waste, and transboundary pollutants.

I no longer recall when I became an environmentalist worrying about such things. Perhaps it was on one of those glorious days out on the Atlantic Ocean with my father. Perhaps it was even the day we nearly capsized as we failed to haul aboard a 2,000-pound ocean sunfish, giving up after our harpoon rope snapped, watching the sunfish sink slowly out of sight, the harpoon jutting up like a flagpole. Since as long as I can remember I've been trying to make sense of what those in charge, now somehow including me, are doing—and not doing—to live in greater harmony with nature. My conclusions in this particular book are tough minded, pointing to serious failings and worrying trends in how we're doing as a species, and highlighting my concern that the interests of those with wealth and privilege are increasingly coming to dominate the demands of environmentalism. Still, I want to be clear that I remain proud to be an environmentalist and continue to see environmentalism as a whole as a progressive philosophy and an important social movement. I'm not throwing environmentalists overboard, but I am wanting to see us make more of a difference.

Over the past few years many colleagues and friends have helped to inform my understanding of the power of environmentalism. In particular I owe my coauthors who have taught me so much over the past few years: Justin Alger, Jen Iris Allan, Jennifer Clapp, Sara D. Elder, Déborah Barros Leal Farias, Jonathan Gamu, Genevieve LeBaron, Jane Lister, Miriam Matejova, Kate J. Neville, and Charles Roger. My books with Lister (*Eco-Business*, MIT Press, 2013) and LeBaron (*Protest Inc.*, Polity, 2014) especially influence my analysis in *Environmentalism of the Rich*, although brainstorming our many journal articles together has been formative, too. I'm grateful as well to my recent graduate students whom I did not have the chance to publish with, especially Priya Bala-Miller, Paula Barrios, Shane Barter, Alice Cohen, Samuel Couture-Brière, François de Soete, William Gochberg, Rama Kiosh Iselin, Meidad Kissinger, Suzi Malan, Frédéric Le Manach, Rumana Monzur, David Seekings, and Edward Thomas. I have also benefited greatly from enduring conversations with my former students Michael Bloomfield, Susan Park, and Hamish van der Ven.

Fieldwork in Southeast Asia (especially the Philippines, Indonesia, and Malaysia) and the South Pacific (especially the Solomon Islands and

Vanuatu) informs this book. So does my time researching and living in Japan (two-and-a-half years) and Australia (seven years). More recently I have been very fortunate to advise—and learn from—a talented team of doctoral and postdoctoral researchers conducting fieldwork far and wide, including on biofuels in Kenya and Tanzania (Neville); wildlife conservation in South Africa, Botswana, Zimbabwe, and Mozambique (Malan); fishing in the Western Indian Ocean (Le Manach); corporate social responsibility in China (Lister and LeBaron); mining in Peru (Gamu); small-scale farming in Nicaragua (Elder); biofuels in Brazil (Farias); forestry in Sweden, Canada, and the United States (Lister); ocean conservation in Palau and Australia (Alger); and civil society groups in climate change negotiations (Allan).

Grants from the Social Sciences and Humanities Research Council of Canada (Global Environmental Politics of Eco-Consumerism, SSHRC reference number 410–2009–1741, and Corporations and the Politics of Environmental Activism in the Global South, reference number 435–2014–00115) provided essential support for me and my research team. I'm further indebted to Beth Clevenger and Miranda Martin at the MIT Press whose astute guidance improved this book immeasurably. I also want to extend a special thank-you to the five anonymous reviewers for this book. It's a genuine privilege to receive such spirited and discerning feedback from so many knowledgeable scholars.

My greatest debt is to my wife, Catherine, and my children Duncan, Nina, and Hugh for supporting my love of writing books. Hugh deserves special mention here for his boundless enthusiasm for the research tales in *Environmentalism of the Rich*.

# 1  Introduction: Is Environmentalism Failing?

More baboons than people may have roamed the earth ten thousand years ago. Back then average life expectancy of the world's roughly 5 million people may have been as low as 10 years. By 1500 CE the human population had climbed to 400–500 million. Since then has been a time of rollicking change for the earth, as the number of people has gone from 1 billion in 1800 to 3 billion in 1960 to more than 7.4 billion today. By the middle of this century 10 billion people could well live on earth. Finding a way to live together without destroying the earth is the most pressing challenge to ever face humanity. Our current way of life is already causing ecological turmoil, with social inequality deepening and the world economy displaying signs of severe instability. Immediate action is clearly imperative for any chance of a sustainable future.

Sweeping changes will be necessary. Simply asking 10 billion people to consume more responsibly will not be enough. Nor will tinkering with government policies and corporate strategic plans. Political leaders will need to act decisively. Societies will need to reorganize; economies will need fundamental overhauls. The sources of our escalating sustainability crisis run deep through the seams of the world order. Centuries of imperialism and colonialism have left festering societal wounds. In much of the world, extreme exploitation, violence, and inequity continue as states and corporations pursue growth and profits. Meanwhile, the globalization of capitalism is bringing particularly grave risks and harms to communities and environments with less power in world politics, such as indigenous peoples, refugees, and tropical ecosystems.

The past half-century has seen environmentalism emerge as a worldwide counterforce to this destruction. No one would question this statement. Yet is the environmental movement actually taking us toward global sustainability? For some the answer is a sharp "no." Disillusioned, in 2004 Americans Ted Nordhaus and Michael Shellenberger pronounced "the death of environmentalism" as a source of innovative ideas, persuasive counternarratives, and genuine solutions, arguing that we need an environmental politics of hope and breakthroughs, not fear. For very different reasons Sunita Narain, head of India's Centre for Science and Environment, also sees a movement in crisis as the developing world rises as a global force, calling for "the birth of a new environmentalism ... to reinvent growth that is affordable, sustainable, and inclusive." Even David Suzuki, Canada's best-known ecologist who once optimistically wrote (with Holly Dressel) *Good News for a Change: How Everyday People Are Helping the Planet*, has become despairing, concluding: "Environmentalism has failed."[1]

But has it?

## Making a Difference

Calls to reduce humanity's impact on nature are louder than ever—and coming from every spot on earth. The courage of activists has never been greater; nor has the desire of ordinary people to live more sustainably. All around the world concerned citizens are uniting to block misguided projects, while tens of thousands of nongovernmental organizations (NGOs) are lobbying governments, fighting for animal rights, and shaming multinational corporations into improving practices. Furthermore, environmentalism extends far beyond the activism of NGOs and the lifestyle choices of consumers. Those who identify as environmentalists work as well across governments and business, enforcing laws, running certification agencies, patenting eco-technologies, conducting environmental assessments for the World Bank, auditing suppliers for Walmart, and of course writing books like this one.

Today's global sustainability crisis would certainly be worse without the spread of environmentalism since the 1960s. More than a thousand multilateral environmental agreements are in place, and across the world governments have set up environmental protection agencies. Wildlife sanctuaries and ocean parks are multiplying; municipal water and sewage management are improving; and markets for products certified as "sustainable" are growing rapidly. Energy productivity is increasing, as is recycling. And corporations are making real efforts to reduce waste and improve environmental efficiencies.

For at least some people and in at least some places, environmentalism has most definitely made life better—as a philosophy offering a way for some people to live with meaning and purpose, and as a movement raising public awareness, safeguarding some ecosystems, and improving some living conditions, especially for affluent citizens. Still, reflecting on the state of the global environment for even a moment, the dismay of activists such as David Suzuki is totally understandable. For all that environmentalism seems to be succeeding, it's failing on the most important dimension of all: global sustainability, even defined simply as not doing irreparable harm to current and future life on earth. Signs of ecological "unsustainability" are everywhere. The last of the old-growth tropical rainforests are disappearing, while the biodiversity of the oceans is crashing. Droughts are intensifying; soil fertility is declining; deserts are expanding; coral reefs are dying; and fresh water is growing scarcer. Megacities and slums are overflowing with rural migrants and desperate people. And garbage keeps piling up, with poisons leaching into waterways and food systems.

Especially worrying, the global climate is becoming increasingly unstable—a "threat" US President Barack Obama in 2014 correctly called "urgent and growing," one that is going to "define the contours of this century more dramatically than any other." Greenhouse gases have been rising steadily since the 1997 Kyoto Protocol was negotiated to bring them under control. Global carbon emissions are now over 60 percent higher than 1990 levels. The international community of states is still hoping to keep the earth from warming by no more than 1.5 degrees above pre-industrial temperatures. On our current path we'll be lucky to keep the increase to 4 degrees by 2100—a fate that will bring fierce storms, severe droughts, rising seas, and possibly a "sixth mass extinction."[2]

How can we reconcile the growing reach and seeming influence of environmentalism with this escalating ecological crisis? Is it perhaps only a matter of time before the global community of environmentalists brings this crisis under control? As every multinational corporation is now promising, is a future of zero carbon emissions, zero waste to landfill, and zero deforestation possibly just a few decades away? I would like to hope so. But my findings in this book suggest a very different future unless humanity changes course. Environmentalism is making a difference, but not nearly enough of a difference.

Partly, the expanding global economy, with more people consuming more goods, is swamping local and sectoral environmental gains. This economy is producing ecosystem collapses, extreme inequality, and over-consumption, with the policies, technologies, and products that serve well-off citizens casting dark shadows onto poorer people, distant ecosystems, and future generations. I made this point in my 2008 book, *The Shadows of Consumption*. Less understood, however, is what has been happening to the nature of environmentalism as the crisis intensifies. Over the past two decades environmentalism in both rich and poor countries has been losing its critical edge—and thus much of its power as a counternarrative to consumer capitalism. Especially since the 9/11 terrorist attacks of 2001, state security agencies have managed to suppress and defuse many of the world's radical, direct-action environmental movements, while the interests and concerns of wealthy citizens, leading corporations, and powerful states have increasingly come to dominate—and moderate—environmentalism as a whole.

This "environmentalism of the rich," as will become clear over the course of this book, is spreading by the day.[3] Its policies, principles, and practices appear under various guises. Governments like to package them as sustainable development, reflecting what Steven Bernstein calls "the compromise of liberal environmentalism," where growth in production remains the top priority.[4] Corporations like to call them corporate social responsibility (CSR)—where "sustainability" is defined as the "eco-business" of pursuing environmental efficiencies and savings to enhance growth and profits, and not as a way of protecting the ecological integrity of life on earth.[5] For NGOs environmentalism of the rich manifests as business partnerships, eco-product fundraising, and market solutions. For individuals it surfaces as a belief in the power of eco-consumerism and small lifestyle changes as forces of progressive change—walking a recycling bin to the curbside, taking shorter showers, and buying eco-products—even as overall consumption continues to rise.

Environmentalism in the West has long had a special interest in preserving wilderness areas and rescuing wildlife. Back in 1872 we saw this when the United States created Yellowstone National Park. And today we see this when citizens rush to protect nesting falcons or beached dolphins. Environmentalism of the rich primarily emerges out of Western environmental thought and institutions. Yet it embraces far more than what some critics disparage as the "cult of wilderness" of Western environmentalism.[6] Equally central has been the pursuit of sustainable yields for renewable natural resources, such as timber, and the prevention of pollution, such as reducing smog. In recent years core goals have also come to include the pursuit of greater energy efficiency, natural resource productivity, and recycling, as well as the pursuit of less waste per product sold.

Sustainable development and eco-business assume that innovative policies, scientific ingenuity, and technology will allow for continuous economic growth. And they reassuringly presume that people can consume more of just about everything and still make progress toward global sustainability. Trust is put in soft regulation, eco-certification, fair trade, and corporate self-regulation, while great promise is seen in corporate responsibility and individual goodwill. Environmentalism of the rich offers a seductive path forward. Yet, as I'll demonstrate in this book, the gains are not adding up to anything approaching global sustainability. Resulting reforms are modest and incremental, rarely scaling up to improve global conditions as firms reinvest efficiency gains, as certification and regulation deflect production into new locations and sectors, as multinational corporations ramp up production in less-regulated markets, and as unsustainable consumption continues to rise. Gains are also highly unequal, with wealthy states and neighborhoods benefiting far more than poor areas, and with hardly any benefits at all in some of the world's most ecologically vulnerable places.

Sustainability policies of governments and corporations may pay lip service to principles of ecology, but the underlying reasoning is almost always ahistorical, fragmentary, and linear, rarely integrating holistic or dynamic understandings of resilience, feedback loops, tipping points, and complex systems. The focus is on preserving patches of nature and improving the production of particular products, not on avoiding ecological risks in situations of high uncertainty, or even on reducing the ecological consequences of individuals or nations. The energy savings from more efficiently producing more bottled water ends up as a measure of progress. Programs almost never address the possibility of savings, efficiency gains, and technological solutions rebounding in a distant place or future time as equally great, if not greater, environmental stresses. And no one in charge seems to ever challenge in any real way the ecological consequences of consuming more nondurable, disposable products. Or expanding industrial cattle and pig

farms. Or paving the world for more Toyotas, Hyundais, and Fords. Or selling more Barbie dolls and Pampers diapers.

To be fair, environmentalism of the rich is improving the administration of nature parks and the management of cities, as well as averting some
known and immediate harms. To some extent it's even making international trade, multinational corporations, and industrialization a little less
exploitative and a little less destructive, especially when nonprofit organizations, rather than governments or corporations, are in a leadership
position, as with some of the international eco-certification organizations.
But it's not working toward the institutional change necessary for global
sustainability. By characterizing mainstream environmentalism as environmentalism of the rich, I'm not dismissing the value of rewilding the
countryside, or freeing whales from aquariums, or relocating wandering
wolves into national parks. Nor am I shunning eco-holidays in the Amazon
or organic groceries at Walmart. Eco-products and eco-tourism are clearly
doing some good. So are sustainable development policies and CSR. And
so are NGO-business partnerships to certify sustainable seafood and raise
money for the conservation of polar bears. But we are deluding ourselves if
we think thousands of tiny environmental cuts into the world market are
ever going to transform the caustic consequences of the globalization of
Western-style capitalism, consumerism, and sources of wealth.

## The Diversity of Environmentalism

Saying mainstream environmentalism now reflects the interests and concerns of the rich is like coming upon a river of spawning salmon and noting
the color red. There are naturally many shades of difference. Not all of the
mainstream, everywhere, has to the same extent come to embrace markets, corporations, and technologies as solutions. Nor does everyone have
equal faith in the value of economic growth, CSR, and eco-consumerism
as ways to move toward global sustainability. And nor is everyone equally
pragmatic, calling for "evolution, not revolution." Environmentalism will
always be a "movement of movements," with a great diversity of values
and visions surfacing out of a turbulent sea of informal groupings and for-
mal organizations. Environmentalists share a commitment to try to protect the environment, yet sharp differences even exist in the understanding
of the word "environment," from those who really mean nature (wildlife

and ecosystems) to those who really mean living spaces for humans (cities, towns, parks, and beaches).[7]

I should also say, I'm not using the phrase environmentalism of the rich as a way to deride environmentalists who happen to have been born into an affluent family or live in a well-heeled neighborhood. Environmentalism of the rich runs far deeper than the solar-paneled mansions and hybrid SUVs of celebrity environmentalists. It is a way of thinking and acting that has come to dominate mainstream environmentalism. As we'll see throughout this book, many well-off environmentalists are continuing to risk their lives to challenge the forces of global unsustainability. Anti-globalization protestors are continuing to take to the streets to demand new international trade and investment rules to protect tropical ecosystems and indigenous peoples. Grassroots activists are continuing to beat back miners, loggers, and poachers, shut down toxic factories and dumps, and block mega-dams and illegal land grabs. And direct-action protestors are continuing to scale oil rigs, burn down ski lodges, and vandalize animal testing labs.

Such acts do not fall within my understanding of environmentalism of the rich, even if pop stars tag along. Nor does living in an eco-village or going on a hunger strike to protest industrial slaughterhouses or celebrating "buy nothing days" and "gift-free holidays"—no matter the personal background of the activists. The defining feature of environmentalism of the rich is not the degree of affluence of the activists. It's much more about the loss of a "spirit of outrage" at the underlying structures of exploitation, inequality, and overconsumption that are causing the global sustainability crisis, and by a spirit of compromise with solutions those at the World Economic Forum in Davos can live with, perhaps even give a standing ovation.[8]

Nor in any way am I suggesting that all poor people or organizations in poor countries are opposing environmentalism of the rich. The ideas, values, and campaigns of environmentalism are too diverse—and the interactions across groups too fluid and dynamic—to capture in a simple dichotomy of rich and poor. Around the world social justice activists, indigenous peoples, and low-income communities have long fought the violence, racism, and corporate injustices underlying the degradation of local livelihoods and environments—what writers such as Ramachandra Guha, Joan Martinez-Alier, and Rob Nixon call "the environmentalism of the poor." Yet many organizations and individuals within poor countries and communities also advocate for the policies and outcomes of what I'm calling environmentalism of the rich, not wanting in any way to undermine the chance of also becoming wealthy one day. At the same time, wealthy countries have a long history of environmentalism of the poor, such as those in the environmental justice movement who have long fought the bigotry of locating incinerators, hazardous dumps, and polluting industries in poor neighborhoods.[9]

Nor am I implying that the beliefs and actions of an individual or organization will always fit neatly into the category of environmentalism of the rich. The views and lifestyles of individual environmentalists naturally change over the years. So do the strategies and tactics of activist organizations. A few organizations have stayed on a strong course of resistance against the world order, such as the Sea Shepherd Conservation Society, the Earth Liberation Front, and the Animal Liberation Front. But far more have been evolving—sometimes under new names, new leadership, and new offshoots—toward more moderate, cooperative organizations.

Over time the local chapters of international NGOs can end up all over the map of environmentalism. WWF, also known as the World Wildlife Fund and the World Wide Fund for Nature, is one of the more prominent NGOs advancing environmentalism of the rich, not only under its own brand, but also by partnering with industry to launch certification bodies, such as the Forest Stewardship Council and the Marine Stewardship Council. Yet even here there's considerable variation across its scores of offices around the world, with the US branch of WWF taking a particularly strong pro-market and pro-business stance. On the other hand the network of organizations under the umbrella of Friends of the Earth is more critical of environmentalism of the rich—and Friends of the Earth International has opposed free trade deals and called for stricter regulation of multinational corporations—but, again, there's considerable diversity across branches, with shifts over time.[10]

Even the seemingly radical group Greenpeace is hard to pin down. Illegally boarding oil rigs or rappelling from a bridge are not examples of environmentalism of the rich. Nor is blockading logging roads or picketing mining sites. Yet even as Greenpeace activists continue to risk their lives and go to jail, the organization is increasingly turning to eco-consumerism as a way to fundraise, recruit supporters, and pressure companies with global brands—a strategy that in recent years is leaving Greenpeace praising Unilever, Nestlé, and Procter & Gamble as "sustainability leaders."

## The Chapters Ahead

My overarching aim in this book is to analyze where, when, and why environmentalism in all of its diversity is (or is not) advancing sustainability. I do not claim to parse out the precise influence of various forms of environmentalism. That would be impossible. The many tributaries of environmentalism crisscross, with individuals and ideas flowing in and out over the seasons. For this reason in the chapters ahead I explore how environmentalism of the rich and radical streams of environmentalism interact, sometimes reinforcing each other, sometimes working at cross-purposes. In doing so I expose what I see as the dangers of the growing dominance of environmentalism of the rich. My point is not that environmentalism of the poor or anti-capitalism or anti-globalization or direct-action environmentalism offer all of the solutions to the escalating sustainability crisis. But I do believe that over the past two decades the pendulum of environmentalism has swung too far toward cooperation and reconciliation with the institutions of capitalism, and to make more of a *global* difference the mainstream of the environmental movement needs to pursue more transformative, ecological, and justice-oriented goals.

This is not to say that environmentalism as a whole has lost all of its power to advance sustainability. Looking at the growing importance of the concept of sustainability for public awareness, government policies, corporate production, and local decision-making it might even seem as if the power of environmentalism is rising. In some respects it is. Examples of grassroots victories over ill-advised development could fill this book. So could case studies of better environmental management. Yet looking across products, sectors, countries, and generations we see far less progress. Particularly concerning, even as the global forces of unsustainability continue to grow stronger, we are seeing the ideas and principles of those individuals and institutions profiting from this unsustainability increasingly dominate the way of thinking in the environmental movement.

Assessing the influence of environmentalism requires first exposing the raw power of these individuals and institutions. Over the next five chapters I'll reveal how the globalization of a politics of more—of more economic growth, of more corporate sales and profits, of more personal consumption—is propelling global unsustainability. To set the stage for later evaluating the consequences of the turn toward markets and consumerism as ways of advancing global sustainability, I focus in particular on what I see as the "problem of consumption."[11] Destroying ecosystems and oppressing peoples on the periphery of power is a defining feature of this politics of growth and consumption. On occasion it looks as if an ecosystem or community has been swept away by a tsunami. But more often despondency and decay build over generations, until situations of extreme inequality, squalor, and desolation seem unavoidable, even acceptable, with no one feeling responsible. This has left much of the developing world in poverty and with little capacity to manage environmental matters. As we'll see in chapters 2–6, European imperialists and colonialists have much to answer for. But so do ruling elites in postcolonial times. And so do contemporary corporations as economic globalization carves out new pathways of exploitation.

I begin my analysis in chapter 2 by sketching the history of ecological imperialism and colonialism after 1600, necessary for understanding the patterns of violence and exploitation within today's globalizing world economy, as well as the depth and scale of today's sustainability crisis. Forced integration into the world economy has traumatized even the most remote places on earth, as I show in chapter 3 with a snapshot of the South Pacific island of Nauru since 1798. Without doubt more people are earning more than ever before as the world economy globalizes. At the height of Nauru's phosphate mining boom in the mid-1970s, average income even reached the world's second highest. But such statistics conceal the misery of unsustainability in places like Nauru, a country now strip-mined, its only bank shuttered, its 10,000 citizens suffering some of the world's highest rates of obesity, alcoholism, smoking, and diabetes, serving as a detention camp for asylum seekers who had been hoping to reach its former colonizer, Australia.

Nauru illustrates how far the global forces of unsustainable production and consumption can disrupt the socioeconomic and ecological sustainability of particular localities, and how, over generations, this can build into an ever-greater crisis. In chapters 4 and 5, I pan out to look globally at the forces of unsustainable production and consumption, showing how, everywhere, inequality is rising—as is excessive, wasteful consumption as corporations pursue more growth and profits. Chapter 4 focuses on what I call "the business of more": of how advertisers capture discourses and manufacture desires, how firms claiming to be CSR leaders market discounted, nondurable products, and how states build infrastructures (e.g., subsidizing highways) to stimulate more consumption. For states this is the business of economic growth; for the world's billionaires this is the business of accumulating even more wealth. Resulting inequalities are truly absurd. Take the Walton family of the superstore Walmart. Christy, Jim, Alice, and Rob Walton were together worth $160 billion in early 2015—an amount a Walmart sales clerk, working 40 hours a week for $10 an hour, would need 7.7 million years to earn (assuming the clerk took no vacations, paid no taxes, never spent a dime, and, well, lived a very long time).[12]

In chapter 5 I turn to document the costs of inequality and unsustainable consumption. The ecological footprint of humanity, which I'll define fully in chapter 5, is already more than 1.5 times higher than the biological capacity of the earth to regenerate renewable resources. And this footprint keeps rising even as the biological integrity of the earth's ecosystems continues to decline. More people are consuming ever more, with disparities rising across and within countries. For high-income consumers, their "fair earth share"—an amount allowing the earth to retain full regenerative capacity if everyone had an equal share—is already at least 3–6 times too high.[13] What would be a fair earth share is growing smaller as the global population rises and the global environment degrades; meanwhile, every trend suggests a future with far higher per capita footprints and even greater disparities in earth-shares. Rising consumption, moreover, is doing more than just depleting natural resources and filling dumps with computers and cell phones. As I recount in chapter 6, the production of consumer products and the introduction of new technologies have long been casting shadows of unsustainability onto vulnerable ecosystems, marginalized communities, and future generations. Some of the resulting calamities are accidental, consequences of arrogance and ignorance. But as chapter 6 brings to light many shadows of consumption are cast by the reckless introduction of new technologies and products in the pursuit of economic growth and corporate profits.

To some extent firms are responding to critics and regulators by greenwashing business as usual and subverting calls for precautionary measures with anti-environmental rhetoric. Over the past decade, however, most multinational corporations have become more proactive in managing critics, avoiding obvious greenwash, and instead partnering with NGOs, offering eco-products and sponsoring third-party certification of production processes and consumer products. The rhetoric of leading business executives can make it seem as if rapid progress is now being made toward global sustainability. As chapters 4–6 confirm, however, the efficiency gains of eco-business are largely lost as firms reinvest energy and cost savings to stimulate even more unsustainable growth and consumption—a rebound effect that's at the heart of the failure of environmentalism of the rich to slow the escalating global sustainability crisis.

As the second half of the book makes clear, however, this is only part of the story of why environmentalism is failing to make more headway against the forces of unsustainability. As I'll discuss in chapter 7, environmentalism as a whole is best understood as evolving out of cultures from around the world, from the pen of the American naturalist Henry David Thoreau in the nineteenth century to Mahatma Gandhi's philosophy of nonviolent resistance in the twentieth century to the animistic beliefs of indigenous peoples over the millennia. This global tradition shapes a wide range of environmental movements, from conservation in North America to environmental justice in Africa to environmentalism of the poor in Latin America. Nonetheless, as chapter 7 underscores, the values and prescriptions of environmentalism of the rich connect most directly to the traditions of moderate Western environmentalism—of preserving nature, enhancing productive yields, and making life safer and more enjoyable for prosperous citizens.

The rise of environmentalism of the rich, however, does not mean that ordinary citizens and dedicated activists no longer resist corporations, organize rallies, occupy city squares, ram whaling boats, or spike trees. Nor does it mean that radical NGOs and activist-scholars have stopped calling for an end to unequal trade, exploitative corporations, and discriminatory global financing.[14] To give some sense of the courage and commitment of these activists, in chapter 8 I reflect on the life of Bruno Manser, who in 1984 trekked from Switzerland to Sarawak, Malaysia, to live with the Penan people and ended up dedicating his life to fighting against the logging of Borneo's rainforests. Manser grew up in a middle-class family in the Swiss city of Basel. His parents were hoping he would go to medical school, but even as a young man he was a nonconformist, at the age of nineteen choosing to serve three months in prison rather than do his compulsory service in the Swiss military, and in his twenties living on the edge of Swiss society as a herder and craftsman in the Swiss Alps.

Manser's decision to journey into the heart of Borneo did emerge out of a romantic vision of living in an unspoiled state of nature. But despite his upbringing and early understandings of the world, his life of activism is not a reflection of environmentalism of the rich. He came to admire the courage and values of the Penan people; he came to love the rainforests; he came to dream in the Penan language. He joined with the Penan to blockade logging roads and for years he hid from Malaysian security forces in the caves and jungles of the deepest recesses of Borneo. After escaping from Sarawak, Manser would then work to raise global awareness of the plight of the rainforests of the Penan people, parachuting into a packed stadium in Rio de Janeiro, nearly dying on a 60-day hunger strike, hurling himself down a gondola cable in the Swiss Alps, and paragliding over Kuching, the capital of Sarawak.

Through the 1990s the moderating tendencies within rainforest activism caused Manser great distress. Like most global environmental causes these moderating tendencies have only become stronger since then, while the fate of those who continue to campaign against exploitation and injustice remains grim. Hundreds of rainforest activists and indigenous leaders, as chapter 8 documents, have been murdered or have "disappeared" over the last two decades. And as we'll see in chapter 9, animal rights activists and more confrontational environmental groups are increasingly being sidelined, facing derision and charges of "eco-terrorism," not only from the mainstream media, business associations, and state security agencies, but also from within the environmental movement itself.

Groups such as Greenpeace are still making headlines by going to the front lines to challenge oil, mining, and timber companies. In recent years, however, Greenpeace has been increasingly targeting well-known brands over social media, including Nestlé's Kit Kat chocolate bar, Mattel's Barbie doll, and Procter & Gamble's Head & Shoulders shampoo, for contributing to tropical deforestation. Drawing in millions of consumers with humorous videos, these "shame campaigns" have managed to push some multinational buyers into discontinuing contracts with suppliers with particularly poor practices. Greenpeace has celebrated these cases as "victories," praising the corporations for changing their ways. As we'll see in chapter 10, however, what is actually changing—getting the toy company Mattel, for instance, to use different cardboard to package its Barbie doll—illustrates just how little influence such campaigns are actually having on global patterns of exploitation, production, and consumption. At the same time, Greenpeace's strategy of dividing companies into sustainability leaders (those willing to bend a little) and laggards (those ignoring them) is legitimizing the sustainability claims of "leaders" such as Nestlé, Mattel, and Procter & Gamble, even though, just like other multinational corporations, their advertising and sales departments continue to manufacture new and ever-larger markets for disposable, nondurable, and environmentally destructive products.

Activist groups that reject or challenge the policies and outcomes of environmentalism of the rich face a whole host of risks, from being labeled "unrealistic" and "naïve" to being treated as subversives. Meanwhile, as the recent history of WWF shows in chapter 11, embracing the discourses of sustainable development, eco-business, stakeholder partnerships, and eco-consumerism opens up many opportunities for NGOs to access new resources, money, and corridors of power. In this context many NGOs are turning to "cause marketing," (tagging the purchase of a product to fundraising) and the cobranding of commercial goods to pay for staff and programs. They are partnering with business to set up eco-labeling and eco-certification organizations, such as the Roundtable on Sustainable Palm Oil and the Round Table on Responsible Soy. And they are turning to consumers as sources and forces of change, urging them to be "consumer activists" and purchase more products to save the planet.[15]

As will become clear over the course of this book, one effect of the increasing dominance of environmentalism of the rich is to mute calls for an overhaul of consumer capitalism even as the global environmental crisis escalates. As the environmental movement increasingly comes to embrace capitalism and consumerism as solutions (rather than as causes) of unsustainability, states and multinational business are progressively capturing ecological discourses and subsuming environmental networks, deploying the language of sustainability to obfuscate, and in some instances even promote, unsustainable and inequitable consumption. The end result is to reinforce a belief in the value of national economic growth, technological diffusion, and the globalization of trade, markets, and investment. Privatization, deregulation, and liberalization end up depicted as valuable for sustainability, said to promote the economic growth so necessary to implement environmental regulations and maintain political stability. State and corporate discourses further reassure people that modest policy reforms will suffice to produce sustainability, while still allowing consumption (and thus revenues and profits) to continue to rise.

At the same time, the discourses of environmentalism of the rich are reinforcing a belief among well-off consumers in the value of small lifestyle changes and eco-product purchases—again, even in the face of an escalating crisis. Such efforts are now a defining feature of environmentalism in wealthy countries. Consumers are being urged to buy green detergents and order sustainably produced seafood in restaurants. And they're being advised to unplug appliances, shut off dripping taps, and air-dry clothes. Although laudable as individual acts, such efforts do not get at the patterns of extraction, production, and consumption that are causing global unsustainability. Recycling a Starbucks cup or a Coke bottle does nothing to address the subjugation and marginalization of the world's least-protected peoples and most vulnerable ecosystems. Nor are sustainable development policies, eco-business initiatives, NGO-business partnerships, and voluntary market-based mechanisms doing much here. At best these manifestations of environmentalism of the rich reduce some of the local symptoms of unsustainability, but do not get at the causes that are spreading like a common cold as the world economy globalizes.

Is there any hope for a sustainable future? Some days while writing this book I did feel like giving up. Yet, at least for me, in the long run saying and doing nothing about the sustainability crisis would be far more demoralizing. "Living at the margins," as the scholar-activist Paul Wapner reminds us, can be invigorating, even uplifting.[16] Defeatism does not motivate my desire to expose the limits and failures of environmentalism of the rich. Just the opposite: as I'll discuss in my concluding chapter, I see confronting these limits and failures as a way to energize environmentalism as a counternarrative to consumer capitalism. In no way, moreover, has this counternarrative gone away. The Occupy movement of 2011 reveals some of the anger of the world's youth at global inequality and injustice, and anti-globalization and anti-corporate movements continue to rumble underneath the institutions of environmentalism of the rich. Protests against modern-day slavery, megadams, chemical poisoning, gas drilling, climate change, and the treatment of indigenous peoples continue to rage. And a spirit of outrage remains strong outside of mainstream environmentalism—an outrage that will surely swell as the costs of failing to live sustainably continue to escalate. In this spirit let's now turn to look at the history of violence, exploitation, and injustice underlying today's global sustainability crisis.

# I  Global Unsustainability

## 2   Sailing into the Anthropocene

Since the beginning of the twenty-first century geologists have been debating whether the Holocene Epoch, which began as the last major Ice Age came to a close some 12,000 years ago, might be over. Like many others, I think we are indeed in a new geologic epoch: the "Anthropocene," defined by the global unsustainability of *Homo sapiens*. Epochs are marked by geologic shifting events—an asteroid striking the earth; sustained volcanic eruptions; continents colliding; drastic climate change—and remain visible in rocks and ocean sediment for millions of years. Some scholars mark the Anthropocene Epoch as starting in the late 1700s when the Industrial Revolution took off. Others see the beginnings in the mid-1900s with the launching and testing of atomic and nuclear weapons. Strong cases can be made for both of these time periods, and, as I'll return to in later chapters, the ecological consequences of human activity did accelerate after each of them, with the last 50 years a period many scholars are now calling the "Great Acceleration."

It's reasonable as well, however, to date the beginning of the Anthropocene around 1600, as by then European imperialism was well on its way to ripping apart the world's social fabric and global ecology, with the population of the Americas, for example, crashing by some 50 million from 1492 to 1650. For centuries after 1600, European armies and commercial allies would continue to subjugate and appropriate lands across the Asia-Pacific, Africa, and the Americas. Explorers and colonists would also continue to transport European diseases, plants, and animals, a process of "ecological imperialism" further devastating societies and landscapes over the next three centuries and continuing to this day to roll over postcolonial societies as the "slow violence" of unsustainability.[1]

Captain Pedro Fernandes de Queirós's voyage across the Pacific Ocean in 1605–1606 provides a glimpse into the mundane terrors of these early years of imperialism. Few of you will have ever heard of this voyage, as most of the historical record is limited to the diaries of the men on board the ships. Entering the history of imperialism through such a seemingly inconsequential moment in time may seem like an odd choice. I do so as a reminder of how far small acts of ignorance can build and extend into the future, and how easy (and tempting) it is to forget that the legacy of European imperialism and colonialism is at the root of what we now call globalization—a fact that environmentalism of the rich tends to push aside.

## The Story of Captain Queirós

Captain Queirós set sail from Peru on December 21, 1605, in command of two ships and a launch. In the service of the King of Spain and for the glory of Catholicism, for the next four months he would navigate the stormy Pacific Ocean in search of the legendary southern land of "Terra Australis Incognita," along the way plundering islands. On May 1, 1606, the fleet sailed into a deep bay off the coast of what Captain Queirós mistook for a vast continent, naming it Austrialia del Espiritu Santo. The land of black sand and coconut palms struck him as a divine spot for a colony. Two days later the *Capitana*, the 150-ton flagship captained by Queirós, and the *Almiranta*, a 120-ton ship captained by his second-in-command Luís Vaez de Torres, dropped anchor in a fine harbor not far from a sparkling freshwater river. Forays over the next week would convince Captain Queirós that his discovery was indeed historic. On the night of May 13 a celebration was held with such a dazzling display of artillery and fireworks that the revelers could hear "great shouts" of alarm from the surrounding hills and valleys.

The next morning, with the Royal Standard of Spain flying, Captain Queirós formally took possession of Espiritu Santo for God and the King of Spain. Following Mass under an awning of branches, he proclaimed the city of "New Jerusalem," appointing his crew to high office as "royal officers" and "magistrates," and vowing that the city would one day rival the capitals of Europe, with gates and sidewalks and houses of white marble, and a marble church as grand as St. Peter's Basilica in the Vatican City.

Captain Queirós was courageous. Yet he was also, in the eyes of many of his men, dithering and pompous. Retaining the respect and loyalty of his officers was never easy for him. Chronically sick, when he did emerge from his cabin he was prone to giving long and sanguine speeches of the splendors ahead, of "hatfuls" of pearls and islands of gold and silver: what one adventurer on board, the Spanish nobleman (and, later in life, a monk of the Order of Saint Basil) Don Diego de Prado y Tovar, would describe in his journal as nothing but "wind." It didn't help that Captain Queirós was Portuguese in charge of a Spanish fleet. The Spanish officers and unpaid adventurers under his command were especially quick to question his orders and navigational judgment, and treachery and mutiny were already in the air a month after leaving Peru. Those loyal to Captain Queirós called for harsh measures to restore discipline. Toss the mutinous lot overboard. Set them adrift. Maroon them on a coral atoll. But Queirós liked to rule with words, not his sword; he chose to transfer disgruntled crew from the *Capitana* to the *Almiranta*, locking up only one of the conspirators, Chief Pilot Juan Ochoa de Bilbao.

Matters grew worse for Captain Queirós after landing on Espiritu Santo. His crew became restless as relations with locals took a turn for the worse after a foraging party under the command of Captain Torres shot and killed a villager, severing the man's head and then, as a warning, hanging the corpse by one foot from a tree branch. Horrified, villagers began to throw stones and shoot arrows and darts. The foraging party countered with a barrage from their arquebuses and muskets, killing at least ten people, including a chief. Captain Queirós was irate. A disciple of the Franciscan Order, he saw himself as bringing peace and religious order, not bloodshed and fear. The tendency of his men to kill without cause infuriated him, as he believed this set back his mission to spread the teachings of Christ.

For many of the crew the response of Captain Queirós to the killings was further proof of his flaccid leadership. The adventurer Prado, a ringleader of discontent throughout the voyage, and whose journal exposes his own vanity and arrogance, was contemptuous of Queirós's "peevish" reaction to the killings: "with such savages it is impossible to use politeness," he scrawled, "in order that another time they should not be so rude to Spaniards." For Prado the reason that Queirós was so soft was obvious: He "could not swallow it, being a Portuguese."

By late May the crew was itching to sail onward. Captain Queirós had forbidden them from bringing kidnapped women onto the ships, and raids were becoming perilous as villagers were now counterattacking. To pass the time the crew decided to ransom three kidnapped boys for all the pigs "in the land." The boys, seeing their fathers on the shore, wept and begged to go home—the eldest, who the crew renamed "Pablo," was around seven years old. Distraught, their fathers quickly handed over fruit and birds and pigs. But the crew never was going to return the boys; they knew Captain Queirós would never permit that. Earlier that week, after a sailor had joked that "thirty pigs would be better eating than three boys," Queirós was indignant, scolding the sailor and praising God for saving "these three souls." I "would rather have one of those children," he said with emotion, "than the whole world besides."

To reassure their fathers on the shore Captain Queirós dressed the boys in silk and paraded them around the ship deck. But his concern for propriety and souls did not translate into compassion for the boys. Reacting to Pablo's weeping pleas to be allowed to go to his father who was calling from the beach, he barked: "Silence, child! You know not what you ask. Greater good awaits you than the sight and the communion with heathen parents and friends." Taking the boys with him, Captain Queirós finally set sail in the *Capitana* five weeks after anchoring off Espiritu Santo, as Captain Torres would log, "without any notice given to us, and without making any signal." Assuming the *Capitana* had either gone its own way or was lost at sea, two weeks later Captain Torres set sail for the Philippines.

Under the command of Captain Torres the *Almiranta* would trade and loot its way through the islands of Melanesia, charting a passage between New Guinea and Australia (known today as the Torres Strait). Along the way Torres would raze villages, in the words of Prado abducting the "youngest women" for "the service" of his crew, and seizing children as trophies and slaves for the Spanish empire, even kidnapping a pregnant woman who, to the crew's wonder, came up on deck during labor, bracing against a cannon as another captive poured buckets of seawater over her (the baby would later die in Manila).

During this time Captain Queirós was sailing to Acapulco, where he would arrive five months later. Bad winds, he would tell anyone who would listen, prevented him from returning to Espiritu Santo to reunite with Captain Torres; heading for Mexico was the best option. Some of the *Capitana* crew would tell a very different story, however, saying officers locked Queirós in his cabin, no longer willing to serve a blustering buffoon. Some officers even urged the Viceroy of Mexico to charge Captain Queirós with incompetence, and, although this was not within the Viceroy's power, Prado, who later met up with crew from the *Capitana*, would say in his account of the voyage that the Viceroy took Queirós to be nothing but a "fool and a madman" who had "deceived" King Philip III of Spain.

For years afterward Captain Queirós would repeatedly petition the Spanish King to finance another trip to Espiritu Santo, comparing his discoveries to those of Christopher Columbus in 1492 and to Ferdinand Magellan's voyage of 1519–1521, and claiming the South Pacific was a treasure chest of riches, where the "clean, lively, and rational" natives would "be very easy to pacify, and teach, and satisfy." But Captain Queirós never would make his way back to Espiritu Santo, in 1614 dying in Panama en route to Lima, still dreaming of a return trip to the "new world." Nor would Pablo ever return home, dying shortly after arriving in Mexico, his captors guessing he was eight years old.[2]

More than a hundred and sixty years would pass before the next European—the French navigator Louis-Antoine de Bougainville in 1768— would reach Espiritu Santo. Six years later, the British explorer, Captain James Cook, would follow, charting Espiritu Santo as the largest island in an archipelago, which he named New Hebrides after the islands off the west coast of Scotland.

## Colonizing New Hebrides

Officers and administrators from France and Britain would come in the wake of Bougainville and Cook to conquer, convert, and "civilize" New Hebrides. Trade in sandalwood took off in the first half of the 1800s. As profitable supplies of sandalwood declined, plantation owners and settlers turned to growing and exporting bananas, coffee, cocoa, and especially copra (dried coconut). Meanwhile, Christian missionaries and teachers built churches and schools, and by the mid-1880s almost every island of New Hebrides had a mission.

Like Captain Queirós, most missionaries—and many teachers—saw themselves as saving a backward and uncivilized people. Like the explorers before them, though, they brought disease and violence and spiritual agony. As was true across much of the world, the peoples of New Hebrides had no history of (or immunity to) a long list of illnesses common in Europe: smallpox, measles, diphtheria, dysentery, whooping cough, influenza, tuberculosis, and sexually transmitted diseases, among others. During this time traders and settlers were manipulating and mistreating islanders. "Blackbirding" was common, where Pacific islanders were kidnapped or tricked into slavery on the sugar and cotton plantations of Australia, Fiji, New Caledonia, and Samoa. By the 1880s more than half of the adult males of New Hebrides were laboring on these plantations. The mortality rate was appalling. Of the 600 people "recruited" from the island of Erromango between 1868 and 1878, for example, just one-third made it home.[3]

The indigenous people of New Hebrides would barely survive European imperialism. When Captain Queirós landed on Espiritu Santo in 1606 as many as 1 million people may have been living on the islands of New Hebrides—roughly equal to 1 in every 550 people on earth. By the mid-1930s just 45,000–50,000 people remained: about 5 percent of the original population. Life in the 1800s on Aneityum, the southernmost island of New Hebrides, illustrates the calamity of contact with Europeans. The population of 5,000 or so fell steadily from the 1830s onwards, with one-third of the people (by then about 3,500) dying from influenza and measles between 1857 and 1863. The population of Aneityum did not stop falling until the 1930s and 1940s, when just 200 or so people remained.[4]

In 1980 New Hebrides would gain independence from France and Britain (who then jointly controlled the colony). The country of 80 or so islands was renamed Vanuatu. Since independence the population of Vanuatu has been crawling back up. Still, if you were to travel to Vanuatu today, you would only find a quarter of the population that existed before the arrival of Europeans.

Yachts now line the docks of Port Vila, the capital of Vanuatu, as captains of leisure explore a life of cocktails and suntanning. Nearby is rue D'Auvergne. Walking along this road a few years ago I could not help but wonder what D'Auvergne did to earn a street name. Did my ancestors colonize the Pacific? I know they were in the first wave of North American colonists. But what was their impact on the Asia-Pacific, Africa, and South America? Were the consequences of my own life, went my wandering mind, really any different from those of my ancestors?

Unlike Captain Queirós I do not brandish a musket when exploring cities like Port Vila. Nor do I kidnap boys or steal pigs—or even pinch souvenirs. Compared to missionaries or traders or settlers my time in such places is short and my purpose very different (or so I believe), as I travel to "conduct research," not to save souls or claim lands for a king. Yet passing by the Chinese embassy and the Vanuatu Association of Nongovernmental Organizations on rue D'Auvergne, I was well aware that my life relies on a world economy emerging out of a traumatic history of imperialism and colonialism, and that in the modern era of globalization the consequences of consuming goods and resources are more far-reaching—and speed across the world at a much faster clip—than was the case during the time of Captain Queirós.[5]

## Being Traumatized

No single book could ever do justice to the environmental histories of imperialism across all cultures, time, and ecosystems. The story of Captain Queirós in Vanuatu reminds us of how the desires, values, and prejudices of European explorers brought horrors for those being explored. More famous captains had sailed the oceans before Queirós, notably Columbus in the 1400s and Magellan in the 1500s; and others would follow, such as Cook in the 1700s. The point of telling the tale of Captain Queirós is not to damn him or his crew in particular. Over the next four centuries even worse captains would invade Asia, Africa, and Latin America. But his voyage does reveal the calamity of early European exploration for indigenous peoples—an important reason for today's global sustainability crisis.

The crew under the command of Captain Queirós was savage by any standard of humanity, murdering and raping and kidnapping islanders with pious impunity. Most of those abducted to serve as slaves or trophies would die within months or years, some of hunger or beatings, but most of raging fevers, in agony and weak from vomiting, coughing, and gasping for air. Other Pacific islanders were equally vulnerable to European diseases. By the 1800s, diseases such as smallpox, the flu, measles, and tuberculosis were causing populations across the Pacific islands to drop precipitously. A single outbreak sometimes killed a third or more of an island's people, and, as in Vanuatu, no culture survived intact. In this upheaval many societies became unstable—a situation that traders and missionaries and colonizers were quick to exploit and almost always make worse.

The indigenous peoples of Australia and the Americas suffered similarly. Australia's first of three smallpox pandemics during the nineteenth century may have killed one-third of the Aborigines. Smallpox killed half of the Huron and Iroquois in the New York area in the 1630s and 1640s; in 1738 alone as many as half of the Cherokee died of smallpox. European imperialism was equally traumatic in South America. At the beginning of the eighteenth century the Chechehets were one of the largest tribes on the Pampas. For generations they had avoided all Europeans as if they were death adders. Panic ensued when smallpox eventually struck in the early 1700s: families fled, shamans were sacrificed, the sick were abandoned.[6] The Chechehets would never recover. By century's end their language had faded away, and today the Merriam-Webster dictionary describes them as "extinct."

European diseases would rampage through societies across the Asia-Pacific, Africa, and the Americas. In North America settlers overran the remaining indigenous peoples. Already in 1634 John Winthrop, the first governor of Massachusetts Bay Colony, was thanking god for killing the indigenous peoples. "For the natives," he wrote, "they are neere all dead of small Poxe, so as the Lord hathe cleared our title to what we possess."[7] Entire indigenous societies in the Americas and Australia were killed off. Centuries of colonialism, racism, land appropriation, and forced assimilation badly wounded the few to survive.

**Being Colonized**

Into these emptying lands European colonizers and settlers brought cows and pigs and sheep while plantation owners bought slaves to till vast estates of tobacco and cotton and sugar. Rats and rabbits invaded the continent of Australia. Fields of grass and clover were sown across New Zealand—with honeybees imported in 1839 to pollinate the new environment. Around the world ranchers razed forests, farmers drained wetlands, and miners dug out gold and diamonds. Whaling and fishing fleets plied the shores of the new colonies. And settlers planted trees and tended gardens to make the new worlds seem more like home.

The tiny Pacific island of Nauru, about 1,200 miles north of Vanuatu, illustrates how steep the trajectory of unsustainability became in some places. Peace had reigned for thousands of years before escaped convicts from Europe introduced rifles and alcohol in the 1800s. It was a lethal mix, and the island was in chaos when Germany annexed it in 1888. The

Germans imposed order, ruling until Australia captured Nauru in WWI. Australia (cooperating with Britain and New Zealand) would then "administer" the island until 1968 (except during Japan's occupation in WWII), after WWI under the "mandate" of the League of Nations and after WWII under the "international trusteeship system" of the United Nations. In theory trusteeship required Australia to prepare Nauru for independence by building political institutions and a stable economy. But, like other colonizers, Australia's primary interest was in exploiting the people and resources of Nauru to grow its own economy, and as in most of the postcolonial world, Australia left behind weak institutions, poorly trained administrators, a boom-and-bust economy, and a volatile political situation.

Few countries are facing a future quite as bleak as Nauru's, as we'll see in the next chapter. Yet many postcolonial states are similarly in crisis: subverted by and indebted to foreign powers, nearly bankrupt, rocked constantly by disease and violence. A need to fit into the world economy—and the power of foreign states and multinational corporations to entice and punish—encourages postcolonial states to keep exploiting their natural resources as fast as possible. Governments across the developing world are exporting untenable amounts of timber, minerals, fish, crude oil, and food (often to former colonial powers) in a bid to earn foreign exchange, service debts, appease donors and bankers, and retain power. Given the importance of economic growth for political stability, few postcolonial states have been able break this cycle of unsustainable development. In many places, as in Nauru, natural resource exports to former colonizers went up after independence, under pressure from organizations such as the World Bank and International Monetary Fund, and as politicians became desperate, as corruption spread, and as extractive industries and transport systems were able to handle larger volumes.

Of course life in places like the South Pacific was far from idyllic before Europeans arrived. Wars, cannibalism, rape, and torture were rife. So were superstition and ignorance. Here and there some truly mad cultural practices had come about: widows in Fiji, to give one grisly example, were strangled or buried alive to accompany their deceased husbands into the afterlife.[8] Yet often, as in the case of Nauru, a vibrant society was in place when Europeans first sailed to their lands. Colonialism similarly shredded the social fabric of Asia, Africa, and Latin America. This helps explain why coups and violence are endemic in so many postcolonial states. This helps explain why corruption and incompetence are so rampant. And this helps explain why so many postcolonial leaders are willing to forsake the future. Unsustainability has reproduced over generations, becoming a way of life, taking on new forms, harming not only ecosystems, but also economies and societies—a process aggravated by globalization.

## Being Globalized

Integrating societies into a world economy has been brutal and wrenching since at least the voyage of Columbus in 1492. This is not to suggest that the globalizing process over the past half-century has not brought opportunities and delicacies and goods to billions of people. It has. And globalization of communication technologies has certainly spread creativity and knowledge, including empowering social movements such as environmentalism. Yet more freedom and wealth for some has come at the cost of adversity and tragedy for many others.

Globalization today is inseparable from the history of men like Captain Queirós pillaging "empty" lands and dislocating indigenous peoples. Wars mark the making of the international society of states; slavery and violence accompanied the rise of multinational corporations and world markets. As during the sailing era of Captain Queirós, curiosity, greed, and zealotry still explain much of why people travel, trade, and resettle to new lands. Even the very idea of "one world"—of one people living on one earth—can only be understood as emerging out of a history of imperialism and colonialism, of bloodshed and cruelty, where Western values and ways of knowing have come to dominate. Forgetting this history can make globalization seem innocuous, as if it's nothing more than the process of new technologies connecting up the world, so people, money, and ideas can travel faster and farther. Being globalized entails far more, though, than just being able to fly from Los Angeles to Sydney in 16 hours, or regularly eating food grown a half-world away, or connecting billions of people on Facebook, Twitter, and Instagram.

Globalization can be violent and exploitative, little different than imperialism. Manifestations include world powers forcing developing countries to deregulate economic affairs, offering grants and demanding loan repayments to open borders to trade, natural resource investors, and foreign manufacturers. One sign of the resulting financial cost is the rising external debt of the developing world, which has gone from $2 trillion in 2000 to more than $5 trillion today. The private sector accounts for more than half of this debt—a debt that reinforces highly uneven and unequal South–North trade flows, with developing countries exporting large quantities of natural resources and low-priced goods (partly to earn foreign exchange to service debt).[9]

Rising inequality and concentrating financial power are further signs of the globalization of unsustainability. Just 1 percent of the world population holds half of global wealth. Around 45,000 people are now worth over $100 million while 124,000 people are worth over $50 million. And the rich keep getting richer. We see this with the thirteen-fold increase in the number of billionaires since the mid-1980s. At the same time around 2.2 billion people were still earning less than $2 a day in 2011—a figure not far off what it was in 1980.[10] This crude measure, moreover, misses much of the hardship in the poorest countries, where monocrop plantations have displaced subsistence farming, where good jobs in rural communities are rare, where working-age adults have left villages, and where hundreds of millions of people live in slums, some even surviving by scavenging for food and recyclables in rancid mountains of garbage.

Also, more income does not necessarily translate into quality food, or better nutrition, or improved health. In the developing world, 1 in 7 people were malnourished from 2010 to 2012. The worst off region is Sub-Saharan Africa, where the UN's World Food Programme estimates that one-quarter of the population is malnourished. Rising consumption of tobacco, liquor, and processed food are causing further health crises across emerging and developing countries. Men in China, for example, smoke 35–40 percent of the world's cigarettes. And more than three-quarters of tobacco-related deaths—around 6 million people a year and rising—are in the developing world. Without tough measures, the World Health Organization predicts that over the course of the twenty-first century smoking will kill up to 1 billion people, with the vast majority in the developing world.[11]

We cannot divorce the process of globalization from past—and continuing—efforts by those with more power and money to gain control, impose beliefs, and extract profits. Nor can we disconnect the process from inequality and gross concentrations of wealth. Nor can we separate it from the exploitation of people and environments in poor and indebted countries. To enslave children to harvest cocoa in Côte d'Ivoire. Or murder striking miners in Peru. Or raze tropical forests in Indonesia. Or overfish the Atlantic and Pacific oceans.

An undercurrent of Westernization has always surged through globalization. And power struggles, resistance, and value clashes are intrinsic to the process, simultaneously stalling, reversing, and accelerating socioeconomic and technological forces of global unity. Back in the 1970s feisty opposition to the globalization of Western brands, international retail, and multinational investors was common. Today, however, only aging Leftists and grassroots activists seem to have any fight left, and they are no match for big business and economic superpowers. Each passing year sees more consumer goods crisscross the world's oceans and highways and airways. And the billionaires of business now have a stranglehold on the world economy.[12]

This globalization of our lives helps explain why so many of us who are trying to live more sustainably so often feel hypocritical. Like the missionaries and explorers of the past five centuries, most of us who call ourselves environmentalists are never quite able to match our actions with our beliefs. Angst is understandable. Yet thinking hard about the consequences of our values, lifestyles, and careers—including those of our ancestors over the last 500 years and our descendants for the next 500 years—is essential for strengthening our sense of personal and collective responsibility for the earth, unquestionably necessary for any chance of global sustainability.[13] At the same time, there's no doubt that it's getting harder, not easier, to live sustainably, as the consequences of our most routine decisions and most basic needs ripple through a complex global system in unpredictable and often untraceable ways, with billions of butterfly effects as we go about our day. Particularly concerning, the gap between the costs of personal consumption and the political capacity to control these costs continues to widen as globalization diffuses, obscures, and deepens the consequences of consumption, over generations gaining the power to destroy even the most isolated places on earth, as the story of Nauru vividly illustrates in the next chapter.

## 3  By No Means Pleasant

Lying between Australia and Hawaii, Nauru is as far from Europe as any place on earth. Its closest neighbor is the island of Banaba, 185 miles to the east. Like Banaba, the island of Nauru surfaced over millions of years as bird droppings and decomposing sea life turned to stone atop a coral reef. Only around 3,000 years ago did Polynesians and Micronesians begin to settle on the 8-square-mile island of Nauru.

Not until November 8, 1798, when the *Snow Hunter*, a British ship en route from New Zealand to the China Seas, was sailing by did any European record seeing Nauru. Hundreds of Nauruans canoed out to greet the sailors. The captain of the *Snow Hunter*, John Fearn, did not permit his men to disembark. Nor did any Nauruans venture aboard. Still, the welcome charmed Captain Fearn, as did the warm winds, the island's green central plateau, the swaying palms, and the white-sand beaches, and seeing "a beautiful little island" he named it Pleasant Island.

The sight (and wafting stench) of the *Snow Hunter*'s motley crew must have come as quite a shock to the Nauruans. At the time, life on the small island was mostly peaceful and predictable. Tensions among Nauru's 12 clans did run deep; and now and then disputes did turn deadly. Any year with light rainfall would cause great suffering too, as the island's only surface water is a brackish and shallow lagoon. Still, for thousands of years, 1,000–1,400 Nauruans had managed to live largely in balance with nature, isolated but self-sufficient, with societal acrimony more or less kept in check. Captain Fearn's naming of the island for the English-speaking world did not upset this stability. But it was an omen of dark times ahead.

## Murder and Mayhem

Born in Britain in 1813, as a young man William Harris was banished to Norfolk Island, a British penal colony about 900 miles east of Australia. Escaping, he would make his way to Nauru in 1842. He did not go there in search of pearls or diamonds or gold. Nor was he looking to trade spices or log sandalwood. He went to live a carefree and easygoing life as a "beachcomber," one of many convicts and deserters then hiding out in the South Pacific. The first beachcombers had come to Nauru in the early 1830s; for them life was not as happy-go-lucky as they were likely imagining. During the 1830s John Jones, like Harris a fugitive from Norfolk Island, had ruled the Nauruan beaches with brutality, murdering at least a dozen beachcombers. Jones stayed on the edges of Nauruan society, brokering deals with passing ships to trade pigs and coconuts for tobacco, liquor, and rifles. Eventually, however, Jones fell out with the Nauruan chiefs (after he blamed them for his murders), and in 1841 they exiled him to Banaba.

William Harris was lucky to arrive in Nauru after Jones had been cast off the island. Like other beachcombers, Harris helped the Nauruans to barter with passing Europeans. But he took a different tack with the Nauruans, integrating into Nauruan society by marrying a Nauruan and raising a large family. Harris would live on Nauru for nearly 50 years. Over this time island life would change in ways unimaginable to any past generation of Nauruans. By the 1870s guns were in homes across the island, and Nauruans were smoking and drinking heavily (especially sour toddy, made by fermenting coconut flowers). In the late 1870s Nauru began to spiral into violence after a chief was shot and killed during a drunken quarrel. Retaliations were swift and deadly. Traditions for resolving conflict did little to slow the escalating feuds among clans and families. Neighbors slew each other; skirmishes turned into bloodbaths. In 1881 the British Royal Navy dropped anchor off Nauru, and Harris boarded the flagship to brief the captain. "A civil war on the island," the captain signaled to his fleet. "An escaped convict is king. All hands constantly drunk: no fruit or vegetables to be obtained, nothing but pigs and coconuts. The present island-king wants a missionary. He was evidently hungry."

Later that decade the British agreed to cede any claim to Nauru to the Germans who were keen to control more of the copra trade in the western Pacific. Germany annexed the island in 1888, dispatching armed marines to enforce a ban on firearms and alcohol. Guided around by the then 75-year-old Harris, on October 2, 1888, German authorities rounded up the 12 chiefs and gave them an ultimatum: Order your followers to surrender all guns and ammunition or go to prison. Within two days islanders handed in more than 750 guns. The decade-long civil war was over. But by then around 500 Nauruans had been killed—more than one-third of the Nauruan people.

At the time Nauru was of minor strategic value for the colonial powers jockeying in the Pacific. Then one day in 1899 the geologist Albert Ellis began to inspect a rock-like object that was propping open a door in the Sydney office of the Pacific Islands Company. He had been told it was a piece of petrified wood from Nauru. But this did not seem right to Ellis, and after investigating he would discover that it was actually high-grade phosphate ore, a super-fertilizer worth a potential fortune if he could locate the source.[1]

## The Phosphate Rush

Sailing to Nauru in 1901 Albert Ellis found that four-fifths of the entire island—the raised central plateau Nauruans call "Topside"—was rich in phosphate of lime. The Pacific Islands Company was renamed the Pacific Phosphate Company, and in 1905 a deal was made with Germany to mine Nauru. A year later the first boatload of Nauruan phosphate would sink in a storm off Australia. But this setback did little to deter miners and, over the next decade, Nauru would export hundreds of thousands of tons of phosphate.

Nauruans had never built homes on Topside, preferring the cooler shoreline; but Topside was home to wild almond and planted pandanus trees, as well as flocks of birds, including terns and noddies and frigatebirds. Miners cleared the scrub, ferns, and trees, scraped away the topsoil, and then dug the ore out of the pits and crevices of the ancient coral underneath. Little care was taken. Photographer Rosamond Dobson Rhone, writing in 1921 for the *National Geographic Magazine*, describes the aftereffects: "A worked-out phosphate field is a dismal, ghastly tract of land, with its thousands of upstanding white coral pinnacles from ten to thirty feet high, its cavernous depths littered with broken coral, abandoned tram tracks, discarded phosphate baskets, and rusted American kerosene tins."

By this time Australia was ruling Nauru, having captured it from Germany at the start of WWI. After the war ended in 1919 the League of Nations put Nauru under the mandate of Britain, Australia, and New Zealand, organized as the British Phosphate Commissioners, with Australia as the administrator. Australia ruled Nauru as an offshore mining site, with Australia and New Zealand importing almost all of Nauru's phosphate. As administrator, Australia's focus was on building mining infrastructure, mechanizing mining, and ramping up exports. In the early 1920s Nauru was exporting some 200,000 metric tons of phosphate a year; by the end of the 1930s it was more than four times that—all priced well below the world average to subsidize farmers in Australia, New Zealand, and Great Britain.

Phosphate mining would grind to a halt after Japan invaded Nauru in 1942. Japanese troops were merciless—with beatings, summary executions, deportations, forced labor camps, and mass drownings (such as of people with leprosy). At war's end in 1945 fewer than 600 Nauruans remained on the island and a quarter of the Nauruan people had died. The United Nations then put Nauru under a "Trusteeship" of Australia, Britain, and New Zealand, with Australia once again administering the island.

By 1946 the Nauruan phosphate industry was restarting; by 1950 exports were higher than ever. Over the next 17 years exports would rise steadily, with Australian and New Zealand farmers continuing to pay far below market prices until 1963. By the time Nauru gained independence in 1968 more than 35 million metric tons of phosphate had left its shores—enough phosphate to fill dump trucks parked end to end from New York City to Los Angeles, and back again.[2]

### Independence

By 1968 one-third of Nauru had been strip mined, and Nauruans were living on a narrow ring around a plateau of jagged, spiky, razor-sharp coral and limestone pillars. During the interwar years and again after WWII Nauruan landowners did receive token royalties, and small trust funds were set up. The mining of Nauru's phosphate was not outright theft; the Nauruan share, however, was tiny considering the profits, damage, and cost of restoring mined land. After independence the Republic of Nauru chose to cash in its remaining phosphate, increasing exports despite knowing that supplies would run out within a generation or two. From 1968 to 1980 Nauru mined on average around 1.8 million metric tons a year, exceeding 2 million metric tons in some years. Production fell somewhat in the 1980s; still, Nauru managed to export on average 1.5 million metric tons a year. Over this time Nauru's total income from phosphate exports exceeded A$2 billion.[3]

On paper Nauruans became wealthy. In 1975 Nauru's Phosphate Royalties Trust was valued at well over A$1 billion and the country's per capita gross domestic product was second only to Saudi Arabia. Nauruans certainly did not live in luxury. But the government did not tax incomes, provided free education and health care, and was the main employer for Nauruans (immigrants generally worked in mining). The government also bought cruise ships, aircraft, and overseas hotels, while politicians were known to charter flights to shop and vacation abroad. Curiously, during this time sports cars became a prized possession in Nauru, even though driving leisurely around the island takes 20 minutes. One police chief even imported a Lamborghini only to discover that he was too bulky to squeeze behind the wheel. "A lot of stupid things happened," recalled Nauruan Manoa Tongamalo in 2008. "People would go into a shop, buy a few sweets, pay with a $50 note, and not take the change. They'd use money as toilet paper."[4]

During this time Nauru was also seeking compensation from Australia, New Zealand, and Britain for the damage done by mining before July 1967. As administrator, Australia knew well that mining was decimating Nauru. By the early 1960s Australia was proposing to resettle Nauruans in Australia, including an offer in 1963 of citizenship and limited self-rule on Curtis Island, just off the coast of Queensland. Yet after independence Australia was unwilling to consider compensating Nauru and, after decades of delays and indifference, in 1989 Nauru took Australia to the International Court of Justice. Australia could see that Nauru had a strong case, and in 1993 the parties settled out of court, with Australia agreeing to pay A$57 million in 1994 as well as another A$50 million (in 1993 dollars) over the next 20 years (later, the UK and New Zealand each contributed A$12 million to reduce Australia's burden). To some extent this settlement was a moral and legal victory for Nauru. But considering the damage the compensation was a financial pittance.

Trying to diversify the economy before phosphate supplies ran out, Nauru turned to offshore banking, licensing around 400 foreign banks by the early 1990s. Tony Audoa, in 1991 in charge of licensing banks, explains the government's reasoning: "After the phosphate industry comes to a close, we have to go into other areas that are sustainable and renewable each year." But "illegal" would be a far more accurate adjective than "sustainable" or "renewable." To open a bank it was not even necessary to visit Nauru, let alone open a branch on the island; even keeping bank records was optional. By the mid-1990s Nauru was also offering "economic citizenship": selling Nauruan passports with little scrutiny. The Nauruan government did earn millions a year in fees. But these schemes turned Nauru into a haven for tax evasion and money laundering, with tens of billions of dollars of criminal profits washing through during the 1990s.

Offshore banking and selling passports could not fix Nauru's economic woes. Desperate for revenue and jobs, with cruel irony Nauru agreed in 2001 to allow Australia to establish a detention center on Nauru to process asylum seekers who'd been trying to reach Australia by boat. By 2002 some 1,000 asylum seekers—mostly Afghan and Iraqi—had been ferried to Nauru, and for a few years Australian aid and processing fees added millions to Nauruan government coffers. Even this scheme, however, could not patch the gaping hole in Nauru's economy as primary phosphate reserves ran out. Through the 1990s phosphate exports had been in steady decline. In 2000 Nauru did manage to export another 500,000 metric tons. But by 2004 Nauru's phosphate boom was truly over, with exports tallying just 22,000 metric tons.[5]

By then Nauru's economy was in tatters. The government still wasn't collecting income tax, while the public service was by far the main employer of Nauruan nationals. State investments had gone awry, and with years of recurring deficits the government had been borrowing heavily from Nauru's sovereign wealth fund to stay afloat. Struggling to pay public service wages and defaulting on loans, in 2004 the Nauruan government agreed to allow Australia to step back in to manage the country's finances. At the time Australian economist Helen Hughes did not see much complexity behind Nauru's fiscal woes: "They have blown close to two billion." From 1968 to 2002 phosphate earned Nauru A$3.6 billion (in 2000 dollars), with about A$1.8 billion in profits. Invested judiciously, Hughes estimated that Nauru's Trust Fund could have been worth A$8 billion by 2004, with each Nauruan family pocketing A$4 million. Yet by 2004 at most Nauru's Trust Fund was worth A$30 million. Hughes did not lay all the blame on local corruption and incompetence. "There's always the sharks that swim in the

Pacific," she would muse. Nauruans "have a long history of being taken to the cleaners by crooks."[6]

Worse economic news was still to come. In 2005 phosphate exports fell to a record low of 8,000 metric tons. That same year Nauru began to require a "physical presence" to license a bank in the country, effectively ending offshore banking. Nauru had been under intense international pressure to stop money laundering and the granting of economic citizenship—the US government even went as far as using the 2001 Patriot Act, which gives it the power to prohibit American banks from dealing with "rogue state" institutions, to go after Nauru for selling its passports.

Today Nauru is still searching for a place in the world economy. Since 2006 it has upgraded mining equipment and refurbished mining infrastructure to dig out harder-to-reach phosphate. But its phosphate industry, mining around 45,000 metric tons a year, is producing nothing like in the past. Below the sprinkling of primary surface phosphate still left on Topside, Nauru does have secondary reserves of phosphate—perhaps as much as 20 million metric tons. Plans are underway to mine this last remaining phosphate. But no one sees this as a long-term solution for its economic troubles.[7]

## A Colony of Refugees

In 2007 Australia shut its detention camp on Nauru, but reopened it again in 2012. "I've been to Nauru and Nauru is quite a pleasant island," then Australian Prime Minister Tony Abbott said on Australia's *Lateline* in 2013. "Nauru is by no means an unpleasant place to live." Another time Abbott even talked of expanding the Nauru camp to hold as many as 15,000 asylum seekers—this, on an island with no natural water supply. By 2015 there were more than 1,000 asylum seekers—Afghans, Sri Lankans, Pakistanis, Iraqis, Iranians—living in tents fenced in on Topside. Dusty and parched in the dry season, the camp is muddy and miserable in the wet season.

Detainees have gone on hunger strikes and sewn their lips together; in July 2013 a riot broke out, destroying much of the camp. It was quickly rebuilt. Amnesty International's Graham Thom describes the camp as "not only extraordinarily ill-conceived, but cruel." Marianne Evers, an Australian nurse who worked at the camp for three weeks in 2012, broke her confidentiality agreement and spoke out on Australian TV in 2013: "There is absolutely nothing to do. There are no trees. There is no grass. There is not even that many birds there. So we live in that heat without air conditioning in tents. It is just desperation that I can't get out of my head. Of all of them."[8]

Desperation seems to pervade all of Nauru. High unemployment is endemic. Even Nauru's only bank on the island—the Bank of Nauru—shut its doors in 2006. Since then Nauru has been a cash economy, and at home Nauruans no longer have credit cards or checks or savings accounts. Even the island's two bank machines, which allow Nauruans to access overseas bank accounts, frequently run out of Australian dollars, the nation's currency. With few restaurants and only two hotels, Nauru has almost no tourism. Landing by air the island looks alluring; up close, you find rusting cars, rundown houses, and rotting garbage. "Nauruan homes are very basic and often seem partly built," Australian journalist Kathy McLeish wrote in 2013. "Rubbish litters roads and yards, while decades-old infrastructure is broken and left to decay."

Australian aid has long been propping up the Nauruan economy. Offshore fishing licenses provide some government revenue, too—as does selling the remaining phosphate. In recent years bingo is the only private sector activity that's been thriving—and the government is finally trying to tax the game. But it is visa fees that are currently injecting millions of dollars into the country's budget, as Australia pays a monthly fee for each asylum seeker held in the Topside camp.[9]

Excluding asylum seekers, some 10,000 people now reside on Nauru. Almost all food is imported; even fresh water is shipped in when the desalination facility fails to meet needs. Processed and canned food makes up much of a diet heavy in salt, sugar, and artificial ingredients. Nauru has the world's highest obesity rates, with more than two-thirds of Nauruan men and three-quarters of Nauruan women obese. And around a quarter of all Nauruan adults suffer from diabetes. Nauru has very high rates of smoking as well, with no other country having a higher percentage of female smokers. Alcoholism is endemic too, contributing to domestic violence and frequent drunk-driving offenses, even though all of the country's roads cover just 19 miles (30 kilometers).[10]

## Turning Back Time

Since the early 1900s Nauru has lost at least four-fifths of its original vegetation. Over this time Nauru has exported around 80 million metric tons of phosphate. If dump trucks could fly, this amount of phosphate could fill enough trucks to link them bumper to bumper from New York City to Tokyo—and then go back. All of this phosphate came from an island one-third the size of Manhattan.

James Aingimea, a minister of the Nauru Congregational Church who in 1999 passed away at the age of 88, dreamed of turning back time in the last years of his life. "I wish we'd never discovered that phosphate," he lamented in 1995. "I wish Nauru could be like it was before. When I was a boy, it was so beautiful. There were trees. It was green everywhere, and we could eat the fresh coconuts and breadfruit. Now I see what has happened here, and I want to cry." Minister Aingimea's wish will never come true. But he knew that. Already in 1995 he was pondering whether it was finally time to abandon the island. "It would be very sad to leave our native island," he said. "But what else can we do? The land of our ancestors has been destroyed."[11] And climate change is bringing even more troubles to Nauru. Droughts and storms are intensifying, and rising seas are eroding the coastline. One day Topside may be all that remains, a reminder of the folly of greed and the irony of Captain Fearn naming the Nauruan land Pleasant Island.

# 4  The Business of More

Nauru is a microcosm of how demand and desire for more economic growth, more money, and more consumption define world politics. Over the past decade business has been increasingly wrapping this politics in the language of sustainability and corporate social responsibility. Doug McMillon, chief executive officer (CEO) and president of Walmart, talks of this time as a "journey" that began by asking: "What if we started listening to NGOs and even our critics more closely?" After what he describes as a series of "awkward conversations" and "frank meetings," the company, he says, is now at "a much different place," where "some of our critics then are some of our best advisors now."[1]

This growing influence of past critics may sound comforting. So might the growing efficiency of Walmart's operations and supply chains. It may seem even more reassuring to know that the eco-efficiency of hundreds of multinational retailers and brand manufacturers is rising. Yet, as we'll see in this chapter, just about every one of these corporations is investing the savings and profits from sustainability programs in opening more stores (especially in the developing world) as well as in making and marketing more consumer goods, much of which is low-quality, disposable, and discounted. Selling less is unthinkable for the vast majority of firms. Even the outdoor clothing store Patagonia, whose brand has long been its commitment to sustainability, is growing ever bigger.

As sales rise and markets continue to globalize, the eco-business of the world's leading corporations is doing little to lower global energy or resource consumption. Nor is it doing much to decrease global waste or pollution. More often than not what these companies call corporate social responsibility is doing more to protect wealth and privilege than advance sustainability in any ecological sense. At the same time the eco-business of

CSR is serving to legitimize unsustainable global production and consumption as NGO and government allies compliment Fortune 500 companies as sustainability leaders. Those who question the benefits of this manifestation of environmentalism of the rich frequently face scorn and derision. Meanwhile, leading legislators, billionaire executives, and journalists generally ignore—or even mock—calls to limit growth or reduce consumption. More consumption of oil and automobiles grows national economies; growing economies help keep politicians in power in both democracies and authoritarian regimes.

Alongside claims of sustainability, brand companies spend trillions of dollars a year to advertise consumer goods, as the case of Pampers in China will show later in this chapter. Samsung alone budgeted a record $14 billion to market its products in 2013: not far off the gross domestic product of Jamaica that year. Advertising is at the core of the business of generating more sales, profits, and growth. Every waking hour direct and subliminal messaging bombards consumers to want more things. A few advertising rebels, however, are playing a very different game, trying to market the idea of buying nothing.

## A Different Game

Kalle Lasn is not your typical ad man. He will never produce a Super Bowl ad. Nor will he ever win an advertising industry award from The One Club. Leading TV networks decline to air his ads, which ridicule gluttony and tear down conceit. MTV, NBC, CBS, ABC, and Fox News have all refused to broadcast "North American Piggy," not wanting to associate with his message that Americans and Canadians "are the most voracious consumers in the world," and having no desire to urge viewers to "give it a rest." Nor have TV networks been keen to show his Autosaurus ad, which tells viewers, "It's coming, the most significant event in automotive history, it's coming, the end of the age of the automobile." To try to get more air time Lasn has even sued broadcasters in Canada for refusing to accept his advertising money.

Now in his mid-seventies, Lasn is an activist who never seems to stop smiling when he talks. Humor is power in his hands, and he has spent the last quarter of a century satirizing advertisements to inspire consumers to buy less, not more. He is the cofounder of Adbusters, a counterculture magazine and global network set in motion in 1989 to "jam" the world capitalist culture with counter-messaging and anti-advertising, from spoofing TV commercials to lampooning brands. Adbusters has set its sights high: "to topple existing power structures and forge a major rethinking of the way we will live in the 21st century." The nonprofit organization sees capitalism as a source of a global "psycho-financial-eco crisis." And it sees corporate advertisers as "tricksters"; multinationals such as Monsanto and Philip Morris as corrupt and "criminal"; and athletes such as Tiger Woods as brand salesmen in need of "subvertising," which it once did by giving Woods a Nike swoosh grin.

In 2011 Adbusters hit the big time after turning to Twitter (#Occupy-WallStreet) to call on artists and activists to descend on Wall Street on September 17—Lasn's mother's birthday—to rise up peacefully against the greed, malfeasance, and cultural dominance of corporations. Adbusters did not organize or lead this protest. Nor did it try to control the focus or outcomes. The genius of the idea was to inspire a spontaneous, chaotic, and leaderless uprising from below, reaching out to the youth who, in Lasn's words, "are looking into a black-hole future."

The Occupy slogan "We are the 99 percent" caught hold and spread, and by November 2011 as many as a thousand occupations were in place worldwide. By then, however, undercover officers had infiltrated the camps, and police and secret service agencies were videotaping gatherings and corralling and arresting protestors. Following harsh crackdowns worldwide, and without specific demands or leaders, the movement soon began to wane.

Lasn nonetheless sees the Occupy Movement as a success, a life-altering experience for millions of young activists not unlike the student protests of 1968 that changed his own life. With this same optimism Adbusters is continuing to spoof ads and run anti-consumerist campaigns. One of its best publicized campaigns is "Buy Nothing Day," celebrated in North America on the Friday after US Thanksgiving (for 2016, November 24) and on the following day in the rest of the world. Buy Nothing Day calls on consumers to "go cold turkey on consumption for 24 hours." During the rest of the year Adbusters urges campaigners to protest excessive, wasteful, and unnecessary consumption. To wander in a mall as a shopping "zombie." To offer shoppers the free service of cutting up their credit cards. Or perhaps "Occupy Christmas" by purchasing nothing for Christmas, instead relaxing, rejoicing, or having a bit of fun by dressing up as Santa Claus and sitting cross-legged in front of a department store as a "Zenta Claus."

Adbusters claims its Buy Nothing campaign reaches across more than 65 countries. Yet not even Lasn would dispute that consumption of branded products continues to rise everywhere. Nor that some of the messaging against consumerism is backfiring. "Somehow," Lasn lamented in 2013, marketers have "stolen our style."[2]

### The Corporate Style of Sustainability

In 2011 on the day after US Thanksgiving (known as Black Friday) the Patagonia clothing chain pulled off an advertising coup with a full-page ad in the *New York Times* urging consumers "Don't Buy This Jacket," and asking them to "take the pledge to reduce consumption." Patagonia's ad was not meant to reduce its sales: the executive team knew the market would crucify such an act. The company saw a comparative advantage in the durability of its clothing as well as a creative opportunity to enhance brand loyalty. Thirty thousand customers signed the pledge; meanwhile, sales of the jacket, priced at $700, went up. Nor was the ad campaign a sign that Patagonia was scaling back. Fourteen new Patagonia stores opened in fiscal year 2012 (ending April 30). That year revenues rose 30 percent, for the first time exceeding $500 million, two times higher than in 2008, and generating three times the profit. By 2014 Patagonia's annual revenues were hovering around $600 million.

Among brand companies Patagonia is a genuine leader in business responsibility and sustainability. The company assures customers that its "products are produced under safe, fair, legal, and humane working conditions throughout the supply chain." These days just about every brand company is making similar promises. But Patagonia's environmental commitment goes further. The mission set by Patagonia's founder, Yvon Chouinard, is to "use business to inspire and implement solutions to the environmental crisis." To achieve this, the company donates at least 1 percent of its sales revenue to "activists who take radical and strategic steps to protect habitat, oceans and waterways, wilderness and biodiversity."[3]

Yet far more powerful brand companies—such as Walmart with around 800 times the sales of Patagonia—are also now competing hard to project an image of sustainability and responsibility. Walmart calls environmental sustainability an "essential ingredient" of business and has pledged to one day rely solely on renewable energy and generate "zero waste." Walmart is further promising to pursue "sustainable sourcing" and is developing purchasing standards, certifying and auditing suppliers, and tracking compliance within its supply chains. In addition, Walmart is partnering with NGOs and government agencies, as well as with mid-size companies with sustainability missions, such as Patagonia. In 2011, for example, Walmart and Patagonia cofounded the Sustainability Apparel Coalition to develop and measure social and environmental standards for the apparel industry, a coalition including firms such as JC Penney, Target, Levi Strauss, Gap, and Nike, as well as government agencies such as the US Environmental Protection Agency, and nonprofits such as the US Environmental Defense Fund, the US Natural Resources Defense Council, and Fairtrade International. Pulitzer-prize winner Edward Hume even went as far as titling his 2011 book, *The Unlikely Story of Wal-Mart's Green Revolution*.

Other multinational corporations with world brands, such as McDonald's, Nike, and Coca-Cola are making equally strong claims of sustainability. Like Walmart, McDonald's is promising to source ingredients and materials more responsibly, pledging to purchase "sustainable" beef, palm oil, coffee, and fish by 2020. Nike is vowing by 2020 to cut energy inputs, water usage, and waste per product sold as well as eliminate "hazardous chemicals." Coca-Cola has pledged to have a zero water footprint by 2020, and is funding hundreds of sustainability projects as well as partnering with organizations such as WWF, The Nature Conservancy, USAID, and the United Nations Development Programme.

Today it's hard to find a brand company *not* promising a future of "zero deforestation," "100% recycling," "zero waste to landfill," "carbon neutrality," "100% renewable energy," "zero water footprint," and "100% sustainable sourcing." At the 2014 UN Climate Summit, for example, 34 companies—among them Procter & Gamble, Walmart, McDonald's, Nestlé, Kellogg's, Johnson & Johnson, and Marks & Spencer—joined dozens of governments and more than 60 environmental and indigenous groups in signing the New York Declaration on Forests: a nonbinding pledge to replant and restore 350 million hectares of forestlands over the next decade and a half, halve the loss of natural forests by 2020, and "strive to end" deforestation by 2030. At first glance the progress can seem compelling. Firms are packaging products and using energy more efficiently. Recycling rates are rising and waste per product is declining. And codes of conduct and certification audits are improving reporting standards and quality controls within global supply chains.[4]

Yet many of these seeming advances are increasing, not decreasing, consumption, moving the world economy away from what Kalle Lasn and Adbusters see as sustainability. This is hardly surprising given the business of more—more revenues, more stores, more profits—is at the core of what these companies are calling sustainability. The same multinational corporations pursuing eco-business and claiming to be CSR leaders are investing savings from "the efficiency gains of sustainability" in expanding markets to sell more Barbie Dolls, more plastic water bottles, and, as the story of Procter & Gamble in China reveals, more disposable diapers.[5]

## The Golden Sleep

Like other brand corporations, Procter & Gamble, the world's largest consumer goods company, is positioning itself as a global sustainability leader, telling customers it's focusing "on making every day better for people and the planet." With fifty or so brands, the company ranked 100th by revenue turnover ($84.5 billion) on the 2015 Global Fortune 500. Its leading brand is Pampers, with annual sales of more than $10 billion in recent years. Other billion-dollar brands include Tide, Crest, Gillette, Iams, Charmin, Duracell, and Pampers. Saying it has a responsibility "to do the right thing and create change," Procter & Gamble has promised to eliminate waste and conserve energy, water, and natural resources per product sold. Doing the right thing for global retailers, however, means selling more, with strong financial incentives to create—and then expand—markets for nondurable and disposable products.

Consider the history of Pampers in China. Procter & Gamble entered China's diaper market in 1998. Back then most parents in China were either not using diapers or were using cloth diapers for their babies. After six months parents would then switch to putting their baby in pants with a split at the back (worn without a diaper). Early toilet training was common; plastic and paper diapers were rare. To try to develop a market for disposable diapers, Procter & Gamble introduced an inexpensive and lower-quality version of Pampers. Sales were poor, however: consumers saw little need for disposable diapers, especially ones with a reputation for being itchy and leaky.

In 2006 Procter & Gamble again tried to develop a diaper market in China with Pampers Cloth Like & Dry, softer and drier than its 1998 version. To market the new-and-improved diaper Procter & Gamble hired the advertising and public relations agency Porter Novelli. "Everything we do at Porter Novelli," the company assures prospective clients, "is designed to achieve one goal: to transform the opinions, beliefs, and behaviors of those who matter most to our clients." Porter Novelli was quick to identify for Procter & Gamble what Chinese parents most wanted: sleep and a healthy, smart baby. In 2007 Procter & Gamble began advertising Pampers as a way to give a baby a "golden sleep": telling parents that P&G researchers, working with the Beijing Children's Hospital, had found that Chinese babies wearing Pampers fell asleep more quickly, slept 30 minutes longer, and slept more soundly (with 50 percent less sleep disturbance). Longer and deeper sleeps, P&G assured parents across China, improves a baby's cognitive development—and of course gives hardworking (and deserving) parents a better sleep, too.

Procter & Gamble spent hundreds of millions of dollars to market Pampers in China. Ads inundated primetime TV and major cities. Store promotions and a social media campaign targeted new mothers in particular. Ingeniously, mothers were encouraged to upload onto the company's Chinese website a photograph of their baby sleeping in Pampers: not only "proving" the sleep benefits of Pampers, but also generating free publicity after Procter & Gamble set a Guinness World Record for the world's biggest photomontage by displaying in a Shanghai store a 7,000-square-foot montage of more than 100,000 babies.

Sales of Pampers jumped more than 50 percent in the first year of the Golden Sleep campaign. By 2010 the Chinese disposable diaper market was worth $3 billion. Ten Pampers factories were built in China to supply the now booming market (and reduce shipping and manufacturing costs). Today Pampers is the top-selling disposable diaper in China, with annual sales of around 5 billion diapers, and in 2013 comprising just over 40 percent of the market share. This market dominance, however, may not last for long. Domestic brands, high-end diapers from Japan and Korea, and traditional rivals such as Kimberly-Clark's Huggies are competing fiercely in a market roughly equal in 2013 to America's and twice the size of Japan's. Such competition is further increasing demand for disposable diapers in China, and analysts are predicting that sales will double from 2013 to 2020—to about 2 billion diapers a month.[6]

**Selling More**

Pampers first went on sale in 1961. Now the world's leading diaper brand, Pampers are made in more than 25 countries, and across more than 100 countries around 25 million babies wear them every year. As in China, Procter & Gamble is striving to expand markets in the developing world. In rural India, for instance, P&G baby-care "advisors" are going door to door to give away samples of Pampers, urging mothers not to see disposable diapers as a "lazy" option, but as the scientifically proven best choice for a baby's sleep and development.

With one of the world's largest marketing and advertising budgets (around $9–10 billion a year), Procter & Gamble is working equally hard to increase sales of its other brands. One example is Bounty, which in 2013 accounted for 45 percent of the American paper towel market. That year the company launched "Bounty DuraTowel" to try to expand this market—a product that P&G's 2013 annual report trumpets "is 3 times cleaner than a germy dish towel and is boldly asking consumers to 'Ditch their dish towels!'" The tests to confirm the cleaning power of Bounty DuraTowels, P&G reassures customers with a "factsheet," was in "a secure P&G lab."[7]

Procter & Gamble's efforts to grow bigger and expand sales are no different than other Fortune 500 manufacturers and retailers claiming to be sustainability leaders. Nestlé's legacy in the developing world of substituting its infant formula for breast-milk is notorious. So is the ongoing strategy of Philip Morris—a company Lasn calls his "mortal enemy" and "vow[s] to take down" in the dedication of his book *Culture Jam*—to sell cigarettes in poor countries to offset lawsuits and declining sales in wealthy ones. But similar marketing stories to manufacture consumption—regardless of need or social and environmental costs—could easily be told of Walmart, Home Depot, Target, and Costco. Or Royal Dutch Shell, ExxonMobil, and BP. Or Apple, Samsung, and Hewlett-Packard. Or General Electric, CVS, and Kroger. Or Coca-Cola, Pepsi, McDonald's, and Starbucks. Or Toyota, Volkswagen, General Motors, Daimler, and Ford. Not growing can quickly take down a company. Even a decline in sales of one leading brand can cause share prices to tumble: a fact that has kept Mattel, the world's biggest toy-maker, scrambling for decades as sales of its Barbie brand keep sliding, from $1.8 billion in 1997 to $1.2 billion in 2013 to $1 billion in 2014.

Still, well over 1 billion Barbies have been sold since the doll debuted in 1959. Other brands are chasing similar sales. As of 2014 Sony had sold more than 340 million PlayStation video game consoles. Apple had sold over 500 million iPhones and 210 million iPads. Sales of Pzifer's drug Lipitor had exceeded $140 billion. And Toyota had sold more than 40 million Corollas. Sales of just about everything keep climbing. About 250 million vehicles—cars, SUVs, buses, light trucks, and motorcycles—were on the world's roads in 1970. By the mid-1980s there were about 500 million vehicles. In 2010 the number of vehicles went over 1 billion—with emerging economies such as China and Brazil leading new registrations. Given trends, the number of vehicles looks set to exceed 2 billion by 2020.[8]

## The Economy of Growth

To survive, capitalism needs to expand production and markets. Karl Marx (1818–1883) made this point back in the 1800s. Over the past two decades we can see this in the growing profits from making, marketing, and retailing consumer goods and services, as well as from supplying the energy to manufacture, transport, and use consumer products. By 2012 the market value of the world's goods and services was at $72 trillion—up from about $32 trillion in 2000, a striking rise even when accounting for inflation. The United States is a giant in this world economy, although China is gaining fast. In 2012 America's gross domestic product (GDP) was $15.7 trillion: that year approximately the same as the combined GDPs of Germany, France, the United Kingdom, Brazil, Russia, India, and Mexico. Still, since 2000 the rise of China as the hub of world manufacturing and as a market for consumer goods and services has been shifting the world economy toward Asia. China's GDP—$8.4 trillion in 2012—grew sevenfold from 2000 to 2012. China might seem to still have a long way to go to catch the United States. Yet at these rates of growth China's GDP could surpass America's within a decade or so.[9]

The burning of oil and gas and coal are powering this growth—as well as, of course, causing climate change. The world's multinational oil companies are turning over record-high revenues. Royal Dutch Shell generated $431 billion in revenue in fiscal year 2015 (ending March 31), ranking as the world's second biggest company on the 2015 Fortune Global 500. Oil and gas companies from the emerging economies have also come onto the world stage. China's Sinopec Group ranked second at $447 billion; China National Petroleum was fourth at $429 billion; Russia's Gazprom was twenty-sixth at a little over $144 billion; and Brazil's Petrobas was twenty-eighth at a little under $144 billion. Most of the world's biggest oil and gas companies, however, still come from Europe or North America. With $383 billion in revenues, America's ExxonMobil ranked fifth on the 2015 Fortune Global 500, while British Petroleum (BP) was sixth with $359 billion. France's Total was eleventh at $212 billion; America's Chevron was twelfth at $204 billion; America's Phillips 66 was twenty-third at $149 billion; and Italy's ENI was twenty-fifth at $147 billion.

The globalization of markets is also allowing for record-high revenues among big-box retailers and brand manufacturers. With record-setting revenues of $486 billion, Walmart ranked first on the 2015 Fortune Global 500. Samsung ranked thirteenth at $196 billion in revenues, while Apple was fifteenth with $183 billion in revenues (with $39.5 billion in profits, making it the world's most profitable company). Many of the best-known automakers are in this pack of corporations, too. Volkswagen was eighth, with revenues of $269 billion; Toyota was ninth at $248 billion; Daimler was seventeenth at $172 billion; the EXOR Group (which includes the Fiat Chrysler brand) was nineteenth at $162; General Motors was twenty-first at $156 billion; and Ford was twenty-seventh at $144 billion.

Sales for the Fortune 500 companies are growing at an even faster rate than the world economy. The combined revenue of the world's top 30 companies for the year 2013 was more than three-and-a-half times higher than it was in 2000.[10]

## The Inequality of Wealth

Comparing the overall wealth of big oil, big retail, and big auto with the wealth of ordinary consumers gives a sense of the inequity of the growing concentration of wealth. Revenues of just the top ten Global Fortune 500 companies in 2014 were three times higher than what the world's poorest 2 billion people lived on that year. Walmart's revenues alone exceeded what the world's poorest 1 billion people lived on that year.[11]

Wealth is concentrating as well among business executives. There were about 140 billionaires in 1986 (excluding dictators and monarchs). That number rose steadily over the next two decades, reaching 1125 in 2008.

The global financial crisis took a swipe at their fortunes, leaving fewer than 800 billionaires in 2009. But this setback did not last long. Since 2010 the surging economies of China, India, Brazil, and Russia have recharged the global economy. A record 1826 billionaires made the 2015 Forbes Billionaires list—with a combined net worth of $7 trillion in March 2015 (up $600 billion from 2014, a year with a then-record 1645 billionaires).

Being American is still a big advantage in accumulating wealth: 536 Americans made the 2015 Forbes Billionaires list. That year 15 of the top 20 billionaires were American. Together, these 15 billionaires were worth more than $647 billion, a total higher than the gross domestic products of more than 170 countries in 2013. This does not mean that some people in developing countries have not become fabulously rich. Mexico's Carlos Slim Helu ranked second on the 2015 Forbes Billionaires list with a net worth of a little over $77 billion.

At the start of 2015, the richest 42 corporate executives were worth roughly what one-third of humanity earns each year. Such inequality and wealth concentration is deeply problematic for global sustainability. Billionaires such as Bill Gates and Warren Buffett both express a desire to help the less fortunate. And both are giving back some of their fortunes. By 2014 Gates had donated more than $28 billion and Buffett more than $25 billion. By then the endowment of the Melinda and Bill Gates Foundation was over $40 billion, with the Foundation providing around $3.5 billion a year in grants. In addition, in 2010 Gates and Buffett officially launched the "Giving Pledge," which "is a commitment by the world's wealthiest individuals and families to dedicate the majority of their wealth to philanthropy."

Yet corporate philanthropy is doing little to correct the extremes of globalization and the escalating sustainability crisis. Consider the salaries, cash bonuses, compensation packages, and stock gains of corporate America a few years after the 2008 global financial crisis. In 2011 the average pay of the top 500 CEOs was over $10 million—16 percent higher than in 2010. In 2012 Apple CEO Timothy D. Cook took home around $144 million; Starbucks CEO Howard Schultz received nearly $118 million. That year no American came close, however, to Mark Zuckerberg, who as CEO of Facebook netted compensation close to $2.3 billion.[12]

Gates and Buffett, moreover, for all of their generosity and leadership on the ethics of billionaires "giving" back their fortunes, remain at or near the top of the world's richest entrepreneurs. And their wealth keeps rising.

In 2015 Gates once again topped the Forbes list of the World's Billionaires, worth $79.2 billion, while Buffet was third at $72.7 billion. Compared to many billionaires Gates lives frugally. He does not own a luxury yacht. But he does own a jet and a vacation island in Belize. And his home on Lake Washington near Seattle does seem to have an excess of bathrooms: twenty-four.

**Buy Nothing**

For environmentalists such as Kalle Lasn, encouraging consumers to take more responsibility for the future is a tough sell. In a rare chance on American primetime TV he spoke with CNN's Carol Costello to plug "Buy Nothing Day," which, as mentioned, in the US falls on the day after Thanksgiving, or Black Friday.

"Black Friday is like a tradition," said Costello. "People love to go out on this day and shop. We absolutely love it. Why do you want them to quit shopping?"

"But, but think about it," said Lasn. "... Those millions of people who went shopping today, I think what they're missing is, they don't quite understand the consequences of their consumption. Because overconsumption has ecological consequences. You know, that, uh, overconsumption is in some sense the mother of all our environmental problems."

"Oh, come on! Environmental problems?"

"Yes, environmental problems! Every single purchase that you make has some kind of an impact on the planet. ... I believe that overconsumption in the rich countries of the world is one of the root causes of terrorism. I believe that this huge inequity ..."

"Oh, come on, come on," Costello interrupted with a smile, "if somebody wants to buy their kid an Elmo doll, what's the harm in that?"[13]

# 5   Consuming the Earth

Tickle Me Elmo first went on sale in the summer of 1996. Children adored how the cuddly Sesame Street Muppet laughed when tickled, and stores across North America quickly began to run out of stock. With Christmas approaching, parents shouted at store staff to find them an Elmo doll; here and there fisticuffs broke out among overly eager customers. Elmo dolls began to sell on the black market for hundreds of dollars. Shoppers trampled one poor Walmart clerk with an Elmo doll in hand, breaking his ribs and knocking him out cold. "The crotch," he would later mourn, "was yanked out of my brand-new jeans." A million Elmo dolls had sold by Christmas. By then Mattel was taking over Tyco Toys, the company that owned Elmo. The following year Mattel was able to sell 7 million Tickle Me Elmos. Other fads would soon overtake Tickle Me Elmo, but the Elmo line of dolls has continued to sell well, even after Hasbro took over production from Mattel in 2011.

Doll sales are of course small change compared to the sales of cars or electronics or condos. Automakers sold more than 87 million new vehicles in 2015: 14 million more than in 2010.[1] What indeed, as CNN's Carol Costello asked Kalle Lasn of Adbusters, is the harm of buying an Elmo doll? After all, as her question was hinting at, any sale of anything is surely a sign of prosperity, of jobs and economic growth—all of which citizens want, and arguably even demand of their political leaders. Yet, as Lasn was trying to ask CNN viewers, are there no ecological limits on the globalization of economic growth and personal consumption? Is no one responsible for overconsumption, wasteful consumption, and intensifying ecological footprints?

Some consumers are certainly trying to take more personal responsibility. Certification and eco-labeling programs, such as Fairtrade and the

Marine Stewardship Council, are helping consumers somewhat. So are NGO campaigns to expose shoddy corporate practices. And so are some government policies (e.g., rebates for installing home insulation) and corporate mechanisms (e.g., websites to trace food supply chains back to farmers). As I'll demonstrate in this chapter, however, rising ecological footprints and unsustainable consumption are causing severe ecological strains—and, as I'll develop even further in my later chapters, the world's unwillingness and inability to tackle the problem of consumption in any serious way explains much of why environmentalism of the rich is failing to rein in the escalating global sustainability crisis.

## Unsustainable Consumption

Humans have always changed ecosystems to support consumption. This is our comparative advantage over other animals, and helps explain why we're so adaptable and prolific as a species. Yet the past 500 years, and especially the last hundred, have seen something different going on, with the range, speed, and power of impacts becoming truly global in scale—what the historian J. R. McNeill describes as "the screeching acceleration of so many processes that bring ecological change."[2]

Consumption began to take off in the late 1700s and 1800s during the British Industrial Revolution. Cheap energy and technological advances spurred economic expansion. Cotton and sugar plantations spread across the colonized world. Fishing and whaling fleets trawled the oceans; miners and loggers plundered the tropics; and European traders traversed the oceans. Clothes and exotic food became more accessible and affordable in cities such as London, Paris, Berlin, and New York. Already by 1899 the American economist Thorstein Veblen was writing of the emergence of a "leisure class" and the rise of "conspicuous consumption."[3] Long before the nineteenth century, emperors and popes had, of course, been seizing foreign lands to appropriate resources; however, by the beginning of the twentieth century capitalism and consumerism had become driving forces of global integration, gaining strength after World War II and then again after the end of the Cold War in the early 1990s. Across the world sustaining economic growth has become necessary for stability and legitimacy: for getting elected and reelected in democracies; for the willingness of military officers to back a dictator; for the endurance of communism without resorting to the tyranny of a North Korea.

This does not mean that the making of one world market is over. At least to some extent states and communities still regulate foreign investors and trade to try to protect local commerce, jobs, and cultures. Yet the politics, ideologies, and institutions of today's world order ingrain a belief in—and the need for—more open economies. To grow these economies, corporate and political interests distort information, limit options, and steer consumers toward particular choices. Meanwhile, increasing numbers of consumers expect, and indeed demand, more goods and services, including both low-priced and luxury options.

Consumers in these economies look more and more alike. They eat chicken, beef, and pork; they drink colas and bottled water; they wear suits, jeans, and sneakers. The better-off own computers and cell phones, and drive cars and regularly fly overseas. The similarity of so many consumers is why the world has more than 20 billion chickens and 15,000 KFC restaurants across more than 100 countries. This is why more than 1.4 billion cattle graze the earth and every day 34,000 McDonald's restaurants serve 69 million customers across 118 countries. And this is why Coca-Cola is able to market 500 different brands and each day sell 1.9 billion servings across every country (although smugglers do the selling in North Korea).

The globalization of Western-style consumerism further explains why in 2012 sales of PVH's Calvin Klein brand earned $7.6 billion across more than 100 countries and its Tommy Hilfiger brand hit $6 billion in sales across more than 90 countries. It explains why Nike can generate annual sales of around $25 billion across 190 countries. It explains why more than 7 billion cell phones are in active use worldwide and why Apple had sold more than half-a-billion iPhones by 2014. And it explains why consumers in China and India are leading the buying charge for Buicks, Volkswagens, Hondas, Toyotas, Hyundais, Fords, Fiats, and BMWs—and why the world is heading toward as many as 3 billion cars on its roads by 2050.[4] The working poor tend to buy more fast food, unbranded products, and discounted goods than high-income earners. Of course many affluent people shop in stores such as Walmart and Costco and Target. But it's mostly the rapid worldwide growth in lower- and middle-class consumers that is allowing discount retailers to prosper.

Walmart is the world's leading discount retailer. Back in 1979 it turned over $1 billion in revenues. Since then it has taken the world by storm. Now, with a workforce of 2.2 million and more than 11,000 retail outlets worldwide, it's by far America's largest private employer. And Walmart is continuing to grow, with, as mentioned, revenues in fiscal year 2015 setting another record high of $486 billion. Walmart is maintaining its position as the world's largest company by expanding especially quickly in China; as of mid-2014, the company was operating more than 400 Walmart Supercenters, Sam's Clubs, and discount stores across 170 Chinese cities, with plans to open another 100 stores in China by the end of 2016. Walmart is working as well to expand across the rest of the developing world—for example, in 2011 acquiring Massmart, which at the time was operating 350 stores in South Africa and Sub-Saharan Africa.[5]

Every week at least 100 million customers go through a Walmart checkout. To stock its stores Walmart relies on a worldwide network of more than a hundred thousand suppliers. Long supply chains provide flexibility and create savings. But these also tend to conceal social and ecological costs. Even more worrying, as consumer goods traverse continents and oceans, and as firms take risks to try to gain competitive advantages and capture new markets, these costs tend to drift into the most fragile ecosystems and vulnerable communities, often with unclear and unknown risks that can last for generations. Most consumers are unaware of, and feel little responsibility for, the environmental risks and damage of consumption in other countries and for future generations. A commercialization of values—reinforced through advertising and branding—is further weakening efforts to promote social justice, economic equality, and ecological integrity.

At the same time, supplying consumer products is increasingly necessary for political success and social stability. Even revolutions must mollify consumers. Consider the politics of Venezuela after Hugo Chávez, leader of the "Bolivarian Revolution," and president of Venezuela from 1998 until dying of cancer in 2013. After promising to continue the revolution President Nicolás Maduro put in place price and currency controls on basic goods when he was elected in April 2013. Just a month later Venezuela was thrown into crisis when toilet paper ran low. Counterrevolutionary forces were causing "excessive demand," grumbled Commerce Minister Alejandro Fleming, then proclaiming: "The revolution will bring the country the equivalent of 50 million rolls of toilet paper. We are going to saturate the market so our people calm down."[6]

Of course the consequences for global sustainability of a person using toilet paper in Venezuela are not nearly as great as a person shopping along London's Oxford Street or New York's Madison Avenue. And the global consequences of consuming depend on where you reside, how much you earn, how much power you wield, and what you actually do. Still, we cannot escape the hard reality that the ecological footprints of individuals and economies are continuing to rise as markets and brands globalize. Nor can we escape the hard reality that humanity's footprint is already well above the earth's capacity to regenerate itself and very few high-income consumers are living within their fair earth share.[7]

## The Footprint of Consumption

Making and transporting so many consumer goods is requiring increasing amounts of timber, minerals, land, food, and water. Using consumer products entails further environmental costs. Consider the consequences for water usage in North American households. An average toilet in North America requires 6–30 liters per flush. Per cycle a washing machine uses 170–190 liters, while a dishwasher uses 40–55 liters. And a typical shower sprays out 5–19 liters per minute. Even a dripping faucet can drain away 280–750 liters of water every week. In total an average North American residence consumes around 350,000 liters of water a year.[8]

Calculating the full environmental costs of consumption is hard to capture in a simple or single statistic. The concept of "ecological footprint," which Bill Rees and Mathis Wackernagel developed at the University of British Columbia, offers some insight. Using United Nations data, ecological footprint analysis tries to assess how much cropland, forestland, fishing grounds, grazing pasture, built-up land, and carbon sinks it takes to support a national economy, converting this into the average "global hectares" of productive land and sea that each person is using to live (a country's per capita ecological footprint).

Ecological footprint analysis is a helpful way to start to understand the consequences of consumption. But we need to keep in mind that it only includes "measureable" resources and waste flows, and doesn't capture the full impact of personal decisions and lifestyle. Doing so in one statistic is

impossible: there are simply too many people, making too many different choices, in too many different settings, with too many diverse consequences. Also, as advocates readily admit, footprint analysis concentrates
on the consequences of consumption of renewable resources and does not
capture well many of the other effects of our lives: biodiversity loss, chemical pollution, and plastic garbage, to name just a few issues. Moreover, as
we'll see in the next chapter, the concept of ecological footprint does not
capture much of the indirect—or unintentional—or unknown—shadow
effects of consumption that can take years, decades, or even generations to
appear, as was the case of chlorofluorocarbons (CFCs) drifting skyward from
refrigerators, air conditioners, and hairsprays to deplete the ozone layer.

Still footprint analysis does help us to compare (very roughly) the environmental impact of consumption across countries as well as get a general
sense of what would be a person's (and country's) fair earth share. Worldwide, the average individual footprint is about 2.7 global hectares. National
averages range widely (as do personal footprints within countries). The
national average across Africa is around 1.5, while it's 4.7 in the UK, 6.4 in
Canada, and 7.2 in the United States. In addition, footprint analysis allows
researchers to compare (again, very roughly) the global ecological footprint
with the earth's productive biocapacity, which, as those who conduct footprint analysis measure it, was around 12 billion hectares in 2010. That year
humanity's ecological footprint was over 18 billion hectares—at least 2.5
times higher than in the early 1960s, and at least 1.5 times above the earth's
capacity to regenerate renewable resources and assimilate waste. Even if we
assume total biocapacity is holding at 12 billion hectares (unlikely given
declining global environmental conditions), at best a person's fair earth
share in 2016 would be around 1.6 hectares; yet high-income earners typi-
cally consume 3–6 times that amount.[9]

The consequences of the rising global footprint for the earth's 8–9 million species have been devastating. Each day another 10 to 500 species of
fungi, bacteria, protists, plants, corals, and insects go extinct, on top of the
at least 600 species of mammals, birds, reptiles, amphibians, and fish lost
over the past 500 years (far above "natural" rates of extinction). The near
future will bring even greater rates of extinction. Already, more than 40
percent of amphibians, 25 percent of mammals, and 13 percent of birds are
under threat of extinction. And some of these are on the brink of extinction. Just four northern white rhinos, for instance, remained after the death

of one in a Czech zoo in July 2015: one in the San Diego Zoo and three in Kenya's Ol Pejeta Conservancy. On our current trajectory some scientists are even warning of the possible loss of three-quarters of all species over the next two centuries.[10]

At the same time the populations of many species have crashed or are crashing. Since 1970 the populations of more than 4,000 species of birds, mammals, fish, amphibians, and reptiles have fallen on average by more than half. Like the Atlantic cod, more than half of commercial fish species are now in biological crisis (exploited to below 10 percent of their initial population). Another one-third of commercial fisheries are nearing this state as overfishing, pollution, and climate change combine to deplete stocks. Ocean life in general is in crisis, with sharks, whales, and dolphins, among many other species, under severe threat. The decline of seabirds is a telling sign of the severity of the crisis. Since 1950 roughly 70 percent of all seabirds have been wiped out—hunted for food, tangled in fishing gear, dying in oil spills, poisoned by plastic garbage and toxic sludge, and unable to adapt to climate change. Blast fishing, inshore pollution, ocean acidification, and climate change are imperiling the coral reefs as well. Already, a fifth of the world's coral reefs are too damaged to ever recover, while around half of what's left is heading quickly toward the same fate.[11]

Tropical rainforests are similarly in crisis. More than half have been cleared since 1950, and, despite some local successes in reducing the loss of tree cover in countries such as Indonesia and Brazil, since 2000 the overall rate of tropical deforestation has continued to rise steadily as forest loss accelerates in West Africa, the Mekong region of Southeast Asia, and the Gran Chaco region of South America. In 2014, as much as 10 million hectares of tropical forest—more than the total area of Hungary—was irreparably degraded or cleared for timber, palm oil plantations, soy plantations, and cattle ranches. Just 15 percent of the remaining rainforests still have the ecological integrity to retain full biodiversity. At least half of all primate species—including apes, lemurs, monkeys, and orangutans—are heading toward extinction. And this is but a small sign of the catastrophic loss of biodiversity as at least half of all terrestrial species are indigenous to tropical forests.[12]

Deforestation more generally is contributing as well to soil erosion, water disturbances, and climate change—with, for example, net annual forest loss accounting for something like 15 percent of total yearly anthropogenic carbon emissions.[13] Overconsumption, dams, and irrigation for industrial agriculture are further stressing global freshwater supplies. So are desertification, droughts, biofuels, and overgrazing—each year leaving another 12 million hectares of land unsuitable for cultivation. And so is the loss of more than half of the world's wetlands. Today, more than 1 billion people do not have sufficient fresh water; another 2–3 billion people go at least one month a year without enough fresh water. Rivers, lakes, and aquifers are drying up around the world; and many are severely polluted from sewage, industrial waste, garbage, pesticides, and chemical fertilizers. The United Nations is projecting an even more severe freshwater crisis by 2025: with 1.8 billion "living with absolute water scarcity" and two-thirds of the global population living with water shortages.[14]

Manufacturing and industrial farming are contaminating every ecosystem with hazardous waste, toxic pesticides, and persistent organic pollutants. The chemical industry has grown by leaps and bounds over the past half century. Back in 1970 chemical output was worth around $170 billion; four decades later output was worth well over $4 trillion. Sales of chemicals doubled from 2000 to 2010 as demand soared across the emerging economies. At least 144,000 chemicals are now in commercial use—and every week companies concoct more compounds to "improve" production processes and consumer products. International agreements and domestic regulations are doing little to slow the rising mountains of hazardous and toxic waste. Every year, for instance, sees another 45–50 million tons of electronic waste pile up as hundreds of millions of consumers upgrade computers, cell phones, televisions, microwaves, dishwashers, and many other electrical products. Of this amount just 6–8 million tons are recycled fully and safely. Much of the world's e-waste ends up in Asia and Africa for disposal and unsafe salvaging.[15]

The garbage from everyday living is reaching even the most remote spots on earth. Vast graveyards of plastic debris now swirl in the North Pacific Ocean, growing bigger by the day as plastic bottles, plastic bags, and plastic toys wash off the lands of North America and Asia, breaking down into tiny plastic beads en route to the calm gyres of the Pacific. The Arctic, already undergoing severe ecological disturbances from global warming, is now polluted with DDT (dichlorodiphenyltrichloroethane), PCBs (polychlorinated biphenyls), and dioxins as these (and other) persistent organic pollutants from pesticides, incinerators, and industrial processes "grasshopper" across the planet on air currents (in a process of evaporation and condensation) until settling in cold climates and then bioaccumulating in wildlife and people.[16]

Over this century, warmer temperatures, melting glaciers, rising seas, and violent storms will inflict even more damage to the world's ecosystems, as well as put the world's poorest and most vulnerable people at even greater risk. How much damage and suffering this will bring is still anyone's guess. The models of leading climate scientists are becoming more intricate and precise, however, and the growing consensus is deeply worrying. One example among many is a 2015 analysis by former NASA scientist James Hansen, who, along with his 16 coauthors, concluded that even an increase of 2 degrees Celsius above preindustrial levels could be "highly dangerous" for the stability of the oceans, possibly causing sea levels to rise as much as 10 feet by the end of this century with consequences far worse than the worst-case scenarios modeled by the Intergovernmental Panel on Climate Change.[17]

Such biological trends and possibilities do not bode well for a world with rapidly rising consumption and where multinational corporations are upheld as sustainability leaders. As the Global Footprint Network calculates, if one day everyone were to consume like Americans do today "we would need 5 planets." Saving our "one planet" has been a rallying cry of environmentalists since at least the 1960s. Progress in the world's wealthiest places, however, has been far greater than in the poorest regions, and when world demand for "natural resources" from a poor or politically weak region is high or rising, as in much of the tropics and high seas, successes have been rare, and often short-lived. Moreover, humanity is not only overconsuming the earth's resources, it's filling the oceans and lands and skies with toxins and waste. One of the greatest failings of environmentalism of the rich, as I explore next, has been controlling the unclear and long-term risks of introducing new products, technologies, and chemicals in the pursuit of economic growth, new markets, and corporate profits.

# 6 Gambling with the Future

Environmentalists have long dedicated themselves to exposing environmental crimes and corruption. Offenses and dishonesty pervade every jurisdiction. Companies dump toxic sludge into rivers, violate air emission standards, and spray banned pesticides onto crops. And criminal gangs poach bear gallbladders, smuggle ivory tusks, fish coral reefs with dynamite, and log wildlife sanctuaries for mahogany. Investigating such crimes is risky work and murders of environmentalists are common—with politicians and police often complicit. Environmental crimes cause extensive damage. But so does legal risk-taking, where firms conceal, disregard, or miscalculate the potential of new products, chemicals, or technologies to harm the health of people and ecosystems. Environmental measures have managed to treat some of the symptoms of legal risk-taking by business, such as through better government procedures and industry technologies to clean up oil spills and handle chemical leaks. Yet, as we'll see in this chapter, more precaution is clearly necessary to stop corporations from "experimenting" on consumers and gambling with the future.

Without a strong precautionary principle, high levels of uncertainty make it very hard for environmentalists to influence legal risk-taking, as is the case, for instance, with the advocacy campaigns for more safeguards when introducing new chemicals, artificial food ingredients, genetically modified organisms, and nanotechnology. The complexity of global systems and the slow process of scientific inquiry mean it can take decades, even generations, before enough certainty forms to enrage citizens and convince regulators to intervene to ban unsafe products and technologies. Over this time vested interests may well fund research to "reconfirm" the value and safety of profitable industries, as well as disseminate misinformation, sponsor anti-environmentalism, lobby politicians, sue critics, ally with moderate NGOs, and appease with philanthropy the concerns and environmental movements of the rich. Moreover, as we see time and again, once one jurisdiction begins to restrict consumer sales or lucrative technologies—as was the case, for instance, with leaded gasoline from the 1970s to the early 2000s—firms profiting from risk-taking tend to react by expanding into jurisdictions with weaker regulations.

Corporate risk-taking in the pursuit of profit and competitive advantages can threaten the future of the earth itself. Few stories illustrate this better than the career of the industry scientist, Thomas Midgley Jr. We've known Midgley's story for many decades now. Yet, as this chapter illuminates, the need for a strong precautionary principle in environmental governance is even more urgent today as even more corporations—with even greater power and global reach—continue to take extraordinary risks with the global environment and people's health, all the while reassuring governments and consumers that they are now responsible and sustainable.

### The Genius of Midgley

No idea was too wacky for Thomas Midgley Jr., born in 1889 in Beaver Falls, Pennsylvania. An avid golfer, he long dreamed of patenting a ball able to sail a mile off the tee. A self-trained chemist, he once tried putting a dollop of melted butter into a gas tank while searching for a way to get rid of engine "knock" for General Motors (at that time partially owned by DuPont). This failed to do much more than give a buttery flavor to the gasoline. Yet null results and setbacks never seemed to discourage him. After testing thousands of more substances, he did eventually find a way to eliminate engine knock, in 1921 creating "ethyl gasoline," for which he was inducted into the American Inventors Hall of Fame in 2003.

During his lifetime Midgley was showered with medals and awards. He won the American Chemical Society's 1923 Nichols Medal; the Society of Chemical Industry's 1937 Perkin Medal; and the American Chemical Society's 1941 Priestly Medal and 1942 Willard Gibbs Award. A degree in mechanical engineering from Cornell University, however, did not prevent him from making some tragic miscalculations. After polio partially paralyzed him in 1940, he built a device of ropes and pulleys to lift himself out of bed. Four years later he would die, strangled by his contraption.

Midgley never did come to know of the full calamity of his genius. Controversy did engulf ethyl gasoline soon after it went to market in 1923. In the end Midgley had put a far deadlier substance into the gasoline than butter: tetraethyl lead, which, as an aghast Erik Krause of Germany's Potsdam Institute of Technology would warn Midgley after hearing of the discovery, was "a creeping and malicious poison."[1] Who would even consider spewing such a lethal poison out of the exhaust of millions of automobiles? The very idea struck some health specialists, including David Edsall, the dean of Harvard's School of Public Health, as sheer folly, if not utter madness.

In response to the controversy, the US government's Bureau of Mines rushed to conduct tests for General Motors and DuPont (with GM providing funds) on the safety of ethyl gasoline. For 3–6 hours a day researchers pumped ethyl gas exhaust into a chamber crammed with rabbits, guinea pigs, pigeons, monkeys, and dogs. One dog did get away. And another dog did die, as did many of the rabbits and guinea pigs. But the exhaust, the Bureau of Mines concluded, did not seem to cause any of these deaths. After eight months all of the surviving animals seemed just fine: for the Bureau of Mines proof enough of the safety of what Frank Howard, a vice president at Standard Oil of New Jersey (renamed Exxon in 1973), told the world was a "gift of god."[2]

The sale of ethyl gasoline continued even as refinery workers grew sick. Public anxiety was already high by the time five Standard Oil workers died in a single week in October of 1924. Before long, the state of New Jersey and the cities of New York, Philadelphia, and Pittsburg had banned ethyl gasoline. To air concerns a conference was held in New York in May 1925. During a break in the conference proceedings, Alice Hamilton, Harvard University's first female professor and a world authority on occupational health and toxicology, did not hold back when spotting Midgley's boss, Charles Kettering. "You are nothing but a murderer," she fumed.[3]

Advocates of ethyl gas fought back. H. C. Parmalee, editor of *Chemical and Metallurgical Engineering*, lashed out at critics in the *New York Times*, calling them "incompetent" and "hysterical" and "misguided zealots." Conference delegates had heard enough concerns, however, to decide to strike a committee under the US Surgeon General to investigate further. In the meantime, the Ethyl Gasoline Corporation, which General Motors and Standard Oil (which held a patent for manufacturing tetraethyl lead) formed in 1923 to market ethyl gasoline, agreed to suspend sales.[4]

This committee was tilted toward the interests of DuPont, General Motors, and Standard Oil. Its verdict, issued in early 1926, was predictable: on the balance of evidence, there were "no good grounds for prohibiting the use of ethyl gasoline." Harvard's David Edsall, a dissenting member of the committee, called the findings "half-baked." But the debate was over. Sales of ethyl gasoline resumed in May 1926. And by the mid-1930s around 70 percent of gasoline in the US was "leaded."[5]

## The Slow Awakening

For the next four decades industry-backed research would repeatedly "confirm" the safety of leaded gasoline. Warning sirens did not go off until the mid-1960s when Clair Patterson, a geochemist renowned for dating the age of the earth at 4.55 billion years, discovered that lead levels of Americans were 100 times higher than was natural. Leaded exhaust, the world would learn by the early 1970s, was not only poisoning soils and the atmosphere, but was the source of a full-blown health crisis, impairing the cognitive development of children in particular. By then more than 90 percent of US gasoline was leaded, with sales taking off in the rest of the world. Over the next three decades the leaded gasoline industry would fight to counter critics and legislators, lobbying politicians, funding research, suing regulatory agencies, and ramping up exports to poor countries as wealthier governments shut down domestic markets.

Back in 1925 Yale's Yandell Henderson had foreseen this future. Putting lead into gasoline, he told the American Society of Safety Engineers and International Safety Council, was really about securing "billions of dollars" in future profits by controlling markets with patents. With so much money at stake, what really was the chance of stopping the sale of ethyl gasoline? "It seems more likely," he brooded, "that the conditions will grow worse so gradually and the development of lead poisoning will come on so insidiously (for this is the nature of the disease) that leaded gasoline will be in nearly universal use and large numbers of cars will have been sold that can run only on that fuel before the public and the Government awaken to the situation."[6]

Seventy-five years after Henderson's speech the historian J. R. McNeill would conclude that Thomas Midgley Jr. "had more impact on the atmosphere than any other single organism in earth history.[7] This might seem a tad unfair, except that Midgley's mark on the earth went well beyond leaded gasoline. Still working for General Motors and DuPont, in just three days in 1928 he would invent Freon to cool refrigerators. His peers hailed Freon as chemical wizardry. At that time, every now and then, the cooling gases in refrigerators would explode: burning down kitchens and hurting sales. Freon was a dazzling solution—nontoxic, odorless, stable, and cheap. Sales of Freon refrigerators were soon booming. And before long manufacturers were discovering many further uses for these versatile chemicals: for air conditioners, solvents, fire extinguishers, aerosol sprays, foam insulation.

For the next 40 years no one ever really questioned the safety of Freon: after all, it's so harmless to people, as Midgley playfully demonstrated at the American Chemical Society in 1930, that you can inhale it as deeply as you like, and then blow out a candle. But the safety of Freon entailed a danger Midgley could never have imagined even if he had lived another 25 years. Freon, the trademark name for the first chlorofluorocarbons, were drifting skyward, and, as the world came to realize in the 1970s and 1980s, were destroying the ozone layer—essential for life on earth.[8]

Compared to Midgley's time, most firms today do a better job of determining risks and avoiding actions that cause immediate harm: like burying waste or selling tainted food. Class action lawsuits, government regulations, and fines for noncompliance help keep firms more in line. So does the importance for profits (and executive bonuses) of consumer and investor confidence. Yet far less progress has been made in the willingness (or capacity) of companies to avoid the long-term consequences of their industrial processes and consumer products.

Companies still routinely introduce new chemicals and technologies with little understanding of the consequences for ecosystems or future generations. Some of these chemicals and technologies will have no discernable implications; but others may entail costs as great as leaded gasoline and CFCs. The reasoning of many industry scientists today is not much different than it was at the Bureau of Mines in 1924: direct, immediate, and measurable harm must be found to deem a product or process "unsafe." Even then, corporate executives might still proceed (or fight government regulations) if profits exceed fines and lawsuits, as was the case for leaded gasoline for decades, and as still occurs in the tobacco and pharmaceutical industries.

## The Need for Precaution

Protecting ecosystems and people requires far more precaution in how and where firms introduce new technologies and products. The benefits of "advances" such as nanotechnology and genetically modified organisms might end up outweighing the social and ecological costs. But at this time our knowledge is simply not great enough to really know. This is the case of many new corporate technologies. Especially worrying is how little scientists still understand about the health and ecological consequences of thousands of chemicals and substances (both organic and inorganic) currently on the world market.

States did manage to phase out CFCs after negotiating the Montreal Protocol in 1987. And many national governments have put controls on some known carcinogens, such as asbestos. International agreements have also been negotiated to try to limit the damage of hazardous waste, pesticides, and persistent organic pollutants: these include the Basel Convention (in force since 1992); the Stockholm Convention (in force since 2004); the Rotterdam Convention (in force since 2004); and the Minamata Convention on Mercury (not yet in force as of 2015).[9] Yet scientists are still unsure of the consequences of CFC-substitutes for aerosols, refrigerants, and foams: some, such as hydrofluorocarbons (HFCs), with emissions rising more than 50 percent from 2007 to 2012, we do know are causing climate change.[10] And there is still little understanding—and minimal regulation globally— of the toxicity of most chemicals, including in our clothing, rugs, pillows, cleaning products, and food. Moreover, as with CFCs, the "solution" to "discovering" that a chemical in commercial use is dangerous is generally to substitute a "new" and "improved" chemical: one with yet again unknown long-term consequences.

Consider the history of Teflon. Back in 1938 the DuPont chemist Roy J. Plunkett accidentally concocted the "slippery" chemical compound for Teflon, unlocking a family of perfluorinated chemicals, or PFCs. In various forms these chemicals would allow for thousands of new consumer products, including nonstick cookware, stain-resistant clothing, grease-resistant pizza boxes, dental floss, and Scotchgard for rugs and sofas. In the 1980s and 1990s evidence would gradually emerge that the manufacturing of Teflon and Scotchgard was generating toxic and hazardous chemical byproducts, and these were turning up in water systems and human blood samples around the world. The chemical industry reacted as it did when confronted with the dangers of leaded gasoline and CFCs: by funding pro-industry research, hiding unwanted findings, fighting lawsuits, lobbying politicians, stalling regulators, and shifting production and sales to developing countries with less regulatory oversight.[11]

Only in 2006 did DuPont finally agreed to phase out "long-chain" PFCs, notably perfluorooctanoic acid (PFOA), which lab tests on animals confirm can cause birth defects and cancer. Agreeing to a phaseout was part of a deal with the US Environmental Protection Agency (EPA) to pay a record-setting $16.5 million fine for concealing for two decades internal research confirming the toxicity of PFOA (also called C8). By the beginning of 2016 the phaseout of PFOA was largely complete in the United States. Yet, as with HFCs and unleaded gasoline, the safety of "short-chain" PFCs is far from clear, and for all we know these may turn out to be just as toxic as the original formulations.[12]

Even diet sodas and sugar-free gum are an experiment on people and the planet. The world market for sugar substitutes, currently worth more than $11 billion a year, is heading toward $14–15 billion by 2020. Artificial sweeteners—sucralose, saccharin, aspartame, neotame, and acesulfame K—are market leaders. The magic of sweeteners such as acesulfame, sucralose, and saccharin is in the human body's inability to metabolize them fully: allowing us to flush calories down the toilet. As scientists are now discovering, however, these sweeteners are surviving waste treatment and pouring into rivers, lakes, and oceans. In one test site in Ontario's Grand River researchers found acesulfame quantities equal to 80,000 to 190,000 cans of diet soda floating downriver every day. What are the consequences? At this point no one really knows, but many scientists are wondering—and worrying—as these sweeteners break down in sunlight, bioaccumulate, and resurface in drinking water.[13]

Generations may well need to pass to see how ecosystems and humans react, adapt, and interact with new chemicals and compounds, a lesson that the histories of leaded gasoline and CFCs teach us. Industry research is aiming for competitive advantages and technological breakthroughs. Speed and daring is what keeps a company "ahead of the curve." And generating scientific uncertainty is a longstanding strategy to delay lawmakers and divide environmental activism.

## The Business of Preventing Precaution

The job of industry scientists like Midgley is to improve the efficiency of production processes and the marketability of products. Some of these scientists are certainly inept or unethical, but pioneering research with broad social benefits is also common—a few industry scientists have even won a Nobel Prize, such as DuPont's Charles J. Pedersen in 1987 for organic chemistry. Yet sales, profits, and patents take precedence in industry. And not all research is objective, on occasion even bordering on farcical, as we saw earlier with Procter & Gamble's "discovery" of the sleep and cognitive benefits of wearing Pampers diapers. To sell products advertisers mislead consumers with select "facts" and "statistics." At the same time corporate executives commission research and spin information with the express purpose of generating scientific uncertainty, delaying regulations, and confusing consumers. As we saw, this was true for the leaded gasoline industry in the 1970s, 1980s, and even into the 1990s. It was true as well for the coal industry's response to acid rain and the CFC industry's response to ozone depletion. And it's the case today for chemical, oil, drug, consumer goods, food, and agricultural companies, among others, as they raise doubts about climate change, health risks (e.g., of artificial sweeteners), and the causes of deforestation, desertification, and biodiversity loss.

Critics of environmentalism lambast books like Rachel Carson's *Silent Spring* as hysterical and irresponsible, and praise (and buy up) books like Bjørn Lomborg's *The Skeptical Environmentalist*, an international bestseller even with its dry prose and 2,930 endnotes. Some of the strongest attacks on environmentalism originate not from within corporate boardrooms, but from economists and pro-industry government agencies. The writings of ecological economists like Herman Daly, for instance, are commonly dismissed as musings of little importance to economic theory or to the practice of micro- or macroeconomics. Flawed theories and failed predictions are a normal, even necessary, part of advancing knowledge in the sciences and social sciences. To this day, however, anti-environmental critics attack *The Limits to Growth* (1972) as unscientific, noting its primitive computer models were "proven wrong." The hyperbole of some bestselling environmental writers like Paul Ehrlich, author of *The Population Bomb* (1968), has also supplied anti-environmentalists with truckloads of ammunition.[14]

The anti-environmentalism of business reaches far and wide. Companies backstop rightwing politicians and conservative think tanks. They lobby world leaders, ally with commerce and natural resource departments, and sue environmental agencies. They intimidate grassroots activists and foment community backlash (for example, representing environmentalism as a threat to jobs or traditions or freedoms). Over the past two decades, multinational corporations have also been increasingly financing and partnering with environmental NGOs with pro-market stances, while continuing to attack radical environmentalists as unscientific, unrealistic, and, especially in countries waging a "war on terrorism," seditious.[15]

Together, industry science and public relations fortify the business narrative of sustainability. As I discussed in the previous chapter, the world's leading brand corporations no longer shy away from presenting environmental problems as real. Nor do they dispute that action is necessary. Instead, they are claiming to be sustainability leaders with the capacity to solve global environmental problems. These same firms are quick to emphasize that the planet is not in crisis; that scientific uncertainty remains high; that rash decisions will only make matters worse. What is necessary is more efficiency, less waste, and better management. Stifling scientific ingenuity with unwarranted precaution or unnecessary regulation will not serve anyone's interests.

Far more effective, brand CEOs are increasingly emphasizing, is for customers to reward "corporate sustainability" by purchasing more products labeled as sustainable. Consumers should buy a CFC-free refrigerator, fill up with "unleaded" gasoline, and drink more Starbucks coffee in "reusable, recyclable, and re-enjoyable" cups. If each person makes these "little changes," folksy CEOs are telling customers, multinational corporations can "save the planet" and still protect jobs, enhance financial security, and respect cultural diversity. This optimistic business message of the combined power of corporate social responsibility and eco-consumerism to advance sustainability is pulling increasing numbers of middleclass consumers into the orbit of environmentalism of the rich. Yet environmentalism remains a diverse and complex political and social force, and although the general trend is toward the growing dominance of environmentalism of the rich, as we'll see over the second half of this book, we should not dismiss the power of citizens and grassroots movements—even those enticed by the small gains of eco-consumerism—to resist corporations, block local projects, and protect natural settings.

# II Global Environmentalism

Many credit Rachel Carson with inspiring the global environmental movement with her 1962 bestseller *Silent Spring* on the hazards of pesticides and herbicides. "Can anyone believe," she wrote while dying of cancer, "it is possible to lay down such a barrage of poisons on the surface of the earth without making it unfit for all life?" Carson, a poet at heart and a scientist by training, merits her renown. But when reflecting on the rise of global environmentalism we also need to remember that she was an American citizen writing in English, and her concerns were a product of a Eurocentric education and a life of bird-watching and beachcombing at her summer cottage in Maine.[1]

Global environmentalism, as Carson knew well, emerges out of a long and rich cultural history, from the practices of hunters and gatherers to the spirituality of indigenous peoples to the intellectuals of China and India. And today ideas and individuals and organizations from around the world infuse environmentalism. So, too, do people living in war zones, poverty, and violence. Moreover, since the release of *Silent Spring* the global environmental movement has moved far beyond worries over industrial pollution, pesticides, and the loss of "nature" to tackle issues of great consequence for developing countries: climate change, desertification, tropical deforestation, water quality, and biodiversity loss, to list just a few.

Nevertheless, even today it's accurate to describe global environmentalism as largely a creation of the West. Environmental NGOs working transnationally—such as WWF, Conservation International, and the Nature Conservancy—have offices, projects, and supporters across the planet. For the most part, however, the goals of these organizations sidestep the traumatic legacy of European imperialism for the peoples, economies, and environments of Africa, the Asia-Pacific, and the Americas. NGOs established to certify consumer products as sustainable, such as the Forest Stewardship Council and the Marine Stewardship Council, have even less interest in raising such thorny issues. Western consumerism and environmentalism of the rich more generally are "solutions" for these NGOs—ones generally at odds with anti-trade, anti-globalization, and anti-capitalist activism.

This chapter sets the stage for a deeper analysis of the rise of environmentalism of the rich in subsequent chapters, as well as my overall assessment in the concluding chapter of the power of environmentalism as a whole to promote global sustainability. The Western origins of environmentalism as a global movement in part explain the growing worldwide dominance of environmentalism of the rich. More important, however, has been the innate power of consumer capitalism to distort and assimilate counter-narratives and countermovements, especially critiques of wealth and economic growth. That said, it's easy to exaggerate the extent of assimilation. A diversity of values and goals, as the next two sections remind us, is the hallmark of environmentalism, and this diversity has always provided the environmental movement with crisscrossing avenues of influence. More-over, as we'll see later in the chapter, citizens everywhere, both rich and poor, continue to speak out, fight local powers, and question the rhetoric of environmentalism of the rich.

## A Movement of Movements

Deep philosophical and policy differences have long characterized environmentalism, including among those with wealth and privilege. The writings of men such as Ralph Waldo Emerson (1803–1882), Henry David Thoreau (1817–1862), and John Muir (1838–1914), who together called for efforts to preserve "nature" and set aside "wilderness" tracts for hiking, exploring, or simply experiencing, still motivate some environmentalists. Others see environmentalism as more about trying to manage renewable "resources" such as fish or timber more "sustainably"—to maximize and maintain yields—or perhaps manage resources to protect biodiversity, or reduce deforestation and soil erosion. Still others emphasize the need to reduce smog or toxic waste or pollution—perhaps with particular worries about crowding, poverty, or disease in the world's slums. And still others focus on endangered species or water quality or climate change.

The diversity of environmentalism goes far beyond just varying interests and concerns. Values, priorities, and assumptions differ widely, too. Some environmentalists see technology as a cause of problems and a reason for an escalating global crisis; others see technology as central to any lasting solutions. Some see humans as one species among many and call for living within natural limits; others see humans as a having special status, with a duty to act as nature's stewards. Some even see humans as a "plague" or "cancer" on the earth, and call for a drastic decrease in the world population—say, down to 1–3 billion people (from the current 7.4 billion). Others do not think the global environment is in crisis, nor do they worry about population growth, perhaps seeing one-child policies as inhumane, or perhaps seeing more people as a source of ingenuity and prosperity.

Distinguishing broadly between radicals and reformers is one way to get a handle on the complexity and diversity of the global environmental movement. Radicals see the globalization of trade, investment, and consumerism as primary causes of global harm—and demand an overhaul of the world economy, sometimes calling for a localization of manufacturing, agriculture, and markets. Reformers advocate for policies and institutions to guide globalization to do good, such as using the power of markets to create win-win-win economic, social, and environmental outcomes: what these days some business-oriented reformers describe as the triple bottom line of sustainability. Sharp differences exist too among radicals—some prioritize ecosystems, others social justice—as well as among reformers—some call for strong institutions and policies, others for every possible effort to eliminate market distortions.[2]

Such diversity has allowed environmentalism to appeal to a wide constituency. Many think of environmentalists as protestors or campaigners or eco-villagers. But increasingly those who identify as environmentalists also beaver away in companies, universities, governments, and international organizations. They invest. They research. They manage. In recent years those who propose measures that do not threaten—and at times advance—the interests of wealthy and powerful elites have gained considerable influence over public policy and within international bureaucracies. The rising influence of environmentalism of the rich, as we started to get a sense of in the first half of the book, has enhanced the general acceptance of markets, trade, and big business within mainstream environmentalism. This philosophical shift is strengthening the overall capacity of environmentalism to advance moderate, incremental reforms, as well as avert worst-case outcomes in wealthy cities and neighborhoods. Yet, even as radical environmentalists continue to block development projects, influence public discourses, and inspire community protests, this shift toward markets and business is weakening the capacity of the environmental movement as a whole to challenge the unsustainability of the world politics of growth.

## The Dynamism of Environmentalism

Mass protests continue to stop the construction of freeways, nuclear power plants, and big-box department stores. Activists continue to prevent logging, fish farming, and the spraying of crops with pesticides. And voters continue to demand bike lanes, public transport, and high-density housing to promote sustainable living. Across the world municipalities now regulate air and water quality, sanitation and garbage collection, and the dumping of hazardous waste. National programs subsidize solar and wind power. And local bylaws protect old-growth trees, beaches, parks, and bird sanctuaries.

Countless scholars have traced the power of environmental lobbying, lawsuits, and political parties to shape national policies and international agreements. They have documented the significance of grassroots campaigns for local decision-making and development. They have zeroed in on the power of environmental norms to alter political and cultural frames. They have shown the importance of NGO pressure on—and partnerships with—corporations for the emergence of certification and environmental codes of conduct. And they have revealed the importance of layers of epistemic communities of scientists with shared policy positions as well as transnational activist networks with shared values and principles. A few scholars, most convincingly Paul Wapner of American University, see the influence of environmentalism as comprising a core part of a "world civic politics," with enough force to constrain states and firms, while gradually transforming cultures. Clearly, even though the world community would seem to be making little headway in slowing the global ecological crisis, it would be a mistake to dismiss the capacity of environmentalism as a whole to change values, discourses, and consumption, as well as to influence politics, from international treaties to local bylaws.[3]

Today, tens of thousands of nongovernmental organizations are running environmental campaigns. The growth of international NGOs since the

1970s is revealing. Greenpeace, formed in Vancouver in the early 1970s to protest American nuclear weapons testing in the Pacific, is now headquartered in Amsterdam, with millions of financial supporters, offices across 40 countries, and thousands of employees. Friends of the Earth International, set up in 1971 to connect four groups from England, France, Sweden, and the United States, has grown into a federation of 75 organizations, employing around 1,200 staff. Worldwide, the federation now comprises more than 2 million members and supports 5,000 or so local environmental groups.

Other international NGOs have seen similar increases in their size and reach. WWF, set up in Switzerland in 1961 to support global conservation, now employs 6,200 staff in offices in over 80 countries (with 5 million or so supporters). Over its history WWF has distributed more than $11.5 billion to finance some 13,000 environmental projects. The Nature Conservancy, established in the US in 1951, now has around 1 million members, and is working to acquire and preserve ecosystems across more than 35 countries, as well as in every American state. With assets of more than $6.5 billion (as of 2015), The Nature Conservancy has helped to protect around 50 million hectares of forests, rivers, lakes, wetlands, grasslands, deserts, and marine ecosystems.

National environmental organizations have also grown considerably since the 1970s. In the United States the Natural Resources Defense Council, set up in 1970 to use scientific analysis and court challenges to fight for environmental causes, now comprises a team of around 500 researchers and lawyers, with a support base of 1.4 million people. The US Environmental Defense Fund (EDF), which began in 1967 as a small group of scientists and lawyers campaigning to ban the pesticide DDT, now has around 1 million members and a staff of more than 500 economists and other professionals. The US Sierra Club, one of the world's older conservation organizations with a founding date of 1892, now has 64 chapters across the United States, with 2.4 million supporters in 2015.

The reach of environmentalism goes far beyond NGO projects and grassroots activism. Just about every country now has an environmental agency, and over a thousand international environmental treaties are in place. As we saw in chapter 4, even big-box stores such as Walmart and Home Depot, brand manufacturers such as Coca-Cola and Nike, and fast-food chains such as McDonald's and Starbucks all now claim to be sustainability leaders, promising to pursue sustainable sourcing, renewable energy, and less waste. And nonprofits have launched hundreds of eco-labeling organizations, such as the Forest Stewardship Council and the Marine Stewardship Council, with something like one-fifth of consumer goods traded worldwide currently certified as meeting an environmental or social standard.

Just about every culture has come to embrace the language of sustainability. "Swamps" have become "wetlands," "jungles" have become "biodiversity hotspots." Sure, some campaigns to reimagine species have flopped: despite the efforts of People for the Ethical Treatment of Animals (PETA), every year the lives of millions of lobsters still end in a pot of boiling water. But environmentalism has altered the cultural frames for hundreds of animals. Much of humanity now sees whales—target practice for the US military a half century ago—as sentient and majestic beings. Harp seal pups, though still clubbed and skinned for their fur in Canada, are now widely portrayed around the world as cuddly and adorable, worthy of "rights" and "status."

The environmental movement can even take some credit for transforming ways of learning and educating citizens. College courses in environmental studies and sustainability have proliferated since the 1960s. Some universities and high schools now mandate sustainability courses as part of the core curriculum. Subfields, such as "global environmental politics" in my own discipline of political science, continue to gain followers. And concepts and theories emerging from scholar-environmentalists—resilience, stewardship, adaptation, environmental justice, and environmental racism to name just a few—are increasingly shaping mainstream academic and policy debates.[4]

Everywhere, people are searching for ways to live more sustainably. Demonstrators in Australia and Argentina are demanding controls on banks and multinational corporations. Campaigners in Bangladesh and Britain are struggling to end modern-day slavery, while ecologists in Malawi and Malaysia are fighting to stop trade in endangered species. Architects are building eco-homes in India and planners are designing eco-towns in Ireland. And across the world citizens are supporting environmental bylaws, voting for green parties, and calling for more action to stop climate change.

Meanwhile, billions of people are recycling and composting. Farmers are marketing fair trade coffee, miners are selling conflict-free diamonds, and consumers are purchasing eco-products, paying eco-taxes, offsetting carbon emissions, and buying locally grown food. Companies big and small are reducing energy use, waste, and packaging per product sold. Governments are regulating parks and rivers and air quality, while communities are reforesting lands and promoting eco-tourism. International agreements are regulating whaling, shipping, and endangered species. And the World Bank and the Global Environment Facility are funding environmental technology transfers to developing countries.

By some measures, in some sectors, and in many places environmentalists are obviously making headway. Look at the progress in reducing air pollution or acid rain or lead poisoning in Western Europe and North America—smog in London during one particularly bad week in December of 1952 may have caused 12,000 people to die prematurely. Consider that since the opening of Yellowstone National Park in 1872 more than 150,000 parks, wildlife sanctuaries, and conservation areas have been created worldwide—not just to promote tourism, but also to protect wetlands, biodiversity, wilderness, watersheds, forests, marine life, and coral reefs. Look at water consumption in the greater Sydney region of Australia, which is roughly the same now as in the early 1970s even with an extra 1.4 million people living there. Or recall from the last chapter the history of the ozone layer—depleting and thinning in the 1970s and 1980s as chlorofluorocarbons drifted into the atmosphere, the international community came together after 1987 to phase out CFCs, at times even exceeding legal commitments, and scientists are now predicting that the ozone layer will repair itself within the next 50 years or so.[5]

These are important gains. A case can even be made that environmentalism is the most significant global movement of the past half century. Countless examples exist as well of influence in the developing world: biodiversity zones in Bolivia and Costa Rica; urban food production in Cuba; community resistance to mining in Peru; conservation areas in Botswana, Zimbabwe, and Mozambique. Grassroots environmentalism has even changed the landscapes of some developing countries, as in Kenya where locals, mostly women, have planted tens of millions of trees since the late 1970s.[6] Moreover, across the world new generations of environmentalists are clearly continuing to rise up in protest even as environmentalism of the rich subsumes the mainstream.

## Citizens Keep Marching and Raising Awareness

September 2014 saw the largest-ever rally to demand action to stop climate change. More than 2,500 marches across 162 countries drew over half a million people, including UN Secretary General Ban Ki-moon and former US Vice President Al Gore who paraded down the streets of New York side by side with the renowned primatologist Jane Goodall (with Leonardo DiCaprio and Mark Ruffalo somewhere in the crowd). Mass rallies and community activism have long been at the core of successful environmental campaigns. Individuals, sometimes alone, sometimes standing together in the millions, continue to raise environmental awareness, advance ecological knowledge, and shift cultural norms and values toward sustainability. It is common for states and corporations to persecute—and at times imprison or execute—those who stand against them. Yet individuals continue to risk their lives and communities continue to unite to fight political corruption and environmental destruction.

Time and again people are coming together to prevent illegal land grabs, poaching, and mega-dams. They are shutting down toxic waste dumps, fighting environmental racism, and restoring degraded ecosystems. And they are continuing to defend old-growth forests and wildlife sanctuaries, to take oil and mining companies to court, and to rally at international environmental negotiations. Together such actions, led not by multinational NGOs but by concerned citizens, can act as a counterforce to states and corporations—a point easy to forget as more and more environmental NGOs applaud eco-business, run eco-labeling programs, and partner with corporations on cause-marketing campaigns. "Our citizens keep marching," US President Barack Obama lectured delegates at the 2014 Climate Summit in New York City. "We cannot pretend we do not hear them. We have to answer the call."

As with the People's Climate March of 2014, with permits and within strict limits, states generally allow peaceful parades of well-off citizens (and celebrities) to go forward, choosing to videotape rather than block them. Security agencies, however, tend to be much harsher on inopportune demonstrations (such as at G20 meetings of heads of government), enduring protests (such as the Occupy Movement in 2011), and challenges to mining, logging, or development projects, especially those in developing countries. Here, protestors routinely face walls of police in body armor, wielding batons, pepper spray, rubber bullets, and water cannons—and on occasion automatic weapons. Look at what happened in northern Peru in 2009. To protest new laws to allow mining on traditional indigenous land, two thousand indigenous and environmental activists were blockading a highway near Bagua city. Police opened fire, shooting at least 80 people and killing ten civilians (fighting and later reprisals also killed 23 police officers).[7]

Ongoing rallies and protests, as we see with President Obama's remarks at the 2014 Climate Summit, raise the profile of environmental causes among world leaders and can spur along international negotiations. Thousands of NGO leaders and frontline activists regularly attend these negotiations as well. Some are accredited as official participants. Some attend parallel events. And some protest in the streets. This was the case, for instance, with civil society attendance at the ten-day United Nations Conference on Sustainable Development (UNCSD) in Rio de Janeiro in 2012 (Rio+20), where around 50,000 people showed up from government, business, and civil society. The UN accredited more than 29,300 of them as official participants; of those accredited, more than 10,000 were from NGOs or civil society organizations. During the conference advocacy groups also ran hundreds of side events.

Civil society attendance is high for international treaty negotiations too, with the annual Conference of the Parties for the UN Framework Convention on Climate Change garnering particular interest. For the 2009 meeting in Copenhagen, the UN accredited a record number of civil society observers for a climate change negotiation: 13,482—nearly 3,000 more than the number of governmental delegates (and five times more than the number of civil society observers at the fourth Conference of the Parties in Buenos Aires in 1998). From 2010 to 2014 the number of official civil society observers at the annual climate change Conference of the Parties fell off, averaging a little over 4,500. Official and unofficial attendance by civil society, however, again soared during the 2015 Conference of the Parties in Paris where delegates negotiated a new international climate change agreement.[8]

Civil society delegates are not only nudging state negotiators to strengthen existing international treaties, but are also influencing negotiations for new ones, such as the Minamata Convention on Mercury signed in 2013. In addition, local conservationists have been instrumental in encouraging states to establish national parks, biodiversity zones, and wildlife sanctuaries. As of 2015 more than 15 percent of the earth's land and inland waters was designated as "protected," up from less than 9 percent in 1990. And around the world conservation officers now patrol old-growth forests, savannas, mountains, and valleys to defend wildlife, endangered species, and pristine nature.[9]

Environmentalists are raising consciousness as well by gathering for events such as Earth Day, celebrated every year since 1970 when 20 million people rallied in the United States alone. Today, Earth Day (April 22) draws over half a billion people into its celebrations, making it, in the promotional language of the Earth Day Network, the world's "largest secular holiday." In addition to Earth Day, every year millions of people attend local environmental marches, as well as join broader public protests, from ones against globalization, inequality, and racism to ones for indigenous rights, social justice, and civil liberties.

Awareness raising occurs too as environmentalists publish thought-provoking articles and bestselling nonfiction books, such as *The Limits to Growth*, cited at least 13,000 times since its publication in 1972. It arises as well from novels, short stories, memoirs, children's books, photography, art, films, documentaries, and comedy skits. How many North American environmentalists started out reading John Steinbeck's *The Grapes of Wrath* (1939)? Or perhaps Farley Mowat's *New Cry Wolf* (1963), or Edward Abbey's *The Monkey Wrench Gang* (1975), or Dr. Seuss's *The Lorax* (1971)? How many have read *The Tree* (1979) by the British novelist John Fowles or the environmental writings of India's Arundhati Roy, winner of the 1997 Man Booker Prize? Who cannot but laugh at the absurdity of denying climate change after watching Jon Stewart on *The Daily Show* skewer Republicans who were participating in 2014 hearings of the US House of Representatives Committee on Science, Space, and Technology?[10]

Awareness of environmental principles and values, as we saw in chapter 4, would even seem to be rising within the business community. All of the world's leading brand corporations are now working hard to reassure governments and consumers of their commitment to corporate responsibility and sustainability. To demonstrate this new commitment, as we've seen, big-box retailers such as Walmart and brand manufacturers such as Coca-Cola are partnering with moderate environmental organizations such as WWF and Conservation International to certify products as sustainable, finance conservation, and market green technologies. At the same time, as I'll focus on in chapter 10, more radical groups such as Greenpeace are gaining influence by shaming brand companies over social media for failing to meet sustainability commitments.[11] Unquestionably, environmental NGOs, mass protests, and ecological knowledge are important political and social forces. So, too, is grassroots environmentalism, especially in its struggles to protect local ecosystems and local communities, as the winners of the Goldman Environmental Prize prove.

## Defenders of the Natural World

Since 1990 the Goldman Environmental Prize has been recognizing community activists who dedicate themselves to protecting "the natural world." As of 2015 the Prize had been awarded to 169 individuals covering every region of the world—with each of the six 2015 winners receiving $175,000. Recipients have fought to save forests, marine areas, wetlands, and inland waters, along the way opposing miners, loggers, and developers, and at times achieving innovative policy reforms. The sacrifices and accomplishments of Goldman Prize recipients are inspiring, as we see with the winners for forest advocacy. One was Wangari Maathai (1940–2011), who received the 1991 Goldman Prize (and in 2004 the Nobel Peace Prize) for founding Kenya's Green Belt Movement in 1977. Her advocacy brought her a lifetime of threats and violence, including the police once beating her unconscious. Her movement, however, has rallied locals, especially women, to plant more than 50 million trees across Africa to curtail deforestation and soil erosion, as well as advance women's rights, create jobs at local tree nurseries, and increase the supply of fuelwood for cooking and heating homes.

The forest and human rights advocacy of Marina Silva, who received the 1996 Goldman Prize, has been equally courageous. Born into a family of rubber tappers, in the 1980s (together with Chico Mendes) she brought together rubber tappers to protest rising deforestation in the Brazilian Amazon. In 1988 a rancher assassinated Mendes. But Silva kept going, in 1994 becoming a senator and helping to establish community-run forest reserves covering more than 2 million hectares of the Amazon. Since then she has held the post of Brazilian Minister of Environment (2003–2008), supporting efforts to reduce Brazil's rate of deforestation, and has run twice for president of Brazil, in 2010 as leader of the Green Party, and in 2014 as leader of the Socialist Party. In recent years she has alienated some of her followers by supporting business investments, biofuels, offshore oil drilling, and hydroelectric dams in the Amazon, although few environmentalists would dispute the daring of her early years of forest and human rights advocacy.

Liberia's Silas Kpanan'Ayoung Siakor, winner of the 2006 Goldman Prize, is yet another example of the bravery of forest campaigners around the world. Risking his life, he compiled evidence for the UN Security Council linking the proceeds from illegal logging and timber smuggling to death squads and human rights violations under Liberian President Charles Taylor. In 2003 the Security Council banned timber exports from Liberia, only lifting the ban in 2006 under the new regime of President Ellen Johnson Sirleaf. During this time Siakor, as director of Liberia's Sustainable Development Institute (the Liberian branch of Friends of the Earth), continued to work hard to promote community forest management in Liberia, including keeping up pressure on the Sirleaf government to protect vast tracts of rainforest.[12]

The 2014 Goldman Prize recipients—India's Ramesh Agrawal, Peru's Ruth Buendía Mestoquiari, South Africa's Desmond D'Sa, Russia's Suren Gazaryan, Indonesia's Rudi Putra, and America's Helen Slottje—give a further sense of the range, scope, and successes of grassroots activism worldwide. Using his Internet café as a headquarters, Ramesh Agrawal founded a grassroots movement to enhance the transparency of development plans and projects in the state of Chhattisgarh in central India. By supplying information to villagers from 2008 to 2012, he mobilized resistance to the opening of yet another huge coal mine in Chhattisgarh. As opposition grew, the government decided to revoke the permits for Jindal Steel and Power, even though a member of the Parliament of India owned the company. Shortly after this victory, thugs, apparently hired to teach Agrawal a lesson, broke into his café and shot him in the leg. This has not deterred him, however, and when he received the Goldman Prize in 2014 he was still working hard to expose environmental illegalities as well as rally the people of Chhattisgarh to demand land rights.

Ruth Buendía Mestoquiari of Peru's Asháninka people received the Goldman Prize for successfully impeding plans to construct large hydroelectric dams in the Amazon. Proposed as part of a 2010 Peru–Brazil energy agreement, these dams would have flooded ancestral lands, displacing thousands of indigenous peoples and destroying pristine rainforests, while offering little compensation or economic benefits for locals (the plan was to export most of the energy to Brazil). Buendía was 27 years old when she was elected in 2005 as the first female president of the Asháninka Center of the Ene River, an indigenous rights organization known as CARE. Distressed at the prospect of mega-dams in Asháninka territory, she trekked through the Ene River Valley to educate—and unite and mobilize—Asháninka communities by screening computer simulations of the dam flooding. Claiming that both domestic and international law require prior consent from indigenous groups before proceeding with development projects on their ancestral lands, she took her case to the Peruvian courts as well as to Washington, D.C., to appeal to the Inter-American Commission on Human Rights. In response to the Asháninka campaign, plans to build the Pakitzapango and Tambo-40 dams on the Ene-Tambo River ground to a halt. Today Buendía and her CARE team are continuing to advocate for the land rights of the Asháninka people as mega-dam proposals continue to wend through government processes, legal proceedings, and community consultations.

The Goldman committee awarded Desmond D'Sa a 2014 Prize for mobilizing residents in the city of Durban, South Africa, to pressure the municipal government into closing a toxic waste dump that was poisoning the community. His advocacy began in 1996 when he cofounded the South Durban Community Environmental Alliance to advocate for environmental justice. In 2009 he launched a campaign to close the Bulbul Drive landfill after the company Wasteman applied to expand operations with a lease to 2021. Residents of this neighborhood of chemical plants, oil refineries, and paper mills—what locals call "cancer valley"—are some of the poorest and most marginalized people in South Africa. D'Sa and his team taught residents to recognize the smells of different poisons and toxins spilling from trucks, drifting from the dump, and leaching out of the ground. Alerting them of their constitutional right under South African law to a clean and safe living environment, he helped blockade highways to protest the illegal trucking of toxic waste. Opposition grew so strong that Wasteman withdrew its renewal application in 2011 and closed the dump in 2012. "We've shown that as a united force, we can stop environmental racism," D'Sa said in 2014. "And we've shown communities that there needs to be a new way of doing business." D'Sa is continuing to fight environmental racism in south Durban, even though his enemies firebombed his home a few years back, and his life remains in jeopardy.

Suren Gazaryan, a zoologist specializing in bats, received a 2014 Goldman Prize for his longstanding campaign to expose political corruption and the unlawful clearing of protected areas along the coast of Russia's Black Sea. Since the 1990s he has been collaborating with the NGO Environmental Watch on North Caucasus to uncover—and try to stop—illegal loggers, tourism developers, and the building of luxury homes in wildlife sanctuaries and protected wilderness, including for top-ranking government officials. After years of campaigning, in 2010 the Russian federal government agreed to give the Black Sea's Utrish Nature Preserve additional legal protections, including halting the construction of a villa for then Russian President Dimitry Medvedev. Environmental advocacy, however, has become increasingly perilous and difficult in Russia since the return in 2012 of Vladimir Putin as Russian president, including new laws to require domestic NGOs with foreign funding, foreign associates, or "political" goals to register as "foreign agents." Russian authorities went after Gazaryan after he accused President Putin of building a luxury villa on protected lands, and as he was campaigning against the illegal clearing of parklands for the 2014 Sochi Winter Olympics. Facing trumped-up criminal charges, in August 2012 Gazaryan fled to Estonia, where he was granted political asylum.

The Goldman committee awarded Rudi Putra a 2014 prize for his work to prevent poaching of the endangered Sumatran Rhino as well as to oppose illegal palm oil plantations in the officially protected Leuser Ecosystem on the island of Sumatra, Indonesia. In 2011 the Indonesian government announced a moratorium on new logging licenses in old-growth rainforests, yet logging and the clearing of peat lands for oil palm plantations continued, including in national parks and protected wildlife reserves in Sumatra. Fighting back, Putra has negotiated with police, banded together local NGOs, mobilized locals, and lobbied palm oil companies. Risking his safety, he also sought out and (with his team) cut down illegal oil palms. Through these actions he has been able to eliminate more than 485 hectares of illegal palm oil plantations in the 2.6 million hectare Leuser Ecosystem. The ability of rhinos, as well as elephants, orangutans, and tigers, to migrate and feed is improving as the Leuser Ecosystem naturally regenerates. It even appears that Sumatran Rhino numbers may be edging upward as conservationists like Putra make some headway. Putra's campaign is still going strong, and as of 2015 he was leading efforts to oppose a proposal by the Indonesian province of Aceh to legally introduce palm oil plantations in the Leuser Ecosystem.

The sixth and final recipient of the 2014 Goldman Environmental Prize was Helen Slottje. Since 2009 she has been providing pro bono legal counsel to townships in upstate New York looking to block plans by oil and gas companies to start "fracking," a process of drilling for natural gas by fracturing shale rock with high-pressure blasts of water, sand, and chemicals. Local governments in New York State do not have the authority to regulate industry. As Helen Slottje and her husband David Slottje revealed, however, the New York State Constitution, through the powers of "home rule," does enable municipalities through zoning ordinances to ban high-risk undertakings, such as hydraulic fracturing. As citizens across New York petitioned municipalities to enact bans, Slottje traveled across the state to offer legal advice and answer questions at town hall meetings. Her campaign is far from over, and her adversaries continue to deride and harass her. Yet town after town has deployed her team's legal analysis of home rule to impose bans and moratoriums on hydraulic fracturing. More than 170 local bans or moratoriums were in place across New York State when in June 2014 New York's highest court upheld the right of towns to ban gas drilling. Meanwhile, other communities, including towns in Ohio, Texas, Colorado, and California, are learning from the local victories in New York, empowering the anti-fracking movement across the United States.[13]

The Goldman Prize is a testimony to the tenacity of environmentalists to fight corruption, greed, and big business. It's also a valuable reminder that individual activists can—and do—sometimes emerge victorious over tough-minded governments, corporations, and ruling elites. Environmental activism, as this chapter highlights, is a complex, diverse, and ever-shifting movement of movements with considerable influence, and even as environmentalism of the rich has increasingly come to dominate the mainstream, the many tributaries of radical resistance and environmentalism of the poor continue to flow.

Enthusiasts cannot escape, however, that even as campaigners rally, lobby, and raise awareness, even as eco-efficiencies rise, and even as reformers and radicals achieve some wins and gain some ground, at the global level biodiversity, oceans, fresh water, rainforests, agricultural lands, and the climate are continuing to deteriorate. Nor can they escape that every year enemies of environmentalism continue to murder hundreds of activists.

Few places on earth are as dangerous as the tropical rainforests. And despite a fearless campaign to expose the political corruption and human rights abuses underlying tropical deforestation, loggers, ranchers, and plantation owners continue to clear tropical forests as fast as ever. Swiss activist Bruno Manser deserves credit for leading the charge in the 1980s and 1990s to raise global awareness of the plight of tropical rainforests. But his story, unlike the Goldman winners, is not one of hope and victory. I tell this story in the next chapter partly to counterbalance the more upbeat stories of the Goldman Prize committee, partly to reveal how already by the 1990s some activists were fighting the trend toward NGO–corporate partnerships, and partly as a tribute to a man who I cannot help but admire having personally investigated the political causes of deforestation in Borneo for many decades now.

Bruno Manser was known as "Penan man" by his admirers and "white Tarzan" by his enemies. On a cloudy day in late March of 1999 he made for a strange sight for the residents of Kuching, Sarawak, on Malaysian Borneo, as he soared overhead in a motorized paraglider. The Swiss activist was carrying a gift for the political leader of Sarawak, Tan Sri Abdul Taib Mahmud. He had wanted to give Chief Minister Taib a live lamb, but friends, animal rights activists, and Singapore Airlines staff convinced him otherwise— so he knitted him a white lamb. Officials were waiting as Manser glided toward Taib's palatial residence on the outskirts of Kuching, not to toast him with cocktails in the shade of the Chief Minister's gardens, but to arrest him. Manser was heading there to protest corruption, human rights abuses, and the destruction of the rainforests on the island of Borneo.

Manser was born in 1954 in Basel, Switzerland. As a young man he moved to the Swiss Alps, working seasonal jobs, hiking and exploring caves, and learning to live off the land. In 1984 his life took an adventurous turn when he journeyed to Sarawak "to live a life without money"—before long looking like your typical European backpacker in his John Lennon spectacles, scraggly beard, and headband to sweep back his long black hair. Manser had gone in search of nomadic Penan people, one of the last of the hunter-gatherer cultures left in the Asia-Pacific. Since childhood, as he told anthropologist Wade Davis, he had dreamed of living in a "jungle," "with a people of nature, to share their traditions, to discover their origins, to become aware of their religion and life, to know these things." Happening to see a picture of the Penan in his local library had convinced Manser that it was his destiny to seek out one of the world's most isolated people.

Manser longed for a simple life among a simple people. His quixotic vision of the Penan people was brimming with ignorance, and back in 1984 he did seem like yet another privileged Westerner heading out on an ill-advised adventure. At one point Malaysia's Prime Minister would even call him an imperialist with an "intolerable European superiority." Yet, as we'll see in this chapter, despite these beginnings his beliefs and actions after arriving in Sarawak did not come to reflect environmentalism of the rich, and by the 1990s the creeping moderation of rainforest activism was causing him great anguish as NGOs such as WWF increasingly began to collaborate with governments and corporations with dubious records—a trend, as later chapters confirm, that since then has only grown stronger as more and more multistakeholder organizations have been set up to certify products originating from tropical rainforest regions as sustainable.

### Saving Paradise

After arriving in Sarawak, finding the nomadic Penan deep in the rainforests of Borneo turned out to be much harder than Manser was expecting. During one early foray into the jungle he became badly lost; during another he became acutely ill after eating a poisonous plant. But he persevered, eventually stumbling upon a couple of Penan who befriended him. Tribal leaders took him under their tutelage, and over the next six years Manser would learn how to wear a loincloth, walk barefoot along thorny trails, hunt with a blowpipe and poison darts, and enjoy a diet of monkeys, snakes, and wild pigs. He cut his hair in the distinctive Penan bowl-style; he grew strong and wiry; he came to think and dream in the Penan language.

His escapades became legendary even among the Penan. Once, he wandered through the jungle for weeks, climbing with his bare hands to the sharp peak of Batu Lawi where he fasted for days. On the way home, alone and having lost his knife, a python happened to cross his path. On a whim he grabbed ahold of the giant snake, wrestling to elude its death-squeeze, nearly losing his grip as he tried to photograph his feat. His life with the Penan, however, was not all fun and games. Malaria would nearly kill him. His closest brush with death would come after a pit viper bit his ankle, leaving him feverous and delirious for weeks, and then on crutches for six months.

Life for his nomadic Penan hosts was also far from idyllic. By the second half of the 1980s only 500–700 of the 8,000 or so Penan people were still fully nomadic; most had settled in towns or longhouse villages. Disease and accidents were common among nomadic Penan, and average life expectancy was less than 40 years of age. Moreover, backed by Chief Minister Taib, industrial logging of traditional Penan lands was expanding quickly during the 1980s, damaging the forests with bulldozers and chainsaws, polluting waterways, and desecrating sacred sites.

Bruno Manser joined with Penan men, women, and children to blockade logging roads, and began to inform the outside world of the malfeasance of Chief Minister Taib. By the late 1980s blockades were costing timber firms millions of dollars in profits. Police and company henchmen threatened, beat, and detained hundreds of protestors. Malaysian authorities blamed Manser for instigating dissent, calling him a communist and a Zionist. Twice, Manser was hunted down. Both times he escaped, taking refuge among Penan tribes and using his spelunking skills to hide in caves. To help conceal his identity from the police and bounty hunters, the Penan began to refer to him vaguely as "Laki Penan," or Penan man. But life on the run wore him down. "My paradise turns into a prison," he scribbled in his journal. "Is this really the end of my life in the jungle? There's still so much I'd like to discover and experience." By 1990 he'd had enough, fleeing Sarawak on a forged passport.[1]

Manser was not giving up his fight. And by this time the world was taking notice of the campaign to save Borneo. In a 1990 speech at the Kew Royal Botanic Gardens, Prince Charles decried the "collective genocide" of the Penan people. In April 1992 Al Gore introduced a resolution in the US Senate to call on Sarawak to do more to protect its rainforests and indigenous peoples, and for Japan to investigate the role of its companies in the over-logging of Borneo. CNN and NBC covered the Penan; so did *Rolling Stone*, the *New Yorker*, *Newsweek*, the *New York Times*, and *Time* magazine. The BBC and *National Geographic* filmed documentaries of the Penan.[2]

Manser was a courageous campaigner—some might even say reckless. In 1991 he landed on the front page of the *Independent* (a UK newspaper) after chaining himself to a streetlight during the 1991 G7 Summit in London. In 1992 he parachuted into a packed stadium during the Earth Summit of world leaders in Rio de Janeiro. Calling for a ban on tropical timber imports into Switzerland, in 1993 he nearly died after a 60-day hunger strike outside of the parliament building in Berne. Three years later, with a banner reading "Save the Rainforest," he careened down a Matterhorn gondola cable on a makeshift contraption, reaching speeds of more than 85 miles an hour.

Two years after that he parachuted into Geneva carrying a live white lamb as a peace offering to the UN's representative from Malaysia.

Manser's campaign infuriated Mahathir Mohamad, Malaysia's prime minister from 1981 to 2003. In a letter to Manser in 1992, Mahathir wrote: "It is fine for you to spend a short holiday tasting the Penan way of life and then returning to the heated comfort of your Swiss chalet. ... What right have you to condemn them to a primitive life forever?" Prime Minister Mahathir saw himself as a spokesman for postcolonial nations, and in his final paragraph he went for Manser's jugular. "Stop being arrogant and thinking that it is the white man's burden to decide the fate of the peoples in this world. ... Swiss imperialism is as disgusting as other European imperialism. It is about time that you stop your arrogance and your intolerable European superiority."[3]

During the 1990s logging in Sarawak proceeded as if Manser were no more than a buzzing fly. Disheartened, Manser summed up the impact of his campaign within Sarawak as "less than zero." By the end of the 1990s, according to Roger Graf who for a time in the mid-1980s lived with Manser in Borneo, Manser was "bitterly disappointed," frustrated to see loggers continuing to bulldoze Sarawak's rainforests, and saddened to see more and more Penan "giving up," accepting token sums from timber firms, wearing Western clothes, drinking Coca-Colas, and moving into towns. Manser was further dismayed to see environmentalists moderating their views and cooperating with corporations, symbolized for him by the founding of the Forest Stewardship Council in 1993 to certify so-called sustainable timber.

"Does this paradise really have to die?" Manser jotted down in his diary of life with the Penan. Activists from around the world would join what he called his fight to "save a dying culture and tradition from its demise." But as time passed more and more fellow activists came to see him as unrealistic. Others began to criticize him for romanticizing a harsh life: how many Penan really wanted to live as hunters and gatherers? Still others worried that his media "antics" were distracting from campaigns to improve the living standards of far larger groups of indigenous peoples in Malaysia—as well as elsewhere in the tropics. "Bruno Manser's story evokes the notion of the Tarzan syndrome," commented Randy Hayes, who cofounded the Rainforest Action Network in 1985. "No one cared about the Penan until a white man came to the scene; they were considered little brown men who needed guidance. While this is not Bruno Manser's fault, he plays into it unwittingly. ... Manser's impact lies in the fact that he brought attention to the issue. But there's a danger in letting the messenger steal the limelight."

On May 23, 2000, Manser slipped back into Sarawak. A few days later he was seen heading into the mountainous Batu Lawi region to meet up with some Penan leaders. He never arrived. At the base of Batu Lawi Mountain a Penan search party would find the end of his trail slashing through the jungle. But searchers could find no trace of him or of his 55-pound knapsack of gear and supplies. Since then no one has ever seen or heard from him, and in 2005 a Swiss civil court declared him legally dead.

What happened to Bruno Manser? Police were pursuing him. Hired thugs were guarding the loggers, and rumors never stopped swirling of a sizable bounty on his head. Was he murdered? Perhaps, but he was facing many other dangers too. Batu Lawi is a treacherous climb. And Borneo's rainforests contain an abundance of mysteries and menaces, a lesson taught to me during a trek deep into Sarawak's jungle when, alone, having slipped the authorities who the day before had warned me to stop asking questions about logging and political corruption, I went rock still, no longer feeling so clever as a 20-foot reticulated python, just inches in front of me, slid slowly past.

The fate of Bruno Manser may forever remain a mystery. It's even possible that he was looking to escape his life. "If he wanted to die," speculated Graf, "it would be somewhere around Batu Lawi. There are many ways of seeking to die."[4]

## Rainforest Activism

Bruno Manser "wanted to study and learn to live like the Penan," explains Penan headman Melai Nah. "He followed the star of the Penan. He was not like other white men—he did not do bad things to the Penan."

Simon Elegant and Long Adang, writing for *Time* magazine in 2001, describe Manser as having "failed utterly" in his campaign to save the Penan and the old-growth forests of Borneo. But this seems too harsh. Manser helped Penan tribes to fight the governments of Sarawak and Kuala Lumpur. He raised global awareness of human rights abuses and biodiversity loss in Sarawak. And his legacy continues to motivate environmental and human rights activists. He can even take some credit for contemporary laws to try to eliminate illegal tropical timber imports into places such as

the EU and United States. The Bruno Manser Fonds, a Swiss nongovernmental organization that he cofounded in 1991, continues to resist destructive logging in Sarawak, including a campaign to expose corruption and
human rights abuses in Sarawak's timber industry. This fund also supports
educational and health services for the Penan, and has financed legal cases
on their behalf.[5]

The global campaign to save the world's remaining rainforests has grown
even bigger since Manser's disappearance in 2000. Indigenous peoples and
environmentalists continue to oppose loggers and organize public protests.
Such resistance remains extremely dangerous for activists. Across 35 countries the NGO Global Witness found over 900 recorded murders of environmental activists from 2002 to 2013, with the average number of killings
each year more than doubling after 2009. Another 116 activists were killed
in 2014. Many more activists "disappeared" or died in what authorities,
after a cursory investigation, dismissed as "accidents." Verified murders of
environmentalists averaged nearly 3 a week in 2012, for a total of 147 that
year (compared to an average of 67 per year during the previous decade).
Indigenous activists are especially vulnerable, particularly those opposing
logging and mining. The most unsafe place for activists is the Brazilian
Amazon, with Brazil as a whole accounting for just over half of all documented murders of environmentalists from 2002 to 2013.[6]

Over this time scores of transnational NGOs have been campaigning to
save the remaining tropical rainforests. These include the Rainforest Action
Network (US, founded 1985), Rainforest Rescue (German, founded 1986),
Conservation International (founded 1987), WWF (founded 1961), Friends
of the Earth (founded 1969), and Greenpeace (founded 1971). Strategies
and tactics range widely, from the tedious to the tantalizing. One Berlin-
based NGO, Fuck for Forest, is raising money for rainforest conservation
through "eco-porn," claiming to donate more than 80 percent of its proceeds from homemade pornography (WWF refuses to take money from
Fuck for Forest).[7]

Thousands of local NGOs work as well to protect rainforests. Many reject
markets and industrial development and continue to challenge greed and
corruption as Manser did. Yet, just as Bruno Manser foresaw, environmentalism of the rich has increasingly come to characterize rainforest activism as more and more environmentalists cooperate with multinational
corporations and growth-oriented governments, endorsing the value of

international trade, foreign direct investment, and privatization, and relying on certification and eco-consumerism as solutions. This environmentalism takes in particular the form of NGOs and nonprofit associations—ones such as the Rainforest Alliance (founded 1987), the Forest Stewardship Council (founded 1993), Forests Trends (founded 1996), the Roundtable on Sustainable Palm Oil (founded 2004), the Round Table on Responsible Soy (founded 2006), and the Global Roundtable for Sustainable Beef (founded 2012)—partnering with corporations to set standards for what they declare is sustainably and responsibly produced timber, palm oil, soybeans, beef, and leather.

## Ending Deforestation?

Together, international programs and agreements to protect rainforests have improved management in some places, but overall progress in slowing tropical deforestation has been frustratingly slow. Loopholes abound and implementation of regulations is generally weak. Debates over how best to end tropical deforestation seem caught in a recording loop with no one listening. Each new international meeting and regional negotiation seems to begin with delegates noting the deteriorating state of the world's forests. Then the conversation starts anew as environmentalists like Bruno Manser rally outside. In places such as Sarawak logging and land-clearing to plant oil palm has continued largely unheeded. Two-thirds of Sarawak's remaining intact rainforests have been fragmented and degraded since Manser launched his global campaign in 1990. And today oil palm plantations cover well over 1 million hectares of Sarawak, with satellite images revealing that just 5–10 percent of Sarawak's rainforests are still intact enough to retain full biological integrity.

Even the same political characters continue to profit from the logging and clearing of Sarawak's rainforests. The world may have lost Bruno Manser. But Taib survives, in 2014 stepping down as Chief Minister after 33 years in power only to become governor of Sarawak (his former brother-in-law became Chief Minister). Taib's family, the Bruno Manser Fund estimates, was worth $15 billion in 2015, with investments across hundreds of firms in at least 25 countries. Environmental and human rights activists have had little influence on politicians or firms inside Malaysia. Campaigns to sway consumers outside Malaysia have gained more traction, but even here the pace of progress has been slow, with seeming gains often lost as new markets and buyers emerge. In the 1980s and 1990s Japan financed logging in Sarawak and was by far the largest importer of logs. Most of this lumber was turned into plywood to mold concrete for building construction in Japan—and then tossed into landfills or burned after being used a few times. Manser made headlines when he joined with activists in Tokyo to call on the Japanese government to ban timber imports from Sarawak. Yet to this day Japan remains Sarawak's biggest buyer of plywood even as NGOs such as Global Witness continue to lobby and protest.

Moreover, China, not Japan, is now the largest overall consumer of tropical timber in Asia. Imports of tropical logs and sawn wood into China rose quickly after Beijing banned logging in China's natural forests in 1998. For activists, influencing politicians, local businesses, and consumers in China is even harder than in Japan. Somewhere between 30 and 80 percent of the timber flowing through China is illegal, as smugglers slip past border guards, forge papers, and evade taxes. In recent years perhaps as much as half of the world's traded timber has been flowing through China as demand soars for housing, furniture, paper, pallets, cardboard, and packaging.[8]

Moreover, consumption of wood and paper products is only one of many causes of tropical deforestation. Logging in the tropics tends to degrade forests, drying them out. A cheap way to clear a logged forest is to burn it down—which in turn helps fertilize plantation crops and grasslands for cattle. Soy plantations, oil palm estates, and ranching are now the three leading causes of tropical deforestation. Soymeal is widely fed to the world's 1 billion or so pigs. And increasingly, firms are growing palm oil as feedstock for biofuel. The growth of fast food and processed food is further stimulating demand for beef, oil palm, and soybeans, with palm oil and soy in thousands of products, from cooking oil, margarine, and potato chips to cookies, cereals, and cosmetics.

Consumption of vegetable oil, including palm oil, has been rising steadily for decades. Palm oil comprises about one-third of global vegetable oil production, and in some supermarkets as much as half of all processed food products contain palm oil. Malaysia and Indonesia are the main producers of palm oil, with output increasing steadily after 1990 (in 2014, they accounted for around 85 percent of global palm oil production). In Indonesia, including in Kalimantan on Borneo, palm oil production rose tenfold from 1990 to 2011. And in Malaysia oil palm plantations now cover more than three-quarters of the country's agricultural land.[9]

Activists are still blockading logging roads and marching to protest the loss of the world's rainforests. National and local governments have passed thousands of forest management laws. Community forestry programs have grown and international donors have set up financing mechanisms to support efforts to curb deforestation. And since Bruno Manser took up the cause of Borneo's rainforests in the mid-1980s, NGOs have partnered with companies and governments on hundreds of initiatives to try to improve tropical forest management. At the 2014 United Nations Climate Summit in New York City, as noted in chapter 4, dozens of governments, multinational corporations, environmental organizations, and indigenous groups pledged to try to cut the loss of natural forests in half by 2020 and end deforestation by 2030. Signatories to the New York Declaration on Forests include the United Kingdom, the United States, Japan, and Indonesia. Also signing were Walmart, Nestlé, McDonald's, and Marks & Spencer, as well as the International Union for Conservation of Nature, the Sierra Club, The Nature Conservancy, and WWF.

Such declarations by such powers might seem like progress. Yet we're not close to ending deforestation. Loggers, plantation owners, and ranchers continue to clear and degrade boreal, temperate, and especially tropical forests. Globally, average deforestation was at least 13 million hectares a year from 2000 to 2010, with two-thirds occurring in Southeast Asia, South America, and Africa—an overall rate of deforestation that has changed little since then. The rate of tropical deforestation, meanwhile, has been rising steadily since 2000, with satellite analysis by the World Resources Institute revealing record levels in 2014. This is a deeply worrying trend. Already, more than half of the world's rainforests are gone and of those remaining the vast majority have suffered significant damage.[10]

The history of the campaign to save the tropical rainforests makes for bleak reading. Was Bruno Manser right? When all is said and done, did his life of activism amount to "less than zero"? The answer is an emphatic "no." Bruno Manser deserves our acclaim and admiration, and to this day his courage and commitment inspire activists. Still, as his life was nearing an end, he could see the raw destructive power of greed and corruption in a globalizing world of ever-rising economic growth, corporate sales, and individual consumption. And he could feel the power of capitalism to assimilate and contain environmentalism, especially the voices and organizations of global environmentalism emerging from the Western world.

I'm sure it wouldn't surprise him that governments and corporations around the world are now claiming that the end of deforestation is in sight, if only we can embrace state-led sustainable development, corporate-led responsibility, and consumer-led demand for sustainable products—three core messages of environmentalism of the rich. It would perhaps dismay him further, though, to see fellow rainforest activist Jane Goodall on this message too. "Oh, yes. I'm hopeful," she said in 2014 as she was contemplating her upcoming eightieth birthday. "I know all the bad things. I do my research and I'm not naive. ... But if a critical mass of us make little changes, we will change the direction of the planet."[11]

Does environmentalism of little changes really have such power? Most radical environmentalists certainly don't think so.

## 9 Radicals and Rebels

Gutsy and audacious, Jane Goodall was the first scientist to ever live as a member of a chimpanzee society, revealing how similar chimpanzees could be to humans: loving, caring, and intelligent; irascible, brutish, and cannibalistic. Guided by a philosophy of what she says is her "curiosity" and "passion" for "all animals," she's dedicated her life to wildlife conservation in Africa. Seemingly indefatigable, in 1957 at the age of twenty-three she left London to live in Kenya, and then later Tanzania, before heading to Cambridge University to complete a PhD in ethology in 1965. Twelve years later she founded the Jane Goodall Institute to advocate for great apes and the value of tropical ecosystems. In the early 1990s she started up Roots & Shoots as a global network to empower and educate young people to respect—and protect—natural systems as integral to improving community life. A few years later she launched a program to support "community-centered conservation" in Kigoma, Tanzania (called TACARE, or the Lake Tanganyika Catchment Reforestation and Education program). In recognition of her service, in 2004 she was made a Dame of the Order of the British Empire.

From 1998 to 2008 Goodall was president of Advocates for Animals, an animal welfare organization headquartered in Edinburgh. A vegetarian, in 2011 she became a patron of Australia's Voiceless: The Animal Protection Institute. Taking on this new role she publicly condemned "factory farming, in part because of the tremendous harm inflicted on the environment, but also because of the shocking ongoing cruelty perpetuated on millions of sentient beings." If this was not already a busy life, along the way she has published more than 25 adult and children books.

Is Dame Jane a radical? Some people certainly think so, seeing her as an animal rights fanatic. Others see her biocentrism—with a belief in the intrinsic value of all life on earth—as sacrilegious. Radicalism in wealthy countries is diverse and fragmented, a characteristic that in recent years security agencies have been exploiting to crack down on more confrontational activism by portraying all direct-action environmental groups as violent extremists and terrorists. As we'll see in this chapter by comparing the acts and beliefs of some of those involved over the years in Greenpeace, the Sea Shepherd Conservation Society, the Animal Liberation Front, and the Earth Liberation Front, deep divisions exist across so-called radical organizations on what are necessary—and acceptable—tactics and reforms, with sharp differences in understanding of what even constitutes a radical act. And as generations collide and individuals age, nasty, bitter disputes have torn apart past alliances of radicals, further undermining the power of more radical environmentalists to challenge the growing dominance of environmentalism of the rich as well as weakening the power of environmentalism as a whole to act as a counterforce to the political and economic forces of unsustainable development.

Today, for instance, very few environmentalists would see Goodall as radical. In 2008 one group even pressed her to resign as president of Advocates for Animals after she described the Edinburgh Zoo's chimpanzee enclosure as "wonderful." Some environmentalists would even say she's a conformist, seeing her philosophy of nonviolence and her ongoing call for little changes to solve global problems as propping up the exploitative structures and institutions that are causing social inequality and biodiversity loss.[1]

### Patrick Moore: The "Greenpeace Dropout"

Would a dame of the British Empire ever deserve the title of radical? Wouldn't a true radical reject the pomp and imperialism of the British monarchy? Describing anyone as radical is always problematic. Was Germany's Petra Kelly—a peace, women's rights, and environmental activist who went on to cofound the West German Green Party in 1979—a radical? What about Japan's Yoichi Kuroda, who in 1987 helped to establish the Japan Tropical Forest Action Network (JATAN), and who for many years coordinated a campaign to end Japan's role in the illegal logging and deforestation of Southeast Asia and Melanesia? Or what about Canada's Patrick Moore, who in the 1970s and 1980s sailed the high seas under the banner of Greenpeace to oppose nuclear testing as well as commercial whaling and sealing?

In some ways Moore is the easiest to classify. In his twenties and for much of his thirties he was most definitely a radical, arrested multiple times as he fought the ruling elites of his day. Sporting a beret atop his long bushy hair, he was on the first "Greenpeace" voyage that left Vancouver in 1971 to "bear witness" to American nuclear tests off the coast of Alaska. Four years later he was on Greenpeace's first anti-whaling voyage, where, off the coast of California, Soviet whalers fired a harpoon over the heads of activists riding in an inflatable dinghy, striking and killing a female sperm whale.

In 1977 Moore became president of the Greenpeace Foundation (renamed Greenpeace Canada when Greenpeace International was established in 1979). Moore did not support sabotage, violence, or damaging property, despite his many scrapes with the law. In the spring of 1978, trying to obtain a government permit to go to the seal hunt on the ice floes off Newfoundland, he was arrested for "loitering" in an office of the Canadian Department of Fisheries and the Environment. Later that spring authorities arrested him for obstructing Newfoundland's seal hunt. His crime? Shielding a startled pup between his legs as a sealer strode over to club and skin it.

For some Greenpeace activists, however, Moore wasn't radical enough. Moore in turn found elements of the hippie counterculture exasperating. Don't "get totally bunkered out on dope and booze as there are complex things to work out," he lectured the board of directors of Greenpeace America at a meeting in San Francisco in 1978. Few on the board seemed impressed. "I have a solid commitment to see that Greenpeace is really revolutionary," Moore added, trying to confirm his radical credentials and convince the directors to help out with the mounting legal costs of Greenpeace's anti-sealing campaign. "I housed draft resisters and deserters. I'm from a radical background. I don't want creeping revisionism or liberalism in Greenpeace. We have to stay peacefully hard line." Still the directors were unwilling to support Moore, vaguely calling on Greenpeace to stay "pure" and "democratic." In the end Moore lost his temper, hollering and storming away empty handed.[2]

In 1979 Moore became a director of Greenpeace International. It was in this capacity that he was visiting New Zealand in 1985 when French secret service agents bombed and sank the *Rainbow Warrior* in Auckland harbor to prevent it from heading to Moruroa (an atoll in the southern Pacific Ocean) to protest French nuclear weapons tests. This espionage scandal would captivate the world, and, as an organization, Greenpeace would emerge even stronger from the publicity. Yet this did not matter for Moore. By then relations between Moore and other Greenpeace leaders had gone from prickly to nasty, and in 1986 Moore and Greenpeace went separate ways.

Since then Moore has most definitely not been living as a radical environmentalist, but has instead been advancing his own form of anti-environmentalism. Now an industry consultant, he portrays environmentalists as emotional and irrational and unscientific. He questions the science of climate change and backs nuclear power, industrial mining, and the chemical and plastic industries. On top of this he advocates for the planting of genetically modified crops, the clearing of tropical rainforests, and the farming of salmon. "At the beginning," explains Moore, "the environmental movement had reason to say that the end of the world is nigh, but most of the really serious problems have been dealt with. Now it's almost as though the environmental movement has to invent doom and gloom scenarios." Today, Moore is a fierce critic of Greenpeace, calling the organization "antiscience, anticorporate, and downright antihuman" on the opening page of his 2010 book, *Confessions of a Greenpeace Dropout*. For its part, Greenpeace dismisses Moore as a "paid lobbyist" and "a paid spokesman for the nuclear industry, the logging industry, and genetic engineering industry."[3]

### Captain Watson: A Life on the "Front Lines"

The lives of radical environmentalists have twisted and turned in many directions over the past half century. Another early Greenpeace activist, Captain Paul Watson, became more militant over time. Like Moore, he was piloting one of the Zodiac boats during the 1975 clash with the Soviet whalers. That day, watching the slaughter of the sperm whales, and knowing the Soviets would use at least some of the whale oil to lubricate machinery to make intercontinental ballistic missiles, he had a "flash" of insight: "We're insane. We're just totally insane. And from that moment on, I decided that I work for whales, I work for seals, I work for sea turtles, and fish, and seabirds. I don't work for people."

In 1977 Watson cofounded the Earthforce Environmental Society to sail the world's oceans to not only disrupt, but also sabotage, whaling and sealing fleets. Two years later Watson piloted a trawler (which he named the

*Sea Shepherd*) to the ice flows off the Magdalen Islands in the Gulf of St. Lawrence where every spring harp seals birth their pups. Here, the crew of the *Sea Shepherd* spray painted a thousand white pups with red dye to ruin the commercial value of the pelts. (Harp pups molt within a few weeks, so spraying red dye on their birthing coat did not hurt their chances of surviving in the wild.) Later that year in Portuguese waters, Watson rammed his first whaling ship, the *Sierra*, which he declared a "notorious prolific pirate whaler" and a "scourge of the seas." The following year, after the *Sierra*'s owners had spent more than $1 million to repair the ship, Earthforce activists slipped into Lisbon harbor and sank the *Sierra* with limpet mines.

In 1981 the Earthforce Environmental Society was renamed the Sea Shepherd Conservation Society. By the early 1980s the Sea Shepherd Conservation Society was also campaigning to save dolphins and sharks, as well as occasionally fighting for animal rights more generally. In 1983, for instance, the crew of the *Sea Shepherd II* broke into Grenada's St. George's zoo to free all of the monkeys. Roundly criticized, Watson was flippant: "These primates cannot possibly do more damage than the primate *Homo sapiens* already has to this island."

During more than 200 voyages, Watson has had many run-ins with coastguards and police. Time and again he and his crew have been arrested. The list of charges is long: scuttling whaling and fishing boats; tossing stink bombs and boarding ships; disrupting seal hunts and shark finning; disabling boat propellers and damaging property; and destroying driftnets and deep-sea fishing lines. To date, however, no Sea Shepherd activist has ever been convicted. And, although minor injuries among Sea Shepherd crew are common, no one has ever been killed. Backing the "outlaw" Watson as he skillfully sails around prosecutors is a company of actors and rock stars—Sean Penn, Daryl Hannah, Mick Jagger, Uma Thurman, Brigitte Bardot, Martin Sheen, Pierce Brosnan, and Christian Bale, among many others over the years. Farley Mowat, the Canadian author of the bestselling book *Never Cry Wolf*, was one of Watson's biggest fans. In 2002 Watson named his flagship the *Farley Mowat* (which the Canadian Coast Guard would seize six years later), and until passing away in 2014 Farley Mowat served as the international chairman of the Sea Shepherd Conservation Society.[4]

In recent years the law has been closing in on Captain Watson. In 2012 Watson skipped bail while in Germany facing Interpol notices for extradition to Costa Rica and Japan on criminal charges for obstructing shark-finning and whaling. For the next 15 months he sailed the high seas as a fugitive, before returning to the United States in 2013 and settling in Vermont. Japan and Costa Rica are still pursuing him, however—as of early 2016 Interpol still listed him as a "wanted person"—and Watson is now concentrating on trying to resolve his legal status, reportedly living at times in Paris. Although no longer at sea, he remains proud of his deeds, and continues to confront his critics head on. Typical is his rebuke of the Canadian Navy for questioning his competence to operate a small submarine that the Sea Shepherd Society had bought. "Since World War II, the Sea Shepherd Conservation Society has boarded more ships, rammed more ships, engaged in more high seas confrontations, and sunk more ships than the Canadian Navy. They are hardly in a position to presume to judge what we are competent or capable of doing."

Like Moore, Watson has been at war with Greenpeace for decades, belittling the organization for being rigid and ineffective, for lacking true commitment (Watson and his crews are vegan), and for being content to accomplish nothing of real consequence. Greenpeace activists are "the Avon ladies of the environmental movement" with "a gigantic self-perpetuating bureaucracy," bristles Watson. "They spend millions of dollars every year on advertising and direct-mail campaigns simply to raise more money. People feel good about giving money to Greenpeace. But holding up protest signs, taking pictures, and 'bearing witness' while whales are getting killed in front of you doesn't achieve anything at all, which is why I abandoned those tactics more than 30 years ago." Greenpeace in turn denounces Watson and, as with Moore, is working hard to purge his presence from the telling of the history of Greenpeace.

Even in the 1970s Watson and Moore never could agree on what was an acceptable act of protest, and shortly after Moore became president of the Greenpeace Foundation, Watson was voted off the board of directors. Today, although Watson still refers to Moore as "Pat," both seem to loathe each other even more than they do Greenpeace. "You're a corporate whore, Pat, an eco-Judas, a lowlife bottom-sucking parasite who has grown rich from sacrificing environmentalist principles for plain old money," Watson emailed Moore in 2004.[5]

## Liberating the Earth: Ecotage or Eco-Terrorism?

The lives of Jane Goodall, Patrick Moore, and Paul Watson remind us of the need to keep in mind that radical environmentalists hold diverse opinions, deploy a wide range of tactics, and over time may become more militant or more moderate. The lives of Kalle Lasn (Adbusters and the Buy Nothing campaign) and Bruno Manser (the Penan campaign) illustrate further the great diversity of views and concerns among radicals. Perceptions of what is an "acceptable" radical act differ widely, too. To some people Watson is courageous and nonviolent, as he targets property, not people; to others he's a dangerous extremist.

Some radical environmentalists are willing to go much further than Watson in risking casualties and collateral damage. According to a 2013 briefing for the US Congress, the two gravest threats are the Animal Liberation Front (ALF), emerging in the UK in the mid-1970s, and the Earth Liberation Front (ELF), emerging in the UK in the early 1990s. ELF formed as more militant activists broke away from Earth First!—a movement of civil disobedience against capitalism founded in the US in 1980. Earth First! began to turn away from direct-action tactics after the FBI arrested five members in 1990, including cofounder Dave Foreman, for conspiracy to sabotage nuclear power and weapons facilities. "I'm not an anarchist," Foreman would later declare, pleading for leniency during his sentencing hearing. "I'm not a terrorist. I'm not a revolutionary. What I did was an attempt to wake people up." Today Earth First! still functions across 20 or so countries. But it's ALF and ELF, with tentacles across dozens of countries, which most worry anti-terrorist agencies (the 2013 US congressional briefing, for example, portrays them as fanatical, lawless, and exceedingly dangerous).[6]

The Animal Liberation Front and the Earth Liberation Front organize in secret cells and urge individuals to "join" by taking direct action to oppose industrial farming, animal testing, and animal cruelty. Such leaderless and underground structures can attract lone-wolf zealots, and differentiating between legitimate and illegitimate acts is nearly impossible. Both movements, however, claim to be "nonviolent," urging followers to take precautions to try to avoid harming any life. At the same time both groups assume that actions will be "illegal," and serving jail time is a badge of honor. Liberation acts include sabotage (commonly called "ecotage"), tree spiking, fire bombing, and harassment.

Since the 1970s ALF followers have "rescued" animals and damaged lab-
oratories, zoos, and fur and factory farms. And since the 1990s ELF followers
(who call themselves "elves") have torched ski resorts, hunting lodges, sub-
urban housing developments, condominiums, fast-food restaurants, and
sports utility vehicles to liberate nature from ever-encroaching humans.
ELF was launched in the UK in 1992 and by the mid-1990s was spreading
across Europe. Its first acts in the United States came in 1996. That year
in Oregon ELF claimed responsibility for vandalizing several McDonald's
restaurants, a Chevron station, and a PR firm working for Weyerhaeuser
and Hyundai; soon afterward a US Forest Service pickup truck and Ranger
Station were set alight.

For ALF and ELF such acts are not theft or vandalism, but rather liberation. ALF contends that it's fighting against "speciesism," a prejudice as bad,
if not worse, than racism and sexism. Only vegans or vegetarians can act in
the name of ALF. And in ALF's view no one has the right to own animals as
property, a practice ALF sees as akin to slavery. The Earth Liberation Front
was named in 1992 to express solidarity with ALF, and followers interact
and overlap. Like the Animal Liberation Front, ELF opposes speciesism, but
also more explicitly fights capitalism, industrialization, and globalization as
forces killing mother earth.[7]

Security agencies have long treated radical environmentalists as potential threats to national security, as we can see from the French secret service
bombing of the *Rainbow Warrior* in 1985 and from the FBI's crackdown on
Earth First! after 1990. Yet, as the crackdown on the Occupy Movement in
2011 shows, many governments are going even further now, increasing
surveillance, infiltrating radical groups, arresting peaceful demonstrators,
and deploying military weapons to subdue mass protests.[8] The US Federal
Bureau of Investigation is taking an especially hard line, and considers ALF,
ELF, and the Sea Shepherd Conservation Society to be "eco-terrorists." The
FBI defines eco-terrorism as "the use or threatened use of violence of a criminal nature against innocent victims or property by an environmentally-
oriented, subnational group for environmental-political reasons, or aimed
at an audience beyond the target, often of a symbolic nature." Under this
definition Watson is an eco-terrorist, and in testimony to the US Congress
in 2002 FBI Section Chief James Jarboe singled out the cutting of driftnets
by the Sea Shepherd Conservation Society as an example of eco-terrorism.

According to the FBI, "eco-terrorists and animal rights extremists" are "one of the most serious domestic terrorism threats in the US today." Animal rights activist Daniel Andreas San Diego, alleged to have bombed a cosmetics/nutrition company and a biotech company in San Francisco in 2003, is on the FBI's list of "Most Wanted Terrorists" (with a $250,000 reward, as of 2015). Arrests and heightened surveillance by the FBI have kept militant environmentalists in the United States largely in check in recent years. In 2007 ten people identifying with ELF and ALF were sentenced to between 3 and 13 years for conspiracy and arson. Other ELF and ALF followers have gone into hiding, such as Rebecca Jeanette Rubin who, after six years on the run in Canada, eventually surrendered and in 2014 was sentenced to 5 years in prison and ordered to pay $13.9 million in restitution.

In 2008 the FBI estimated that since 1979 environmental extremists had committed more than 2,000 crimes in the US, with damage exceeding $110 million. Sporadic attacks do still occur in the United States. In 2013, for instance, saboteurs destroyed genetically modified crops in Oregon. Animal rights and earth liberationists are the main ideological sources of such acts in the US, although now and then environmental sabotage occurs as well in the name of anarchism, eco-feminism, anti-globalization, anti-capitalism, anti-technology, and biocentrism.[9]

Militant environmentalists have committed similar acts across Europe as well as in countries such as Canada, Australia, and New Zealand. Agendas and tactics range widely. Three people, for instance, were arrested in 2010 for conspiracy to bomb an IBM nanotechnology plant in Switzerland. Swiss police would later link them to Italian anarchists who claimed responsibility for bombings in Switzerland, Italy, and Greece. A loose collection of environmental extremists and anarchists—sometimes expressing allegiance to Italy's Informal Anarchist Federation—seems to be linking across Europe. The group first hit the UK in 2012. And actions are ongoing. In 2014, for example, websites for the Informal Anarchist Federation and the Earth Liberation Front took credit for arson attacks on mobile phones towers in Bristol, England.

## Radical Environmentalism

Violence and sabotage gain headlines and trigger harsh state responses. Yet such acts comprise a tiny fraction of what most environmentalists would call radical environmentalism. Breaking the law is acceptable for most radicals—say trespassing or sleeping overnight in a public park—but the vast majority would never support bombs, violence, or sabotage. Most eco-radicals, as we see with frontline activists for Greenpeace or the Rainforest Action Network, categorically reject such acts, understanding "nonviolence" as never risking the lives of others. For most environmentalists, radicals are men such as Daniel Hooper, who at the age of twenty-two earned the nickname "Swampy" after tunneling under a highway excavation site in southwest England, eluding police and delaying construction for a week. Radicals are women such as Julia Butterfly Hill, who at the age of twenty-three climbed a thousand-year-old California redwood where she would live for two years to keep the chainsaws at bay. For most environmentalists, radicals should bear witness and stand in the line of fire. They should chain themselves to bulldozers and occupy city squares. They should "reclaim the streets" with throngs of cyclists and throw "road parties" to delay highway construction. And they should "guerilla garden" public lawns and boulevards with native flowers and local vegetables.[10]

Just about every day, radicals of this kind come out in force somewhere in the world. Passions run deep for saving wildlife and preserving wilderness. So does sympathy for chimpanzees, whales, dolphins, and seals. Yet much of what more militant environmentalists oppose—speciesism, industrial farming, suburbs, highways, and automobiles—rarely ignite large-scale uprisings. Nor are many people in any culture inspired to revolution by pleas for biocentrism, animal rights, less consumption, or the valuing of all life equally. On occasion concerns over exploitation and inequality—and slogans such as Occupy's "We are the 99%"—do resonate globally. Even then, however, the vast majority of people do not seem willing to change their lifestyles fundamentally, let alone live for two years in a tree to fight for global justice.

Jane Goodall accepts this. But as we saw she also sees a critical mass of young people willing—indeed, even eager—to make little lifestyle changes in the name of environmentalism. For her this trend holds the potential to generate real and lasting change in the way firms exploit natural resources and supply consumer goods. This is why, like so many environmentalists these days, she's putting so much hope in the environmentalism of the rich. Certainly, NGOs such as Greenpeace continue to challenge the interests of big business with daring acts of protest and targeted media campaigns. Yet, as we'll see next, even Greenpeace is now embracing eco-consumerism in many of their campaigns, a strategy that is producing some minor reforms to industry practices, but is doing little to advance global-scale sustainability and runs the risk of legitimizing the very political and corporate processes that are causing the overall rate of unsustainable consumption to escalate.

# 10 Mindbombing the Wealthy

*Time* magazine chose Canadian journalist Bob Hunter as one of the most influential "eco-heroes" of the twentieth century, alongside the likes of Rachel Carson, Jane Goodall, and Paul Watson. A Greenpeace cofounder and its first president, Hunter liked to call on his comrades to "mindbomb" global consciousness with media images of environmental wrongdoing. Hunter died of cancer in 2005 but his influence lives on as Greenpeace continues to mindbomb consumers and policymakers with ideas and images, relying on the daring acts of "eco-warriors" (another of Hunter's colorful expressions), the backing of music and movie stars, and the shaming of iconic brands to capture the world's imagination.

Such campaigns have been able to rally protestors and voters, as well as push towns, cities, and states to pass environmental regulations. They have further influenced millions, at times even billions, of citizens to consume more responsibly. In recent years campaigners have even managed to influence some of the world's best-known brands through social media. As this chapter charts, as part of a campaign to push multinational brands to cancel contracts with suppliers linked to tropical deforestation, Greenpeace shamed Mattel into changing its Barbie doll packaging, as well as Nestlé (for its Kit Kat chocolate bar) and Procter & Gamble (for its Head & Shoulders shampoo) into switching palm oil suppliers. Seeing these outcomes, other global brands have been quick to revise their own policies for sourcing and certifying palm oil and pulp and paper—with, for example, Pepsi, Mars, Cargill, L'Oréal, General Mills, Kellogg's, and Johnston & Johnson all announcing new commitments in 2014. Even a few of the suppliers, such as Asia Pulp & Paper (the source of Barbie's cardboard packaging), are now claiming to embrace sustainability to try to convince multinational brands to once again purchase their products.

The power of Greenpeace to influence global supply chains and certification processes would appear to be increasing as multinational brands and local suppliers try to avoid becoming a target. In particular, Greenpeace seems to be gaining leverage by pitting corporations against each other, praising some as leaders and critiquing others for lagging behind. Greenpeace is proud of these campaigns. But it's easy to exaggerate the value of the resulting corporate reforms and, as we'll see in this chapter, mindbombing middle-class consumers over social media is doing little to alter the world politics of ever-rising revenues, growth, and consumption.

If anything, brand companies such as Nestlé, Mattel, and Procter & Gamble are now trumpeting what are relatively minor reforms as examples of sustainability and corporate responsibility, using savings and feel-good rhetoric to sell even more products (as we saw firms doing in chapter 4, too). This outcome helps explain why, even as eco-consumerism of the middle classes continues to gain in strength, per capita ecological footprints continue to intensify (as we found in chapter 5). At the same time, as I'll show next with the Greenpeace campaign to stop multinational oil and gas companies from drilling in the Arctic, those who call for far-reaching reforms to the environmental practices of corporations continue to face violent resistance from both states and business.[1]

### Eco-Warriors of the *Arctic Sunrise*

Greenpeace has been detonating mindbombs since first campaigning in the 1970s against nuclear weapons testing, whaling, and sealing. Typical are the exploits of the Greenpeace ship *Arctic Sunrise* to protest oil drilling in the Arctic. In September 2013 the *Arctic Sunrise* sailed to the Pechora Sea where two Greenpeace activists scaled like mountaineers up the towering walls of a Gazprom oil platform. Torrents from the rig's fire hoses blasted the climbers. In the freezing and choppy sea below, four Greenpeace inflatable dinghies tried to evade Russian Coast Guard agents who, wearing balaclavas and wielding knives and guns, were trying to ram and slash the dinghies. Warning shots were fired as agents seized the two activists who were retreating from the fire hoses.

The next day armed Russian agents rappelled from a helicopter and stormed the *Arctic Sunrise* in international waters. The captain and 29-person crew (including 2 freelance journalists) were arrested and the *Arctic*

*Sunrise* was towed to Murmansk in northwest Russia. Kumi Naidoo, at the time the executive director of Greenpeace International, rushed to their defense. "Greenpeace International has a 40-year history of taking peaceful action to protect the environment," he said, "and last week's protest against dangerous Arctic oil drilling was carried out in line with these strong principles. Our activists did nothing to warrant the reaction we've seen from the Russian authorities."

In no way was Russia contrite, however, and prosecutors upped the ante by charging the 30 activists with "piracy": a crime carrying a sentence of up to 15 years. "Any claim that these activists are pirates," Naidoo retorted, "is as absurd as it is abominable. It is utterly irrational, it is designed to intimidate and silence us, but we will not be cowed." Outrage swept the global environmental community, and more than 50 environmental groups signed a letter to Russian President Vladimir Putin demanding an immediate release of the "peaceful" protestors. The piracy charges were a lead news story around the world, with interest particularly high in the eighteen countries of citizenship of what the media was now calling the "Arctic 30."

For the next two months the Arctic 30 would languish in a detention center in Murmansk. Over this time Greenpeace did not ease up in its campaign against Gazprom. In Germany, activists chained themselves to a Gazprom gasoline pump. In Italy, they disrupted a regatta sponsored by Gazprom. During a Champions League soccer match in Switzerland, they unfurled a giant banner: "Gazprom: Don't Foul the Arctic." And in Copenhagen, they hung a banner down the side of a building proclaiming, "872 Oil Spills in One Year: Stop Gazprom."

Declaring the Arctic 30 "prisoners of conscience," Greenpeace appealed to the world for help. To try to free them, the Netherlands, as the flag state of the *Arctic Sunrise*, launched international arbitration proceedings against Russia under the Law of the Sea Convention. Hundreds of pro-Greenpeace rallies erupted across scores of countries. Letters of support for Greenpeace inundated Russian embassies worldwide. City mayors signed a joint letter appealing to Russia to set the charges aside. National leaders, including UK Prime Minister David Cameron, German Chancellor Angela Merkel, and Brazilian President Dilma Rousseff, pressured Russia on behalf of Greenpeace. Madonna, Paul McCartney, Ewan McGregor, and Jude Law put their names behind Greenpeace. And 11 Nobel Prize laureates called on Russia to free the activists. "Arctic oil drilling is a dangerous, high-risk enterprise," the laureates wrote to President Putin. "An oil spill under these icy waters would have a catastrophic impact on one of the most pristine, unique, and beautiful landscapes on Earth."

In late October Russian prosecutors decided to reduce the charges from "piracy" to "hooliganism," a crime carrying a maximum of 7 years in prison. This did nothing to appease critics, however, and the European Parliament immediately issued a press release calling the charges of both piracy and hooliganism "disproportionate." A few weeks later authorities transferred the Arctic 30 to a prison in St Petersburg. By then support for the Arctic 30 was widespread, and a "global day of solidarity" saw rallies across hundreds of cities, mostly in Europe, but also reaching as far as India, where 30 rallies were held. Shortly afterward, Russia began to release some of the activists on bail.

On November 22, 2013, the International Tribunal for the Law of the Sea ruled on the Netherlands's arbitration request. The tribunal ordered the Netherlands to post a bond of €3.6 million (which Greenpeace agreed to cover) and ordered Russia to release the *Arctic Sunrise* and 30 activists. Russia did not comply with the arbitration decision, however— and a breakthrough did not come until mid-December when the Russian parliament granted the Arctic 30 amnesty. "We may soon be home," reacted *Arctic Sunrise* Captain Peter Willcox, "but the Arctic remains a fragile global treasure under assault by oil companies and the rising temperatures they're driving. We went there to protest against this madness. We were never the criminals here." By the end of the year all of the non-Russian Greenpeace activists had left Russia; the *Arctic Sunrise* would follow in mid-2014.[2]

For Greenpeace, the Arctic 30 mindbomb was a resounding victory. The courage and sacrifice of these activists raised awareness of Arctic oil drilling and the risks of oil spills. In particular the campaign highlighted the readiness of leading oil and gas companies such as Gazprom—a company ranking seventeenth in the world on the 2014 *Fortune* Global 500, up from twenty-first in 2013—to go anywhere and do anything to drill for more oil and gas. By 2014 more than five million people had signed a Greenpeace petition against oil drilling in the Arctic, and Greenpeace campaigns to oppose Gazprom and Shell were going strong.

## Greenpeace International

Many Greenpeace activists, as the Arctic 30 confirm, still battle in the tradition of eco-warriors. Yet, as the title of a 2012 *Al Jazeera World* documentary suggests—"Greenpeace: From Hippies to Lobbyists"—the organization has become far more complex, even bureaucratic, since the 1970s when Bob Hunter was first calling on eco-warriors to toss mindbombs. Now headquartered in Amsterdam, Greenpeace has more than two dozen branch offices and employs thousands of people. The annual income of Greenpeace as a whole sits at around €300 million (roughly $330 million in February 2016): although, unlike most multinational NGOs, 98 percent of this income comes from individual donors. In 2013 the budget of Greenpeace International was just under €73 million. That year, however, a Greenpeace finance clerk lost €3.8 million after speculating on the euro weakening in the second half of the year, and Greenpeace ended up with a budget deficit of €6.8 million.

In recent years Greenpeace International has been reorganizing staff and finances to shift resources away from the Amsterdam headquarters and toward campaigns in developing and emerging economies. "This restructuring is not about reducing the number of people working full time on Greenpeace campaigns," explains Kumi Naidoo, who stepped down as executive director at the end of 2015; "it's about making sure we have people where we need them, and increasingly that's not in Amsterdam. The big environmental issues are increasingly in the southern hemisphere, be it Indonesian or Amazonian deforestation, Chinese coal plants or overfishing in the Indian and Pacific Ocean[s]."[3] Central to reaching into the developing world are campaigns to shame multinational brands into raising standards within their global supply chains.

In recent years Greenpeace has been increasingly employing humorous social media to expose questionable corporate practices. These campaigns aim to devalue corporate images and raise consumer awareness, which Greenpeace tracks through online petitions, Twitter, and Facebook, as well as to encourage "supporters" to donate to Greenpeace (90 percent of Greenpeace revenues come from small donations of less than $150). The threat of falling sales and the potential for reputational gains of taking action tend to make multinational manufacturers and retailers with global brands the most responsive to shame campaigns. Campaigns to discourage consumers from purchasing a product until the manufacturer modifies a particular practice have tended to achieve the most traction. Firms have generally offered the least resistance when it's relatively easy and inexpensive to appease campaigners, and when doing so does not look likely to hurt long-term revenues, profits, or market control, as was the case with the 2011 Greenpeace campaign to push Mattel to change its Barbie doll packaging.

### Greenpeace's Barbie-Box Campaign

In June 2011 Greenpeace activists abseiled down the side of Mattel's corporate headquarters in California to hang a four-story pink-and-blue banner of a frowning Ken doll, announcing, "Barbie: It's Over: I Don't Date Girls That Are Into Deforestation." Through DNA testing and on-the-ground investigations, Greenpeace had found Indonesian rainforest fibers in Barbie's packaging box. Shortly after hanging the banner, Greenpeace posted on multiple Internet sites a video of Ken "breaking up" with Barbie after he discovered that she was deforesting the outer islands of Indonesia, home to orangutans, elephants, and Sumatran tigers, and a significant carbon sink to mitigate climate change.

Greenpeace released the video in twenty languages, including Mandarin and Arabic, and over Facebook and Twitter publicized its campaign to "stop MATTEL packaging toys with destroyed rainforest." Consumers were urged to email Mattel's CEO, post messages on Barbie's Facebook page, and contact Mattel executives to demand immediate action. Three days into the campaign Mattel disabled the comments wall for Barbie's Facebook page. Treasure hunts across the UK for "Chainsaw Barbies" kept up the pressure on Mattel. So did a staged Twitter fight between Ken and Barbie. "Did you know there are only about 400 Sumatran tigers left in the wild?" Ken tweeted. "Feel a bit sick:{"

The culprit was Mattel's supplier Asia Pulp & Paper, one of the world's largest paper producers, and a core company within the Chinese-Indonesian conglomerate Sinar Mas. For years Greenpeace had been campaigning against APP, in 2010 releasing an investigative report on how Sinar Mas was "pulping the planet." In this report Greenpeace was careful to compliment brands such as Office Depot, Staples, and Australia's Woolworths for no longer sourcing from APP. At the same time the report highlighted other international brands that were still buying from APP, including Walmart, KFC, France's Carrefour, and the UK's Tesco. Greenpeace did have some quick successes, including a decision in 2010 by Tesco to stop sourcing from APP. But APP was fighting back, in 2010 even hiring former Greenpeace Foundation President Patrick Moore—now, as we saw in the previous chapter, a corporate spokesman—who, predictably, evaluated APP's practices as "world-class sustainable forest management." The campaign against Barbie was part of an effort by Greenpeace to step up the pressure on multinational brands.

Greenpeace was calling on Mattel to kick APP out of its supply chain as well as develop a global policy to stop sourcing from tropical rainforests. Greenpeace was not only targeting Mattel as the world's largest toymaker, but was also delivering a message to Disney, Hasbro, and Lego. The Danish company Lego quickly promised to stop sourcing from suppliers causing deforestation (including APP), as well as increase the recycled and certified content of its packaging (with preference for certification by the Forest Stewardship Council). A few months later Mattel also jettisoned APP from its supply chain, in October 2011 announcing a new policy for sustainable sourcing similar to Lego's. Greenpeace celebrated this "victory," and appealed to consumers to step up and donate so the organization could "continue to investigate, track, and document forest destruction, link it to corporate practices, and pressure them to clean up their act." By 2013 a long list of multinational brands had discontinued their purchase orders from APP, including Hasbro, Disney, Danone, KFC, Adidas, Staples, and Kraft.[4]

By this time Asia Pulp & Paper was in crisis. In February 2013 APP announced sweeping reforms to its forestry practices—a "Forest Conservation Policy" that Greenpeace declared a "major breakthrough." The rhetoric of APP's sustainability director, Aida Greenbury, became docile and resigned: "It is time to stop talking and fighting—it is time for us to show real action on the ground." APP said it would no longer log natural forests or damage peatlands and committed to a policy of zero deforestation. In response Greenpeace called on multinational brand manufacturers and retailers to wait and watch to ensure that APP's commitments were genuine.

Since then APP does seem to be conducting business a bit differently, doing more, for example, to track wood sources and report on sustainability criteria. In early 2014 Staples announced that it would once again source from Asia Pulp & Paper. The conclusion of the leader of Greenpeace UK—that the approach of APP underwent a "seismic shift"—would seem rather hyperbolic, as APP's management team remained in place. But certainly the company is now more willing to admit its past mistakes. "We are the largest pulp and paper manufacturer in the world right now and we want to expand to other markets as well," Greenbury explained in 2014. "We couldn't have this rubbish hanging around our neck, to be known as the forest destroyer. We had to adopt a much higher standard."[5]

### Greenpeace's Palm Oil Campaign

Greenpeace's Barbie-box campaign is just one of many to pressure global brands to dump suppliers causing deforestation—and more recently to praise suppliers such as APP for reforming policies. For years Greenpeace, for example, has been shining a spotlight on the unsustainability of palm oil plantations in cleared (often burned down) tropical forests. In March 2010 Greenpeace called on Nestlé to stop sourcing Indonesian palm oil from Golden Agri-Resources, the world's second biggest palm oil corporation, and like APP part of the Sinar Mas conglomerate. A mock video was posted (and reposted) online of a bored office worker taking a break from shredding paper to eat a Kit Kat chocolate bar, his co-workers watching in horror as he unwittingly chews on the finger of an Orangutan, blood smearing his chin and spewing onto his keyboard. "Ask Nestlé to give rainforests a break," went the tagline. Nestlé was indignant. The company claimed the video violated copyright and strong-armed YouTube into removing it. But it was too late. The video went viral with more than a million views. Emails deluged Nestlé. And hundreds of thousands of Greenpeace supporters demanded action on Facebook and over Twitter. Greenpeace activists followed up by dressing as orangutans and protesting at Nestlé's 2010 Annual General Meeting.

Just weeks into the campaign Nestlé was backtracking. Ties with Sinar Mas were severed. Nestlé reiterated its promise that by 2015 the company would only purchase palm oil that was certified as "sustainable," as well as map its supply chain to ensure full traceability of all of its products. Executives met with Greenpeace organizers and in May 2010 Nestlé became the first multinational consumer goods firm to partner with The Forest Trust to audit suppliers for responsible palm oil practices. In addition, Nestlé revamped its digital media strategy, hiring a new team to engage the online world. Today, the company portrays NGOs as allies, not adversaries. Activists are, in the words of Nestlé's Chris Hogg, the company's "eyes and ears on the ground. And if they find something, we take it seriously and look into it."[6]

Since 2010 Greenpeace has kept up pressure on brand manufacturers and retailers to stop sourcing uncertified palm oil. In early 2014, following a year-long investigation, Greenpeace took on Head & Shoulders shampoo for sourcing palm oil from plantations linked to deforestation in Indonesia. As with Kit Kat, Greenpeace's strategy was to shame a leading brand into jettisoning a supplier, with reforms then rippling through global supply chains. "If a well-known company like Procter & Gamble can show leadership to clean up supply chains, we expect other companies will follow," explained Bustar Maitar, who is leading Greenpeace's Indonesia Forest Campaign. Greenpeace was also keen to expose the weaknesses of the Roundtable on Sustainable Palm Oil, of which P&G is a member. Speaking in 2014, Maitar was blunt: "RSPO, from my perspective, has been used for greenwashing by companies who want to expand their plantations into the forest."[7] As with Nestlé, P&G folded within a few months of the launch of the Greenpeace campaign, in April 2014 announcing a zero deforestation policy and pledging that by 2020 none of its suppliers would have links to the loss of natural forests. Greenpeace International called on its supporters to monitor commitments, but also "take a moment to celebrate" P&G's policy shift.

Tactically, Greenpeace is aiming to divide and conquer multinational brands, classifying some as leaders and others as laggards. As Greenpeace was chastising Head & Shoulders, it was praising Nestlé for its leadership on palm oil sourcing. To encourage uptake Greenpeace now publishes a list of brand companies committing to zero deforestation and sustainable sourcing of palm oil. In mid-2014, for example, Greenpeace's list of "forest-friendly companies" included P&G, as well as other notable brands such as Colgate-Palmolive, Kellogg's, Mars, Nestlé, L'Oreal, and Unilever. At the other end of the spectrum—what Greenpeace calls "non forest-friendly companies" was Pepsi. In the first half of 2014 Colgate-Palmolive was on the non-friendly side, but was moved after reforming its policies.

Greenpeace is further trying to leverage its mindbomb victories to pursue more ambitious reforms to palm oil certification. In 2013 Greenpeace joined with WWF, Rainforest Action Network, and the Forest Peoples Programme to partner with "progressive" palm oil companies and initiate the Palm Oil Innovation Group (POIG). POIG describes its mission as pushing for more "responsible" palm oil—not only "sustainable," but also "conflict-free"—aiming for "innovations" to advance the standards of the Roundtable on Sustainable Palm Oil. According to POIG's "launch statement" a central goal is "to explore ways to increase the market demand for palm oil products that are produced by innovators within the industry."[8]

Activist campaigns over social media have clearly damaged brand reputations and influenced large numbers of consumers. As in the cases of Barbie, Kit Kat, and Head & Shoulders, when activists demand small, simple, and low-cost reforms, it's proving more effective—and in the end cheaper—for multinational corporations to pledge sustainability (and sacrifice suppliers) than to ignore or defend themselves against campaigns. In this context more brands are also now trying to appease activists and sidestep potential campaigns against them.

This is one of the reasons why more and more brand corporations are promising to source products certified as forest-friendly, with many now committing to timelines to end deforestation. In 2010 the more than 400 companies in the Consumer Goods Forum, which together turn over about $3 trillion in sales annually, called on members to eliminate by 2020 products and processes causing deforestation from their supply chains. In 2013 Singapore's Wilmar International, the world's biggest palm oil producer with 45 percent of the market, committed to zero deforestation. In 2014 alone, besides Procter & Gamble, scores of brand manufacturers and retailers committed to zero deforestation: L'Oréal, Kellogg's, Mars, General Mills, Safeway, Colgate-Palmolive, Danone, Johnston & Johnson, Pepsi, Cargill, Dunkin' Donuts, and Krispy Kreme. The 2014 New York Declaration on Forests was effusive: "Taken together, the share of palm oil under zero deforestation commitments has grown from 0 to about 60 percent in the last year."

Will such efforts slow deforestation? Divisions within rainforest activism run deep over the value of business pledges, CSR and certification, eco-products and eco-tourism, and using forests as carbon sinks. Many activist campaigns continue to appeal to governments, firms, and consumers to respect the rights of indigenous peoples and the biological value of old-growth rainforests as the lungs of the earth. As is typical across the environmental movement, however, more and more campaigns are also now appealing to the self-interest of consumers, business, and wealthy states, portraying rainforests as a climate change solution that demands no significant changes to middle-class lifestyles.[9]

## The Power of Eco-Consumerism

Consumers are the foot soldiers of today's middleclass environmentalism. Governments urge them to use energy and water smartly. Advertisers tell them to buy eco-products and eco-services. And NGOs recruit them to punish and reward business. Across the world consumers are responding to the sustainability call as environmental mindbombs continue to explode all around them. They are buying Chiquita organic bananas and Toyota Priuses. They are trading in old refrigerators and installing low-flush toilets. They are seeking out eco-tourist adventures and purchasing carbon offsets when flying. And, as we just saw, they are boycotting products—from Barbie dolls to Head & Shoulders—that cause tropical deforestation.

Julia Hailes, author of *The New Green Consumer Guide*, sees eco-consumers as the most powerful way to get firms and governments to act. Like Jane Goodall, she has faith in the combined power of little lifestyle changes. "The savings made from doing things like turning off the stand-by button on your TV, buying a more energy-efficient washing machine or taking the train rather than driving your car, may seem trivial. On their own they are pretty insignificant, but if millions of people—or even billions—make these changes the cumulative impact can be huge."[10]

Yet how effective is eco-consumerism? Certainly, green consumers are doing much good. The recycling trade, for example, is worth more than $500 billion a year and is racing toward $1 trillion. Yet consumers worldwide are a diverse group. And individual choices, decisions, and actions are inconsistent. Given this, eco-consumerism tends to be a weak force of global environmentalism, especially when it comes to reusing products or reducing consumption worldwide.[11]

Look at plastic production. Many supermarkets are now charging for plastic bags, and around the world villages, towns, cities, and even a few states have banned or restricted the use of plastic grocery bags, including various cities in India since the late 1990s, the country of Bangladesh since 2002, the country of China since 2008, and various American cities since San Francisco took the lead in 2007 (including Los Angeles, Seattle, and Chicago). Regulations in China have reportedly decreased consumption by as much as 40 billion plastic bags a year.

Everywhere, shoppers would seem to be going back to using paper or reusable bags, as was the norm before retailers began offering free plastic bags in the 1970s. At the same time billions of consumers are clearly working hard to rinse and recycle plastic milk jugs, yogurt containers, and margarine tubs. Such trends would seem to be good news. And in some ways they are. Yet plastic production went up fourfold from 1980 to 2010, and every year manufacturers are continuing to churn out another trillion plastic bags. Already, the oceans contain at least 5 trillion pieces of plastic. Another 5–13 million metric tons goes into the oceans annually, an amount on track to rise many times over by 2025, according to a 2015 study in the journal *Science*. Meanwhile, plastic production is continuing to rise, with manufacturers now rolling out 300 million tons or so each year, most of which still eventually goes into landfills, dumps, rivers, lakes, and oceans.[12]

Eco-consumerism is also doing little to reduce global energy consumption. Around the world governments are offering rebates to those who renovate homes to lower electricity and heating usage (and thus energy bills). Yet gains are often soon lost as households purchase new electronic products. By global standards my own province of British Columbia has done fairly well: average household electricity usage is roughly the same today as it was at the end of the 1980s. Worldwide, however, consumption of oil and natural gas have been rising steadily since then. The world has not even managed to reduce its reliance on coal, a highly-polluting and carbon-emitting energy source. Coal consumption within countries in the Organisation for Economic Co-operation and Development has gradually fallen since 1973. Yet coal-fired supply chains and corporate networks, over the past few decades increasingly running through China, continue to supply OECD consumers. And for at least the foreseeable future the International

Energy Agency is predicting a worldwide rise in coal consumption of more than 2 percent annually.[13]

Partly, increasing energy consumption since the late 1980s reflects growth in the world economy, and partly it reflects a rise in individual purchasing power (as well as another 2 billion people). Yet it also reflects the general increase in the global ecological footprint of consumers—even as environmentalism of the rich spreads. This trend exposes some of the innate limits of advancing global sustainability through eco-products, eco-services, cause marketing, as well as, as I turn to in the next chapter, through NGO-corporate partnerships and product cobranding.

# 11   Million Dollar Pandas

WWF is a leading advocate of NGO-corporate partnerships as a way of conserving forestlands, protecting wildlife, and preventing illegal trade in endangered species. "License the panda logo and WWF name to secure revenue and to build brand awareness," the US office of WWF advertises on its website. The US WWF awards the title of "Million Dollar Panda" to any firm donating "$1 million or more." Bank of America, Avon, Gap, Domtar, and Coca-Cola are all Million Dollar Pandas.

Corporate money and partnerships are financing environmental projects, programs, and technologies. And they are paying for NGO staff, supplies, buildings, and campaign costs. Since 2009, for instance, the Bank of America has been offering World Wildlife Fund VISA cards and checking accounts, with a donation going to WWF when a new client signs up. Every year Domtar Corporation, one of North America's largest paper and fiber-product manufacturers, contributes $350,000 from sales of its "EarthChoice" products to WWF offices in Canada and the United States. And since 2008 the Gap clothing chain, as part of a sales promotion it calls "Give & Get," has been offering customers the opportunity to donate 5 percent of the price of a purchase to WWF, earning WWF more than $1.8 million as of 2015.

Such partnerships with business are also offering NGOs the chance to monitor, and even manage, certification and eco-labeling programs. And they are opening up opportunities for environmental activists to advise—or perhaps work alongside—business executives and state regulators. It's understandable why so many environmental NGOs are embracing market solutions and partnering with business, especially, as we saw earlier, with just about every multinational corporation now seeking out nongovernmental allies as part of their new sustainability policies.

We should not discount the benefits of corporate funding and partnerships for the capacity of environmental NGOs to support programs and projects. We can see this with WWF, Conservation International, and The Nature Conservancy. And we can see this with nongovernmental organizations specializing in standard setting, responsible trade, and supply-chain auditing, such as the Forest Stewardship Council, the Marine Stewardship Council, Forest Trends, Rainforest Alliance, the Roundtable on Sustainable Palm Oil, the Round Table on Responsible Soy, and the Global Roundtable for Sustainable Beef. Marketing and trade partnerships are definitely enhancing the technical and administrative capacity of NGOs to influence global environmental governance. And, as with WWF, the extra funds do seem to be improving the management of some species and some natural resources, as well as enhancing the capacity of NGOs to influence international and domestic laws and initiatives. Yet at the same time such partnerships, now at the forefront of environmentalism of the rich, are ceding authority to global business by diffusing criticism of the growth, sales, and profit models of multinational investors, manufacturers, and retailers. These partnerships, as we'll see later in this chapter with the WWF-Coke partnership, are also doing little to lighten ecological footprints and nothing at all to reduce the extreme inequalities, unrelenting violence, and unsustainable growth underlying the world economy. Such an outcome was hardly the hope of the conservationists who signed the Morges Manifesto, the founding document of today's WWF.

## WWF

In 1961 sixteen leading conservationists, including the UK biologist Sir Julian Huxley (1887–1975) and the UK ornithologist Sir Peter Scott (1909–1989), signed an international declaration in Morges, Switzerland, imploring the world to save its "fine and harmless wild creatures" from "an orgy of thoughtless and needless destruction." The authors of the "Morges Manifesto" saw "ignorance, greed, and folly" at every turn. Hunters and poachers were killing indiscriminately; factories were poisoning rivers and lakes; developers were draining wetlands; plantation owners were clearing forests; and dams were flooding vast ecosystems. For these authors "the eleventh hour" had already "struck" for nature. Yet they saw hope, too. For them the solution to the "emergency" lay not in more resolve or knowledge, but in additional "support and resources" for scientists and wildlife advocates. Conservationists "need above all money," they implored.

The Morges Manifesto called for the creation of an international "war room" to highlight trouble spots, provide rapid-response assistance, and coordinate—and boost—fundraising for wildlife protection. In response, later that year the World Wildlife Fund was set up in Switzerland as a non-profit charity and international secretariat. Peter Scott designed a logo: a giant panda, in black and white to save on printing costs. National offices would soon follow, with the first opening in the UK in November 1961 and the second in the US shortly afterward.[1]

The World Wildlife Fund, or WWF, was soon raising hundreds of thousands of dollars a year. Early financing went to save bald eagles, red wolves, and Hawaiian seabirds in the United States, Tule geese in Canada, and Atitlán (giant) grebes in Guatemala (now extinct). It went to protect birdlife in Columbia and pink flamingos in Kenya; conduct research in the Galápagos Islands off the coast of Ecuador; introduce southern white rhinos into Kenya; and conduct wildlife surveys and train rangers in Africa. As the 1960s drew to a close, the World Wildlife Fund had raised more than $5.5 million. And by the late 1960s and 1970s, with its reach and fundraising capacity expanding, the organization was progressively pressing for—and financing—nature parks and wildlife sanctuaries, such as Spain's Coto Doñana National Park (established in 1969) and Costa Rica's Corcovado National Park (established in 1975).

Also over this time the World Wildlife Fund was increasingly lobbying for stronger environmental laws (both national and international), campaigning to conserve species (e.g., tigers, whales, and dolphins), and forming new environmental networks and organizations. Its advocacy and research helped to bring into force in 1975 the Ramsar Convention on Wetlands of International Importance as well as the Convention on International Trade in Endangered Species of Wild Fauna and Flora (CITES). To further these efforts, in 1976 the World Wildlife Fund partnered with the International Union for Conservation of Nature and Natural Resources (IUCN) to establish TRAFFIC—a "wildlife trade monitoring network" to investigate illegal trade in endangered species as well as to advocate for more biodiversity-friendly legal trade. Around this time WWF further launched a global campaign to preserve tropical rainforests.

By then WWF was also highlighting the consequences of economic development for conservation, although crisis interventions to save species and advocacy for forest and marine parks remained front and center in its everyday work. Notably, in the late 1970s WWF joined with the UN Environment Programme to finance and shape the IUCN's *World Conservation Strategy* (published in 1980), advancing the importance of conservation for what the strategy called "sustainable development," and laying the groundwork for the 1987 World Commission on Environment and Development's definition in *Our Common Future*: "development that meets the needs of the present without compromising the ability of future generations to meet their own needs."[2]

In 1986 the World Wildlife Fund changed its name to the World Wide Fund for Nature to reflect the broadening of its mandate over its first 25 years. The branches in Canada and the US did not follow suit, however, and for the next 15 years, rather confusingly, the organization ran under both names (yet used the same acronym) before agreeing in 2001 to brand the organization simply as WWF, with the Swiss headquarters called WWF International.

Since the mid-1980s conserving biodiversity and wildlife through parks, sanctuaries, and nature corridors has remained a top priority for WWF. In the second half of the 1980s WWF helped to establish the Manas Wildlife Sanctuary in Bhutan, the Cockscomb Basin Wildlife Sanctuary & Jaguar Preserve in Belize, and the Guaraqueçaba Ecological Station in Brazil. In the 1990s WWF helped to convince the Philippines and Malaysia to create the Turtle Islands Heritage Protected Area to conserve the nesting grounds of green sea turtles; additionally, it began to work with the Chinese government to protect giant pandas as well as helped to convince the Ecuadorean government to establish a marine sanctuary around the Galápagos Islands. That decade WWF also helped to put in place a marine conservation plan off Canada's Pacific Coast (home to orcas), a nature "corridor" between Argentina and Brazil, and community-run conservation programs in Namibia. Among thousands of other activities, since 2000 WWF has further helped to develop the Tumucumaque National Park and the Chandless State Park in the Brazilian Amazon; finance region-wide reef conservation off the coasts of Mexico, Belize, Guatemala, and Honduras; protect freshwater habitats in Brazil, China, and Mexico; establish new parklands in Russia to protect tiger habitats; and create Bhutan's Wangchuck Centennial Park.

Over the past 30 years WWF has also been a leading advocate of "debt-for-nature" swaps. Back in 1984 Thomas Lovejoy, then WWF vice president, called on donors to forgive (or for conservationists to pay off) Third World debt in exchange for protecting biodiversity and wildlife. In the late 1980s WWF put in place multimillion dollar debt-for-nature swaps in Costa Rica ($3 million), Madagascar ($2.1 million), the Philippines ($2 million), and Ecuador ($1 million). In 1993 it helped to negotiate a $19 million debt-for-nature swap in the Philippines, one in Madagascar in 1996 worth $3.2 million, then one in the Peruvian Amazon in 2002 worth $10.6 million (with funding from The Nature Conservancy, Conservation International, and the US government). In 2004 WWF facilitated a $10 million debt-for-nature swap to protect old-growth forests in Columbia, with the Global Environment Facility contributing another $15 million, then in 2008 assisted with a $20 million debt-for-nature swap involving France and Madagascar.[3]

This is just a sampling of the thousands of WWF conservation projects and financing agreements since 1961. Over this time WWF also conducted research and advocacy, such as campaigning for a ban on trading ivory under CITES (passed in 1989), exposing the dangers of pesticides and industrial waste (backing, for instance, the 2001 Stockholm Convention on Persistent Organic Pollutants), and lobbying in the 1990s to convince the US Congress to approve the 1994 North American Free Trade Agreement, or NAFTA (WWF saw the environmental clauses as valuable). Once again teaming up with IUCN and UNEP, WWF authored the 1991 report *Caring for the Earth*, which influenced international discussions at the 1992 UN Conference on Environment and Development (UNCED, or what is commonly called the Earth Summit) in Rio de Janeiro. WWF was a leader as well in the international campaign for a Convention on Biological Diversity (signed in 1992, with 195 parties as of 2015) and a proponent of the 1997 Kyoto Protocol on climate change.[4]

Since cooperating with Unilever to launch the Forest Stewardship Council (FSC) in 1993, WWF has also been a leading advocate of timber certification, eco-labeling, and sustainable trade, partnering, for instance, with the World Bank in 1997 on a strategy to designate 200 million hectares of forests as "well managed." By 2013 more than 180 million hectares of forest were FSC-certified, with approximately 8–10 percent of timber traded internationally stamped with an FSC logo. Similarly, WWF has been at the forefront of "sustainable seafood," partnering with seafood companies to establish the Marine Stewardship Council in 1996. By 2015 more than 250 fisheries and 25,000 seafood products were MSC-certified, covering 9–10 percent of the world's annual wild seafood catch (by weight).

WWF has worked as well with producers to market "sustainable palm oil," helping to launch the Roundtable on Sustainable Palm Oil (RSPO) in 2004. In 2012 WWF joined with Cargill, McDonald's, Walmart, and four other businesses to found the Global Roundtable for Sustainable Beef. In addition, it has cooperated with agricultural corporations to market "responsible soy," helping to establish the Round Table on Responsible Soy (RTRS) in 2006. By 2015 more than 1.3 million metric tons of soy was RTRS-certified, while more than 3 million hectares of oil palm estates were RSPO-certified, covering 12 million metric tons of palm oil and capturing 18 percent of the world market. These programs have not been without controversy for WWF. For instance, environmental activists have criticized WWF for supporting the very idea of sustainable oil palm plantations and sustainable beef, and for cooperating with the Round Table on Responsible Soy, which includes Monsanto despite the company's use of genetically modified crops. WWF has not backed down, however, arguing that "refusing to participate" in the Round Table on Responsible Soy would only undermine its influence over agricultural development.[5]

As this brief history shows, WWF has long cooperated with communities, businesses, and governments on conservation. Since the mid-2000s, however, it has been partnering more and more with multinational brand manufacturers and retailers. Starting in 2006 WWF began to work closely with Walmart on forest, mining, and agricultural purchasing guidelines and supply-chain certification. In 2007 WWF partnered with Coca-Cola to promote freshwater conservation, with Coke donating $20 million to WWF in 2007 and $3.75 million in 2008. That same year WWF partnered as well with Dell, IBM, Google, and Intel to launch the "Climate Savers Computing Initiative" to promote energy efficiency and reduce greenhouse gases in the computer industry.

In addition, WWF has become an increasingly strong advocate of corporate sponsorships and cause marketing, where shoppers can donate to a cause by buying certain products. The US chapter of WWF, for instance, provides a link on its website called "SHOP TO SUPPORT." Here, Amazon.com offers customers the opportunity to shop within "smile.amazon.com" where 0.5 percent of the purchase price goes to WWF (or another charity of the customer's choice). Potential customers also learn on WWF's website that 13 cents from each can of Wild Selections (an MSC-certified brand of Bumble Bee Foods) tuna, salmon, sardines, and shrimp is now going to WWF, promising to donate a minimum of $1 million by 2018.[6]

WWF in the US continues to tell the world that it's aiming to conserve biological diversity, support renewable resource use, and reduce "pollution and wasteful consumption." WWF International, meanwhile, says the organization as a whole is pursuing the "twin goals of conserving biodiversity and reducing humanity's Ecological Footprint." As we've seen, with offices spanning scores of countries and by raising billions of dollars, WWF has funded thousands of wildlife rescues, nature conservation sites, and community forest programs. Many examples exist too of successful WWF-funded research and advocacy campaigns as well as WWF-supported certification and eco-labeling programs for consumer goods and fresh food.

But is WWF actually helping to reduce pollution and wasteful consumption or lower humanity's ecological footprint? Are all of its efforts really stopping what the Morges Manifesto called "thoughtless and needless destruction … in the name of advancing civilization"? The answer is "no," as is clear with the outcomes of its partnerships with Coca-Cola.

## Coca-Cola Pandas

In 2011 Coke and WWF expanded their 2007 freshwater partnership to include an "Arctic Home Campaign" to raise funds in North America for the conservation of polar bear habitats in the high Arctic above Greenland and Canada. A year later this fundraising campaign was extended to Europe. Besides giving WWF $2 million up front, Coca-Cola agreed to match (with limits) online donations to WWF's campaign to conserve polar bears. As well, consumers could donate to WWF using "Coke Rewards points," which consumers earn by purchasing Coke products. The first two years of the partnership saw the "Arctic Home Campaign" raise more than $3 million.

Coke-WWF projects now cover more than 50 countries. Calling its partnership "transformative," in 2013 Coke and WWF announced that they would extend the partnership until at least 2020. "Our work with Coca-Cola has proven that collaboration can amplify and accelerate the impact we need," explained Carter Roberts, President of WWF in the US. "Working with WWF," Coke CEO Muhtar Kent added, "will continue to challenge our company to advance our sustainability programs, and WWF's expertise will be instrumental in reaching our environmental performance goals, some of which they help us set."[7]

Appointing Neville Isdell as chairman of WWF's US Board of Directors cemented this partnership, as before retiring he was a career Coca-Cola executive who served as CEO from 2004 to 2008. Millions of dollars of ongoing revenue are now flowing to WWF from this partnership, including $66 million for freshwater conservation from 2007 to 2014. In 2014 Coke once again matched donations (up to $1 million) of $10 or more to the Arctic Home Campaign, including donations of Coke Rewards points. Funding from Coca-Cola since 2007 has mostly gone to support WWF campaigns to protect river basins and catchments, such as in the Amazon, Mekong, Yangtze River, Mesoamerican Reef, and Great Barrier Reef. The WWF-Coke partnership has also helped Coca-Cola's 300 or so bottling plants to improve water efficiency and recycling rates, as well as decrease packaging, waste, and greenhouse gas emissions.

In isolation this might look like progress toward global sustainability. Yet we need to judge the value in the context of the growth and profit ambitions of the Coca-Cola Company. With a relatively small investment, Coca-Cola is gaining favorable publicity, including a chorus of compliments and thank-yous from WWF leaders. Already the company has 17 brands worth more than $1 billion, including the bottled water brand Dasani. Coca-Cola's revenues in 2014 were $46 billion, netting a tidy profit of more than $7 billion. And its marketing budget exceeds $1 billion, with, for instance, $4.5 million spent on each 30-second advertising slot during the 2015 Super Bowl.

The partnership with WWF is clearly a good deal for a company protecting a brand worth $82 billion in 2014, behind only Apple ($119 billion) and Google ($107 billion), and ahead of IBM ($72 billion) and Microsoft ($61 billion). In total, Coca-Cola markets more than 500 brands, such as Fanta, Sprite, and Diet Coke. In 2013 Coke sold nearly 700 billion "servings," or roughly 98 drinks per person (assuming we include the 400 million babies and toddlers around that year). Granted, to make these drinks Coca-Cola bottlers are now using energy and water a bit more efficiently, yet it still takes 150–300 liters of water to produce a typical half-liter of sweetened soda pop—and this, we should recall, is occurring in a world where billions of people live without adequate fresh water for at least part of every year.

At the same time Coke is pushing hard to expand production and markets. From 2010 to the end of 2013 Coke and its bottlers invested more than $50 billion in factories, brand advertising, and acquiring local businesses, including in China, which is on its way to becoming Coke's largest market. Already in 2010 Coca-Cola ranked first in the world among buyers of aluminum and sugarcane, second for glass, third for citrus, and fifth for coffee. Coca-Cola set new company records in 2013 for selling the most servings, reaching the most customers, and owning the most billion-dollar brands. That year the volume of Coke, Fanta, and Sprite all grew by 2 percent, while non-carbonated beverages grew by 5 percent, allowing the company to sell hundreds of millions of additional cases of soda and sports drinks. Coca-Cola's "2020 Vision" is particularly telling for the capacity of the WWF-Coke partnership to promote global sustainability. For the "planet," the company says it's aiming by 2020 to "be a global leader in more sustainable water use, packaging, energy, and climate protection." For its "portfolio," meanwhile, it's aiming by 2020 to "more than double our servings to over 3 billion a day."[8]

## The Rise of Corporate Partnerships

WWF is certainly not alone among environmental NGOs in pursuing corporate financing and partnerships. The Nature Conservancy trumpets its recent partnerships with Dow Chemical, Cargill, and 3M. It calls its partnership with Dow Chemical since 2011 a "breakthrough collaboration" that's helping "Dow and the business community recognize and incorporate nature's value into global business goals, decisions, and strategies." And it praises Cargill for promoting sustainable soy production and reducing deforestation in the Brazilian Amazon, and 3M for "building sustainable communities, through environmental giving."[9]

Conservation International, set up in 1987 to protect global biodiversity and natural resources, is another leading advocate of corporate partnerships. Today, Conservation International has around 1,000 staff and works across more than 30 countries to conserve rainforests, marine life, and endangered animals. To pay for projects, campaigns, and staff, Conservation International has partnerships with dozens of the world's biggest multinationals, including Bank of America, Coca-Cola, Disney, ExxonMobil, Gap, McDonald's, Monsanto, Nestlé, Shell, Sony, Starbucks, Toyota,

United Airlines, and Walmart, among many others. Since the early 1990s, for example, Bank of America has been working with Conservation International on debt-for-nature swaps, cause-marketing campaigns (such as donating 50 cents to Conservation International for each box sold of its "Vanishing Species" checks), and biodiversity protection during the production of oil and gas.

Conservation International has also worked closely with McDonald's. In 2008, for example, Conservation International set up "panda-cams" in China to support "Kung Fu Panda" Happy Meals, which DreamWorks Animation was using to publicize its *Kung Fu Panda* film. The promotion aimed to generate "panda-mania," as well as, of course, sell more Happy Meals. Free with this meal was one of eight plastic Kung Fu Panda toys, one of which was the movie's title character Po the Panda (which Conservation International declared was the "cousin" of the endangered giant panda). That year Conservation International also partnered with McDonald's Europe on an "Endangered Species" Happy Meal promotion, displaying on the box the logo of Conservation International, a website link to learn more, and pictures of eight endangered animals. Such promotions, in the words of CI staff, "empower kids to make conservation part of their everyday lives and to create positive environmental solutions for our planet." The CEO of Conservation International, Peter Seligmann, was equally enthusiastic to have McDonald's on board: "we're pleased to align with a leadership company like McDonald's who is not only supporting our work to protect pandas, but helping us deliver this important message in a unique way to inspire and empower the next generation of conservation leaders to take action to protect our environment."[10]

Yet another champion of corporate partnerships is the US Environmental Defense Fund. EDF first partnered with a multinational corporation in the early 1990s when it teamed up with McDonald's to increase recycling and reduce packaging and waste. Since then EDF has been a strong advocate of corporate partnerships, and today the NGO calls them "the key to lasting solutions" and "a cornerstone of [its] approach." EDF continues to work closely with McDonald's, as well as with other multinational companies such as Walmart and FedEx. Like WWF, The Nature Conservancy, and Conservation International, EDF is quick to boast of its influence. "Our partnerships," claims EDF Vice President Tom Murray, "drive sustainability leadership at top corporations, creating ripple effects across entire industries."[11]

But is this really true? How could the branding of Happy Meals with Kung Fu Pandas be a "solution for our planet"? Most NGO partnerships with business are well intentioned and many outcomes are laudable. At least to some extent these partnerships are offering some opportunities to reform the sourcing and auditing practices of multinational corporations. Still, the need to finance nonprofit bureaucracies, including paying staff who fundraise, is clearly motivating many NGOs to partner with corporations. These partnerships, moreover, are doing little to redress the legacy of ecological imperialism or challenge the underlying structures of unsustainability, and in some ways are doing more to legitimize a highly unequal and exploitative world economy by reassuring consumers of the sustainability of multinational companies such as ExxonMobil, McDonald's, and Walmart. Far greater political and economic reforms than those arising out of environmentalism of the rich are clearly necessary to make real headway toward global sustainability.

# 12 Conclusion: The Allure and Illusion of Riches

As we've seen, environmentalism as both a social movement and a philosophy of living has long challenged the excesses of capitalism and consumerism. The degree of influence has varied widely across the world, and certainly in some places at some points in time the ideas and energy of environmentalism have hardly mattered. Moreover, environmentalism is neither a unified nor uniform force, as we see, for instance, with the bitter conflicts over windmills and biofuels. Still, looking globally over the past fifty years, environmentalism in all of its diversity has clearly been an important counterforce to the reckless pursuit of economic growth, corporate profits, and personal consumption. Historian Joachim Radkau is right: the Anthropocene is also "the age of ecology."[1]

The age of ecology is a spirited uprising of ecological sensibility. Activists are sabotaging shark finning, scaling oil rigs in the Arctic, going on hunger strikes on the steps of legislatures, and skydiving into packed stadiums. To stop highway construction, they are tunneling underground like moles; to stop logging, they are living in trees like squirrels. "Buy nothing" campaigns are jamming popular culture, and demonstrators are occupying city squares to oppose inequality. Anti-corporate coalitions are fighting agribusiness and open-pit mining. Anti-globalization activists are disrupting finance and trade summits. Nonprofits are forming to advocate for environmental justice in poor, marginalized neighborhoods.

And this is just a sampling of the dynamism of today's environmental movement. Campaigns are opposing fracking and coal mining, as well as the construction of hydroelectric dams, oil pipelines, and nuclear power plants. Thousands of activists are risking their lives to stop poaching and big-game hunting, and millions are calling for more action against climate change. At the same time, nonprofit organizations are setting up bird sanctuaries, wildlife parks, and vast forest reserves as carbon sinks. Meanwhile, average citizens are celebrating Earth Day in the hundreds of millions, as well as recycling, buying environment-friendly products, and donating money to advocacy groups. As all of this is happening, people who identify as environmentalists are also modifying their lifestyles: eating organic fruit and locally grown vegetables; purchasing Fair Trade flowers, soccer balls, jewelry, and wine; riding bicycles and driving hybrid cars; installing triple-pane windows and solar panels in their homes; composting food scraps and carrying around reusable coffee mugs; and gathering together to replant trees and clean up litter.

The age of ecology, however, goes even deeper than eco-activists and eco-consumers, with those who identify as environmentalists working across government, academia, the media, and business. Within national governments, lawmakers are passing stricter domestic regulations and ratifying new international environmental agreements. As this is going on, environmental agencies are battling economic departments, standing up to politicians, and fining corporations such as BP and Volkswagen for violating regulations. In some countries, such as Germany and New Zealand, green parties are even winning seats in elections. Within cities, mayors and councils are voting to add walkways and biking lanes, tear down viaducts, restrict lawn watering during droughts, and contain landfill emissions. Within academia and the media, professors, students, and journalists are collaborating with community leaders, nongovernmental researchers, industry managers, government scientists, and city planners to challenge conventional thinking and shape public opinion. Within industry, environmental researchers are developing new technologies and reengineering industrial processes. Middle managers with degrees in business and sustainability are implementing new standards in the name of corporate social responsibility. And the CEOs of Fortune 500 companies are rewriting strategic plans around a triple bottom line of financial, social, and environmental sustainability.

The crisis of the Anthropocene would certainly be worse without all of these efforts. Especially since the early 1970s environmentalism has made a real difference in how governments regulate, how corporations operate, and how people live. In this sense environmentalism is succeeding. Yet, even as environmentalism continues to spread, the global environmental crisis continues to escalate. In this sense environmentalism is failing. The sheer force of the crisis of the Anthropocene partly explains this failure. So does the sheer difficulty of solving this crisis, as ecosystems interact and react in unpredictable ways to pollution, degradation, overexploitation, species collapse, and climate change.

Still, environmentalists must accept some responsibility for the escalating crisis. Especially since the 1990s, as I've argued in this book, environmentalism has increasingly come to reflect the interests and comforts of those with the most money and the most power. Of course, to some extent environmentalism has always mirrored the concerns of affluent individuals. After all, in wealthier countries environmentalism emerged from a desire to preserve nature for trail hiking, birdwatching, game hunting, and sustainable yields—then later gained strength following calls to clean up pollution in high-income neighborhoods. Yet in recent years, the priorities of big business, powerful economies, and well-off consumers have taken center stage, while calls for frugality, quality of life, community wellbeing, social equality, corporate controls, limits on growth, and sustainable consumption have been pushed into the wings.

The various manifestations of environmentalism of the rich—such as the sustainable development of governments, the eco-business of multinational corporations, the NGO partnerships with business, the cause marketing of nonprofit organizations, and the eco-consumerism of citizens—do have considerable power to produce small-scale, local successes. Yet, as I've further argued, environmentalism of the rich does not have the innate capacity to aggregate into global-scale solutions or transform the political, economic, and societal structures causing overconsumption, extreme inequality, and ecological decay. The growing dominance of environmentalism of the rich, moreover, is having insidious consequences, weakening the power of environmentalism as a whole to function as a counternarrative and counterforce to consumer capitalism, while opening up opportunities for ruling elites to coopt aspects of the movement to enhance the legitimacy of business as usual.

Resistance to the extremes of wealth and exploitation underlying environmentalism of the rich does rage around the world. One example among many is the World Social Forum, which regularly brings together thousands of social justice, indigenous, anti-capitalist, and alter-globalization activists under the vision of "another world is possible."[2] Anger clearly rumbles just below the surface of the world order, as we saw in 2011 when Adbusters ignited the Occupy Movement with a few tweets. And the future could well see many more citizen uprisings as political elites fail to act and as the sustainability crisis worsens. Yet, at least in the near term, the reach of environmentalism of the rich looks set to deepen even further, and understanding its appeal, limits, and dangers is therefore essential for anyone striving for a more sustainable future.

## The Appeal of Environmentalism of the Rich

It's easy to see the allure of environmentalism of the rich. It exudes optimism and pragmatism and realism, appealing to the understandable desire to move beyond pessimism and cynicism—a common charge against "old-style" environmental activism. Solutions arise from business innovation, wealth creation, new technology, eco-markets, free trade, more foreign investment, and faster development, not from new rules to contain excesses and change lifestyles. All that is necessary are small steps and small changes, allowing people to feel like they're advancing sustainability without sacrificing anything of note.

Governments and corporations are touting the net gains from eco-technologies, eco-markets, and soft regulation as progress toward global sustainability. Such claims almost always exaggerate the value of these gains; yet it would be a mistake to dismiss them as unimportant. A major appeal of environmentalism of the rich is its capacity to produce measurable, if incremental, improvements for some issues, in some firms, in some locales, for some periods of time—what advocacy groups can tell supporters are "victories." On some markers environmentalism of the rich even looks like a resounding success. City air in North America, Europe, and Japan is cleaner than it was fifty years ago, and air quality is starting to improve in some developing countries. More than a thousand international environmental treaties are now in place, and more are on the way. There are more than 209,000 "protected" marine and terrestrial areas and over a seventh of the earth's landmass has now been officially set aside to protect wetlands, lakes, and forests. At the same time international certification bodies are offering more reliable environmental labeling standards, as well as supporting the growth of eco-markets, such as certified timber, seafood, and palm oil. The Marine Stewardship Council, as mentioned in the last chapter, now certifies around 10 percent of wild seafood consumed, while the Forest Stewardship Council certifies around 10 percent of traded timber.[3]

The eco-business of multinational corporations is clearly producing results too, even taking into account that CSR managers are presenting gains in the best possible light. The energy efficiency of buildings, appliances, and automobiles is rising, as is the recycling of cans, computers, and cardboard. Walmart, for instance, is now diverting more than four-fifths of its waste (such as plastic bags, glass, cardboard, and paper) from going into landfills, with stores in Japan and the UK over 90 percent. Measured on a per product basis, many firms have even managed to decrease energy and natural resource inputs. Corporations are achieving this through a variety of means. Just-in-time delivery and technological advances are cutting waste and inefficiencies. Codes of conduct and sustainability programming for supply chains (such as audits and reporting requirements) are enhancing the power of multinational corporations to control suppliers. Waste is powering factories and cycling back into production. Lightweight technology and smart packaging are cutting per unit fuel costs of shipping and trucking goods. Solar panels are being installed on redesigned buildings.[4]

Adding further to the appeal of environmentalism of the rich is its increasingly "aspirational" tone. As we saw in the first half of the book, brand retailers and manufacturers have set remarkably far-reaching aspirational goals: water neutrality, zero waste, zero deforestation, carbon neutrality, 100 percent sustainable sourcing, and 100 percent renewable energy, among others. In some cases aspirations have even sped across industries. Companies pledging zero deforestation, for example, accounted for just 5 percent of the world trade in palm oil in 2013; two years later the figure was 95 percent.[5]

For some analysts—let's, for convenience, call them "eco-modernists"—these gains confirm that the world economy is now heading toward sustainability. The Breakthrough Institute, which Ted Nordhaus and Michael Shellenberger founded the year before publishing *The Death of Environmentalism* in 2004, define eco-modernists as those who "are optimistic about humanity's ability to shape a better future—a 'good Anthropocene'."[6] Their optimism, which they call "eco-pragmatism," arises out of the belief in the value—and the possibility—of technology "decoupling" economic growth from nature. Eco-modernists see the possibility of even more intensive land use; of growing more crops and raising more livestock on less land; of moving even more people into environmentally friendly megacities. They further see an opportunity for even more efficient use of materials, of making more products with less inputs, of substituting scarce natural resources and further reengineering suboptimal production processes. Some optimists, such as Ronald Bailey, go so far as seeing an "environmental renewal in the twenty-first century" as ingenuity, technology, and economic growth combine into solutions. Others, such as William McDonough and Michael Braungart, see a redesigning of our products, homes, neighborhoods, and offices as bringing a future of "abundance, proliferation, delight."[7] For sure such optimism is appealing. But it's not warranted, as it underestimates the extent and force of the global sustainability crisis and ignores the limits and dangers of environmentalism of the rich.

### The Limits of Environmentalism of the Rich

Wealth is often said to give citizens the luxury, and governments and industry the capacity, to conserve nature and clean up pollution. Yet, as the first half of this book highlighted, much of today's wealth is a product of the globalization of an unsustainable world economy of ever-higher extraction, growth, and consumption, where violence, extreme inequality, and ecological risk taking are the norms. Why does 1 percent of humanity control half of the world's financial wealth? Why has the number of billionaires more than doubled since 2009? Why do the top eight billionaires together control more than what a billion people manage to earn in a year?

Those who put their faith in environmentalism of the rich do not account adequately for the sources and consequences of such extreme wealth. Nor do they sufficiently integrate into their analysis the legacies of imperialism, colonialism, and the globalization of consumer capitalism. Moving toward global sustainability will require the rich to confront the violent, unjust, and risky sources of their wealth. Being colonized—and later globalized—has traumatized peoples across the developing world, causing many societies to spiral into ever-greater crises, as in the Pacific island of Nauru. The ongoing exploitation and devastation of Africa, Latin America, and the Asia-Pacific is causing these crises to escalate further, as the damage from imperialism, colonialism, and globalization compounds, as inequality and financial instability rise, and as deforestation, biodiversity loss, overfishing, chemical pollution, and climate change intensify. Humanity's ecological footprint, as we saw in chapter 5, "Consuming the Earth," is already well over the earth's biocapacity—and it's growing bigger by the day as consumption soars and more and more people exceed their fair earth share.

Alone, eco-efficiencies, eco-technologies, and eco-markets will never suffice to solve this crisis. Nor can we resolve it by intensifying agriculture, or getting more people to migrate to cities, or substituting untested technologies and products. Matters could even get worse as the rush for technological fixes supersedes the need for precaution. Efficiencies are quickly lost as companies reinvest savings to ramp up production and stimulate even greater levels of unsustainable consumption. Certification benefits are lost as investors find new buyers, as buyers purchase from new locations, and as new markets emerge for uncertified products. Even seeming regulatory successes are often lost in the shadows of global trade as firms increase exports to places with lower standards.

Yet, as we've seen in this book, the limited gains of environmentalism of the rich are nonetheless enticing more and more NGOs to take a more restrained, pragmatic stance with business and governments. This does not mean radical environmentalism has gone away. The second half of this book was filled with examples of people rising up to fight land grabs to make way for plantations, national parks, and hydroelectric dams, as well as to oppose the clearing of forests and the pollution of waterways. As we saw, however, states have long treated both environmentalism of the poor and the direct action of radical activists as security threats, suppressing uprisings and jailing leaders. And challenging the wealth and values of ruling elites has become even harder since the Al Qaeda attacks of 2001, with countries such as the US now classifying direct-action environmentalism as eco-terrorism.

Furthermore, as economies grow and consumption rises, increasingly it is NGO campaigners (with fundraising in mind) and affluent consumers (living far above their fair earth share) at the core of mainstream environmentalism. More and more campaigns are targeting brand corporations and middle-class consumers, focusing on raising money to support small-scale projects and modest policy reforms. Few large NGOs are working to overhaul trade, multinational corporations, or state governance. Even calls to lighten ecological footprints and move toward consuming fair earth shares are rare. Instead, the talk is of the value of partnering with business, of cause marketing and leveraging markets. Of eco-certification and eco-tourism. Fair trade logos and green products. Recycling and composting. Rewilding and wilderness preservation. Carbon offsetting and green technology. And the charity of billionaires and celebrities.

All of these solutions share a common trait: they fail to confront the politics of producing (and desiring) ever-more wealth and consumption. Recent social media campaigns have been able to embarrass brand companies such as Nestlé, Mattel, and Procter & Gamble into modifying some sourcing practices and some manufacturing processes. Nonetheless, as this book brings to light, such campaigns are doing nothing to alter the forces of exploitation or inequality, and very little to reduce the overall consequences of consumption. Look at livestock, which contributes around 15 percent of greenhouse gas emissions—more than the entire US economy. Rarely do governments or NGOs ever suggest lowering the consumption of meat or dairy products as a solution for climate change. And few consumers are even aware of the environmental consequences of livestock.[8]

Once again, I'm not denying that industrial processes, including manufacturing, transportation, and food production, are improving somewhat as governments regulate and corporations pledge sustainability. Nor am I disputing the efficiency gains from smart packaging, recycling, or smart buildings. As this book highlights, however, efficiency gains and savings from corporate sustainability are going straight back into churning out more nondurable and disposable products, building more big-box stores, and producing more billionaires. At the same time little progress has been made in getting states or corporations—let alone consumers—to truly believe in limits, or even in restraint. Direct-action campaigns to save cute or majestic creatures, such as seal pups and whales, have met with some success, but these have done little to stop the accelerating biodiversity crisis as plantations and cattle ranches replace tropical forests. Buy Nothing Day has a few devotees, but no discernible impact on reducing total consumption as retailers from Walmart to Patagonia continue to sell, sell, sell.

Nor are consumers reusing more, as engineers design products for rapid obsolescence and as advertisers manufacture new needs and new desires, from Elmo dolls to Barbies to Pampers. The corporate style of sustainability, as P&G's campaign to market Pampers in China exemplifies, is one where a company boldly pronounces that "sustainable thinking is in everything we do," yet consciously and determinedly reengineers entire cultures to sell billions of cheap, disposable products.[9] The corporate style of sustainability is advancing green technology, as eco-modernists are quick to point out. But low-flush toilets and energy-efficient appliances do not take us very far in the quest for global sustainability; nor will hybrid and electric vehicles once 3 billion cars, SUVs, and trucks clog the world's roads in 2050. And, as the histories of leaded gasoline, CFCs, and Teflon remind us, relying on corporate research and technology is itself risky. Firms have long introduced dangerous chemicals and products in the pursuit of profits and growth, while "next-generation" substitutes entail a host of new health and environmental risks.

Furthermore, although some international environmental treaties (notably, the 1987 Montreal Protocol to phase out ozone-depleting substances) have been effective, most are stunningly ineffective, reflecting political rather than ecological priorities, with obtuse language and few, if any, penalties for non-compliance. Local bylaws and national policies are generally more effective, although many governments struggle to enforce regulations, and some are even using environmental policies to suppress indigenous peoples and insurgencies, what Berkeley's Nancy Peluso calls "coercive conservation."[10] Few local regulations anywhere in the world, moreover, are doing much to rein in damage to the global ecology, with many practices in wealthy countries and neighborhoods casting ecological shadows onto peoples and places with less power, both at home and abroad.

In short, environmentalism of the rich is doing little to scale back the global ecological damage of states, corporations, or markets, primarily addressing symptoms of unsustainability, not root causes. Calls for degrowth, appropriate technology, localization, and steady-state economies do continue to echo from the past, with each year bringing more books and conferences envisioning ways to remake the world economy.[11] And some activists are decrying environmentalism of the rich as a sell-out, at best ineffectual, at worst reinforcing a growing global crisis as outcomes do more to validate unsustainable economies and lifestyles than protect vulnerable ecosystems and exploited peoples. Nonetheless, as we've seen, environmentalism of the rich is continuing to spread and deepen, marginalizing those calling for equity, prudence, and sufficiency as guiding principles of social and economic life, and leaving fewer and fewer people willing to even consider the idea that consumption matters for global environmental change.

## As If Consumption Matters

The myopic morality of Captain Queirós in 1606 in exploiting places with less power clearly continues, now with even greater speed, inequalities, and damage as the world economy globalizes. As in the past, even what might seem compassionate or right to those trying to help may well look like interference or arrogance to those being "protected" or "saved." Our descendants in 2406 will surely remember us as crass, ignorant, even barbaric. As we act in the name of sustainability, we should not forget this.

Without a doubt, consuming sustainably is wildly challenging as global production and supply chains obscure and deflect responsibility, with the result that few people feel responsible for global sustainability and even fewer live sustainably. What is the global environmental consequence of a businessman in Moscow lunching on a Brazilian steak? Or a construction worker in Japan eating a Snickers chocolate bar? Or a London lawyer buying an iPad or driving a BMW? Or honeymooners from Utah sipping French champagne in Tahiti? Given my own childhood of fishing the waters of Nova Scotia, do I have any responsibility at all for the collapse of the Atlantic cod? What responsibility do each of us have for the sustainability of the earth?

Is this last question not pure hubris? Isn't one person too inconsequential to matter? After all, humanity's total biomass may not be much different than all the ants on earth.[12] Already, one of the weaknesses of more critical environmentalism is its pessimism, with many followers wracked by guilt, anxiety, and despair. Should we perhaps repress the idea that our life matters for global sustainability, like thoughts of death?

Yet people do matter for global change. E. F. Schumacher knew this, as he elegantly argued in his 1973 classic *Small Is Beautiful: Economics as if People Matter*. Generally, those of us who study global change tend to think in big, abstract categories. We discuss world systems and global forces. We analyze states and economies and corporations. We lecture on capitalism and empires and globalization. And we debate the value of international law and market governance. Subsuming people into analytical concepts can—and does—allow for many insights. It helps us see the importance of structures and ideologies for constraining and influencing decisions. And it rightly emphasizes the power of governments and firms to direct global affairs. But it also risks limiting our inquiry and leaving us feeling powerless.

My analysis in *Environmentalism of the Rich* has put people front and center. Doing so shifted my emphasis toward the consequences of lifestyles, desires, needs, and especially consumption. And it moved my focus toward individual activists who have struggled to reform the world around them. Claiming people matter for global sustainability may seem obvious. Yet rarely do states or international organizations or multinational corporations engage fully with the impossibility of sustaining 10 billion American-style consumers without doing great harm to the earth. In the search for feasible and measurable objectives, even NGOs hardly ever pursue global sustainability as if rising and unequal consumption matters.

One consequence is a tendency of most books on the politics of global sustainability to concentrate on international treaties and organizations, multinational corporations and state policies, and trade and markets. These certainly constrain people's choices. And understanding them is absolutely necessary for analyzing the consequences of consumption and lifestyles for global sustainability. But institutions also comprise and serve people. Ignoring this runs the risk of thinking about responsibility in rather intangible and vague ways—with concepts like capitalism, rather than the people who make up and run the institutions of capitalism, somehow accountable for unequal and unsustainable outcomes.

My premise here is in no way surprising, although it is surprising to me how often people across every culture ignore it: careers, choices, and every-day consumption matter greatly for the sustainability of the earth. Care must be taken, however, when making this argument. As we've seen, calling on consumers to change the world risks playing into the hands of clever marketers, and given the diversity of needs and desires across cultures, consumers will inevitably act at cross-purposes, with some never caring, some never understanding, and some, both rich and poor, doing far more than others. Most importantly, asking consumers to act sustainably must not substitute for firms and governments regulating and changing production. As political scientist Michael Maniates rightly reminds us, some people who recycle or buy eco-products or purchase carbon credits to offset travel will see such efforts as their fair share, and leave to others the much harder work of demanding—and then building—the institutions for more balanced consumption.[13] A danger of despair replacing hope exists too, as those consumers taking more personal responsibility fail to see progress toward global sustainability, as they see others ignoring responsibilities, and as feelings of hypocrisy gnaw at them.

Still, as Kalle Lasn of Adbusters tried so hard to explain to CNN's Carol Costello at the end of chapter 4, getting people to consume less and differently is crucial for global sustainability. The value of getting more people to consume less goes beyond lowering demand for unsustainable products. For some citizens it will one day lead them to rally for action on climate change, or volunteer for an environmental cause, or vote for a green party. For some college students, it will lead them to join campus sustainability clubs. For some workers, it will lead them to advocate for more responsible sourcing practices or better workplace conditions. And for some politicians it will lead them to call for the greening of cities or trade or finance.

But of course capitalism frames today's world. Culture and politics constrain people's options and shape the consequences of their decisions. So do economic circumstances. A few individuals are living in radically different ways, as we saw with Bruno Manser during his time in Sarawak and with Captain Paul Watson of the Sea Shepherd Conservation Society. Yet no one can get around the fact that corporate, societal, and political forces—from advertising to consumerism to legislation—amalgamate our consequences, guiding the ecology of our collective lives like dry riverbeds channeling storm waters.

Moving high-consuming lifestyles toward a fair earth share will therefore require far-reaching political and economic reforms that put in place new social rules and institutions: a point Paul Steinberg makes especially well in his book, *Who Rules the Earth?*[14] Stricter international and domestic laws to protect ecosystems and human rights are necessary. So are measures to end extreme inequality and stop corporate pillaging. So are far higher levels of precaution when introducing new technologies and chemicals. And so is a new energy base for our economies: carbon-neutral, with fairer distribution. Most challenging of all, we will need more people, especially those with power and money, to accept more responsibility for the consequences of the sources of their wealth, owning up to historical wrongs and to contemporary inequities so new rules and institutions can be put in place.

At the same time we can and must measure progress toward sustainability, however rife with hazards. A politics of global sustainability will not be possible without a world economy of less waste, less resource exploitation, and less biological disruption—and thus less greenhouse gases, deforestation, overfishing, biodiversity loss, desertification, and pollution. It's simply not good enough for a country or company or community to produce more efficiently, or recycle more effectively, if *overall* damage is continuing to increase. Such a world economy must also generate more well-being for more people, and not simply produce higher gross domestic products for nations.

Going beyond profit-oriented development, corporate-run solutions, and consumer-led responsibility is vital. Controls must be placed on the institutions of overconsumption and wasteful consumption, including the automobile industry, the chemical industry, the construction industry, the fossil fuel industry, the mining industry, the fishing industry, the timber industry, the advertising industry, the fast-food industry, the discount retail industry, and the agricultural industry. And investments must be shifted into green jobs, local food production, and more sustainable ways of living. Expecting government-led sustainable development, corporate-NGO partnerships, CSR, eco-consumerism, and feel-good rhetoric to transform the world economy is not only naïve, it's downright dangerous. Both states and firms, as this book reveals time and again, tend to advance unsustainability even as part of sustainability efforts, with governments growing economies of overconsumption to retain supporters and appease critics, and firms increasing sales and profits by manufacturing even more consumption.

Prioritizing wealth creation for the wealthy is not going to get us anywhere close to global sustainability. Much deeper reforms are necessary across all international structures, all nations, all businesses, all cities, all towns, all factories, all universities—and, yes, all households. Sustainability must be seen as a value like justice or liberty, with a new politics within all institutions and across all cultures. A politics of global sustainability must respect nature, demand intergenerational equity, advance environmental justice, and promote fair economics without irreparably harming present or future life. It must restrain corporations as well as unbalanced growth and consumption. And it must recognize that socioeconomic and ecological systems interlock, putting in place measures to balance systems that are interacting with increasing speed and volatility.

To begin, moving toward global sustainability will require more people to take on more responsibility for transforming the rules and institutions causing our current environmental crisis to keep escalating. Not everyone is equally responsible, of course. Those with power, education, and money consume far more of the earth's resources, and have far more responsibility for solving the crisis. Progress will require way more of these well-off people to think globally and act responsibly, making big changes as consumers *and* as citizens to reduce ecological footprints toward a fair earth share. Critics will dismiss this conclusion as unrealistic and impractical. I'm not aiming, however, to offer a practical guide to sustainability or a blueprint for a new environmentalism. Rather, I'm underlining the need for big changes, and making a case for the value of challenging the complacency of environmentalism of the rich with an energetic, critical questioning of the sleight-of-hand illusions of sustainable development, corporate social responsibility, business-NGO partnerships, and market solutions. A spirit of outrage at the world order is necessary to move toward sustainability, not shrugging acceptance of extreme inequality, destructive growth, excessive business power, and a growing problem of consumption.

# Notes

## Chapter 1

1. J. R. McNeill compares the number of baboons and humans in 8,000 BC in *Something New Under the Sun: An Environmental History of the Twentieth-Century World* (W.W. Norton, 2000), p. 8; the estimate of life expectancy in 8,000 BC is from Carl Haub, "How Many People Have Ever Lived on Earth?" *Population Today* (February) (1995). For human population projections, see United Nations, Department of Economic and Social Affairs, Population Division, Population Estimates and Projections Section, *World Population Prospects: The 2015 Revision*, as of July 2015, at http://esa .un.org/unpd/wpp.

For the Nordhaus, Shellenberger, Narain, and Suzuki quotes, see Michael Shellenberger and Ted Nordhaus, "The Death of Environmentalism: Global Warming Politics in a Post-Environmental World" (2004), and Ted Nordhaus and Michael Shellenberger, "The Long Death of Environmentalism" (February 25, 2011), both at www.thebreakthrough.org; Ted Nordhaus and Michael Shellenberger, *Break Through: From the Death of Environmentalism to the Politics of Possibility* (Houghton Mifflin, 2007); Sunita Narain, "Environmentalism of the Poor vs. Environmentalism of the Rich," Wrigley Lecture, Global Institute of Sustainability, Arizona State University, March 27, 2013 (https://schoolofsustainability.asu.edu/media/video/sunita-narain); and David Suzuki, "The Fundamental Failure of Environmentalism" (May 1, 2012), at www.straight.com.

2. The scientific and technical reports of the International Panel on Climate Change (IPCC) are particularly sobering reads. See, for example, IPCC, *Climate Change 2013: The Physical Science Basis* (Working Group 1, Fifth Assessment Report of the Intergovernmental Panel on Climate Change, 2013), at http://www.ipcc.ch/report/ar5/ wg1. President Obama's 2014 speech was at the United Nations Climate Summit (New York City, September 23, 2014), and is available at www.youtube.com. The estimate of the increase in global carbon emissions is from the Global Carbon Project at www.globalcarbonproject.org.

Even a rise of 2 degrees Celsius above the pre-industrial average may prove "highly dangerous" as sea levels undergo "non-linear change." For evidence, see J. Hansen et al., "Ice Melt, Sea Level Rise and Superstorms: Evidence from Paleoclimate Data, Climate Modeling, and Modern Observations That 2°C Global Warming Is Highly Dangerous," *Atmospheric Chemistry and Physics* 15 (2015), pp. 20059–20179, DOI: 10.5194/acpd-15-20059-2015. The phrase and idea of a "sixth extinction" coming this century comes from Richard Leakey and Roger Lewin, *The Sixth Extinction: Patterns of Life and the Future of Humankind* (Doubleday, 1995). Also see, however, Elizabeth Kolbert, *The Sixth Extinction: An Unnatural History* (Henry Holt and Company, 2014).

3. With slightly varying meanings and emphases, others in recent years have also used the expression "environmentalism of the rich," including Sunita Narain for the title of her 2013 Wrigley Lecture at Arizona State University, "Environmentalism of the Poor vs. Environmentalism of the Rich" (see above for details), and Patricia Ávila-García and Eduardo Luna Sánchez, "The Environmentalism of the Rich and the Privatization of Nature: High-End Tourism on the Mexican Coast," *Latin American Perspectives* 39 (6) (2012), pp. 51–67. On occasion, the scholarship on "environmentalism of the poor" (for examples, see below) also refers to environmentalism of the rich (sometimes called the "ecology of affluence"). See, for instance, Joan Martinez-Alier, "Distributional Conflicts and International Environmental Policy on Carbon Dioxide Emissions and Agricultural Biodiversity," in Jeroen C. J. M. van den Bergh and Jan van der Straaten, eds., *Toward Sustainable Development: Concepts, Methods, and Policy* (Island Press, 1994), pp. 235–264 (see p. 259 in particular).

4. Steven Bernstein, *The Compromise of Liberal Environmentalism* (Columbia University Press, 2001); Steven Bernstein, "Liberal Environmentalism and Global Environmental Governance," *Global Environmental Politics* 2 (3) (2002), pp. 1–16.

5. The term "eco-business" is from Peter Dauvergne and Jane Lister, *Eco-Business: A Big-Brand Takeover of Sustainability* (MIT Press, 2013); this book analyzes why, and in what ways, big-brand companies are using sustainability tools and programs to enhance reputations, growth, and profits.

6. For reference to the "cult of wilderness," see, for instance, Ramachandra Guha and Joan Martinez-Alier, *Varieties of Environmentalism: Essays North and South* (Earthscan, 1997), p. xxi.

7. The phrase "movement of movements" is more often used to describe the global resistance to capitalism and globalization than to characterize global environmentalism. I use the phrase, however, to emphasize the diversity of environmentalism, which itself overlaps with movements against capitalism and globalization (and for global justice). For a discussion of this phrase in relation to anti-globalization activism and alter-globalization campaigns (offering social justice alternatives to globalization), see Tom Mertes, ed., *A Movement of Movements: Is Another World Really Possible?* (Verso, 2004). For a sense of the great diversity of environmentalism, see

Further Readings, "Environmental Activism ("insider" critiques of)," "Environmental Discourses and Movements (varieties of)," "Environmental Justice Movements," "Environmental NGOs and Transnational Networks," "Environmentalism (developing countries)," "Environmentalism (overviews)," and "Voluntary Simplicity, Localization, and Eco-Villages."

8. The phrase "spirit of outrage" comes from J. M. Coetzee, *Waiting for the Barbarians* (Vintage, 2000; first published by Martin Secker & Warburg, 1980), p. 110.

9. For environmentalism of the poor, see Rob Nixon, *Slow Violence and the Environmentalism of the Poor* (Harvard University Press, 2011); Joan Martinez-Alier, *The Environmentalism of the Poor: A Study of Ecological Conflicts and Valuation* (Edward Elgar, 2003); Guha and Martinez-Alier, *Varieties of Environmentalism*. For analysis of the environmental justice movements in developing countries see David V. Carruthers, ed., *Environmental Justice in Latin America: Problems, Promise, and Practice* (MIT Press, 2008); and David Naguib Pellow, *Resisting Global Toxics: Transnational Movements for Global Justice* (MIT Press, 2007). For environmental justice movements in developed countries, see, for example, Gwen Ottinger and Benjamin R. Cohen, eds., *Technoscience and Environmental Justice: Expert Cultures in a Grassroots Movement* (MIT Press, 2011); Ronald Sandler and Phaedra C. Pezzullo, eds., *Environmental Justice and Environmentalism: The Social Justice Challenge to the Environmental Movement* (MIT Press, 2007); David Naguib Pellow and Robert J. Brulle, eds., *Power, Justice, and the Environment: A Critical Appraisal of the Environmental Justice Movement* (MIT Press, 2005); David Naguib Pellow, *Garbage Wars: The Struggle for Environmental Justice in Chicago* (MIT Press, 2002); Daniel Faber, ed., *The Struggle for Ecological Democracy: Environmental Justice Movements in the United States* (The Guilford Press, 1998).

10. See Brian Doherty and Timothy Doyle, *Environmentalism, Resistance and Solidarity: The Politics of Friends of the Earth International* (Palgrave Macmillan, 2013).

11. Peter Dauvergne, "The Problem of Consumption," *Global Environmental Politics* 10 (2) (2010), pp. 1–10.

12. Unless otherwise noted, all $ signs in *Environmentalism of the Rich* refer to the US dollar. The estimate of the Walmart family wealth is from the 2015 Forbes list of billionaires, at www.forbes.com/billionaires/list.

13. See William E. Rees and Jennie Moore, "Ecological Footprints, Fair Earth-Shares and Urbanization," in Robert Vale and Brenda Vale, eds., *Living within a Fair Share Ecological Footprint* (Routledge, 2013), p. 16.

14. For examples, see Further Readings, "Capitalism (critiques for a general audience)" and "Globalization (critical accounts)."

15. For an analysis of the growing influence of corporate funding and worldviews on international NGOs, see Peter Dauvergne and Genevieve LeBaron, *Protest Inc.: The Corporatization of Activism* (Polity, 2014); Julianne Busa and Leslie King,

"Corporate Takeover? Ideological Heterogeneity, Individualization, and Materiality in the Corporatization of Three Environment-Related Movements," *Journal of Environmental Studies and Sciences* 5 (3) (2015), pp. 251–261. Also see Further Readings, "Activism (corporatization of)," "Eco-Certification," and "Eco-Consumerism."

16. Paul Wapner, "Narrative: Frames: Living at the Margins," in Simon Nicholson and Sikina Jinnah, eds., *New Earth Politics: Essays from the Anthropocene* (MIT Press, 2016).

## Chapter 2

1. Simon Lewis and Mark Maslin make the case for two logical start dates for the Anthropocene: 1608 (seen in the geologic record as carbon uptake as vegetation and trees grew over abandoned agricultural land after tens of millions of people perished in the Americas) and 1964 (when the ban on testing nuclear weapons under water, in outer space, and in the atmosphere went into force). See Simon L. Lewis and Mark A. Maslin, "Defining the Anthropocene," *Nature* 519, March 12, 2015, pp. 171–180 (see p. 176 for the research sources and overall estimate of the population decline in the Americas from 1492 to 1650).

The idea of "ecological imperialism" is from Alfred W. Crosby, *Ecological Imperialism: The Biological Expansion of Europe, 900–1900,* new edition (Cambridge University Press, 2004). Also see Further Readings, "Ecological Imperialism." The idea of understanding environmental degradation as "slow violence" is from Rob Nixon, *Slow Violence and the Environmentalism of the Poor* (Harvard University Press, 2011).

2. Queirós was born in Portugal, but was under the authority of the King of Spain; the Spanish spelling of his name is Quirós.

Don Diego de Prado y Tovar wrote a derisive account of Queirós's leadership, first published in 1615–1616 as a collection of Spanish, Portuguese, and Latin documents; the Prado quotes in the opening section of chapter 2 are from an untitled English translation by George F. Barwick in 1922, available from the State Library of New South Wales (www.sl.nsw.gov.au). Other crew would also tell scathing stories of life under Queirós. For example, in a letter dated March 25, 1607, Juan de Iturbe, the accountant aboard the voyage to Espiritu Santo, mocked the founding of New Jerusalem, arguing Queirós was unfit for command.

For Queirós's recollections of the voyage to Espiritu Santo, see Captain Pedro Fernandez de Quir (Queirós), *Account of a Memorial Presented to his Majesty, Concerning the Population and Discovery of the Fourth Part of the World, Australia the Unknown, Its Great Riches and Fertility, Discovered by the Same Captain,* translated from Spanish by W. A. Duncan (Thomas Richards, 1874) (original Spanish text published by Charles de Labayan, 1610) (see p. 21 and p. 28 for Queirós's remarks "clean, lively, and rational" and "be very easy to pacify ..."; see as well Duncan's opening essay, "Notice by the Translator," especially pp. 8–10). Duncan portrays Queirós as "the

last of the great Spanish discoverers," "second only in rank" to Christopher Columbus (quotes at p. 10 and p. 3).

Besides Queirós's and Prado's accounts, my understanding of this voyage also
draws on Clements Markam, editor and translator, *The Voyages of Pedro Fernandez de
Quiros, 1595 to 1606*, Volumes I and II (Hakluyt Society, 1904). Markham brings
together four accounts of the voyage to Espiritu Santo: personal reflections by
Queirós, as recorded by Belmonte Bermudez, his devoted Secretary during the
voyage (and later in life a poet of some renown); the log and remarks of one of the
fleet's pilots, Gaspar Gonzalez de Leza; a telling of the voyage by Juan de Torque-
mada, a Franciscan Friar who spoke with Queirós and his crew in Acapulco in late
1606, first publishing his account in 1614; and a short letter by Torres to the King of
Spain. (In his Introduction, Markham also summarizes, but does not include,
Iturbe's letter mentioned above.) For the quote "great shouts," see p. 248 of Volume
1; for the quotes, "Thirty pigs ...," "these three souls," and "would rather have one
of those children ...," see p. 256 of Volume 1; for the Queirós quote "Silence, child!
..." see p. 277 of Volume 1; for confirmation of the death of Pablo in Mexico, see
p. 311 of Volume 1.

In addition, my account reflects a reading of more recent scholarship on Queirós,
including Margaret Jolly, "The Sediment of Voyages: Remembering Quirós, Bougainville and Cook in Vanuatu," in Margaret Jolly, Serge Tcherkézoff, and Darrell Tryon,
eds., *Ocean Encounters: Exchange, Desire, Violence* (ANU E Press, 2009), pp. 57–111;
Miguel Luque and Carlos Mondragón, "Faith, Fidelity and Fantasy: Don Pedro
Fernández de Quirós and the 'Foundation, Government and Sustenance,' of La
Nueba Hierusalem in 1606," *The Journal of Pacific History* 40 (2) (2005), pp. 133–148;
and Brett Hilder, *The Voyage of Torres: The Discovery of the Southern Coastline of
New Guinea and Torres Strait by Captain Luis Baéz de Torres in 1606* (University of
Queensland Press, 1980).

3. The estimate of the number of New Hebrides adults laboring overseas in the
1880s is from James S. Olson, ed., *Historical Dictionary of European Imperialism*
(Greenwood Press, 1991), p. 443. See also Kalkot Matas Kele-Kele, *New Hebrides: The
Road to Independence* (Institute of Pacific Studies, University of the South Pacific,
1977). R. W. Robson, *Pacific Islands Year Book and Who's Who*, 9th edition (Pacific
Publications, 1963), p. 432, is the source for the estimate of the number of Erroman-
gan laborers lost between 1868 and 1878.

4. You should treat the "1 million" population figure for New Hebrides in 1600 as a
reasonable, but very rough estimate, as it extrapolates from a patchwork of archeo-
logical surveys, anthropological observations, the diaries of early explorers, and oral
histories of the islands. Depopulation in other Melanesian societies was similarly
catastrophic. A measles epidemic in 1875, for example, killed one-quarter of the
Fijian population (which in the 1840s was between 200,000 and 300,000).

You can have more confidence in population estimates for the island of Aneityum (where the demographer Norma McArthur and the archeologist Matthew

Spriggs did extensive fieldwork) as well as the 1935 and 1960 population estimates for New Hebrides. For a summary of McArthur's work on Aneityum and for the estimate of measles deaths in Fiji in 1875, see Brij V. Lal and Kate Fortune, eds., *The Pacific Islands: An Encyclopedia* (University of Hawai'i Press, 2000), p. 84. For details on the population of New Hebrides in 1960, see Robson, *Pacific Islands Year Book and Who's Who*, p. 431.

For a seminal and contentious analysis of the depopulation of Melanesia and Polynesia after contact with Europeans, see Norma McArthur, *Island Populations of the Pacific* (Australian National University Press, 1967). For an analysis of the difficulties of making such estimates, see Patrick V. Kirch and Jean-Louis Rallu, "Long-Term Demographic Evolution in the Pacific Islands," in Patrick V. Kirch and Jean-Louis Rallu, eds., *The Growth and Collapse of Pacific Island Societies: Archaeological and Demographic Perspectives* (University of Hawai'i Press, 2007), pp. 1–14. The research in this edited collection provides further confidence in the "1 million" estimate for New Hebrides in 1600. In particular see chapter 14, Matthew Spriggs, "Population in a Vegetable Kingdom: Aneityum Island (Vanuatu) at European Contact in 1830," pp. 278–305.

5. For example, a letter from Captain Torres updating King Philip III of Spain on the progress of the voyage, penned in Manila on July 12, 1607, did not reach the King until June 22, 1608.

6. Crosby, *Ecological Imperialism*, pp. 202, 204–206. See also Bruce G. Trigger, *The Children of Aataentsic: A History of the Huron People to 1660* (McGill–Queen's University Press, 1987, first printing 1976); Richard Grove, *Green Imperialism: Colonial Expansion, Tropical Island Edens and the Origins of Environmentalism, 1600–1860* (Cambridge University Press, 1995).

Crosby focused on three biological sources of environmental change—European diseases, plants, and animals—as European imperial powers explored, conquered, and settled the lands of the Asia-Pacific, Africa, and South and North America from 900 to 1900. His great insight was to extend our understanding of imperialism beyond the cultural, political, economic, and military forces of devastation already well exposed by critical (especially Marxist) scholars, such as Vladimir Lenin in 1917 in *Imperialism, the Highest Stage of Capitalism*, Eric Hobsbawm in 1987 in *The Age of Empire: 1876–1914* (Pantheon Books), and Edward Said in 1993 in *Culture and Imperialism* (Knopf).

My analysis is also influenced by the Marxist-inspired literature on ecological imperialism, including those who analyze within the frame of "world-system theory" and a "theory of metabolic rift." For a sampling, see John Bellamy Foster and Brett Clark, "Ecological Imperialism: The Curse of Capitalism," *Socialist Register* 40 (2004), pp. 186–200; James Petras and Henry Veltmeyer, *Globalization Unmasked: Imperialism in the 21st Century* (Zed Books, 2001); James Petras and Henry Veltmeyer, *Extractive Imperialism in the Americas: Capitalism's New Frontier* (Brill Academic Publishers, 2015).

Jason W. Moore, "Environmental Crises and the Metabolic Rift in World-Historical Perspective," *Organization & Environment* 13 (2) (2000), pp. 123–157. Jason W. Moore, "The Modern World-System as Environmental History? Ecology and the Rise of Capitalism," *Theory and Society* 32 (3) (2003), pp. 307–377; Jason W. Moore, "Transcending the Metabolic Rift: A Theory of Crises in the Capitalist World-Ecology," *Journal of Peasant Studies* 38 (1) (2011), pp. 1–46; Ariel Salleh, "From Metabolic Rift to Metabolic Value: Reflections on Environmental Sociology and the Alternative Globalization Movement," *Organization & Environment* 23 (2) (2010), pp. 205–219; Alf Hornberg, J. R. McNeill, and Joan Martinez-Alier, eds., *Rethinking Environmental History: World-System History and Global Environmental Change* (AltaMira Press, 2007).

7. John Winthrop, *Winthrop Papers, 1631–1637* (Massachusetts Historical Society, 1943, III), p. 167, quoted in Crosby, *Ecological Imperialism*, p. 208.

8. Cema Bolabola, "Fiji: Customary Constraints and Legal Process," in Institute of Pacific Studies at the University of the South Pacific, ed., *Land Rights of Pacific Women* (University of the South Pacific, 1986), p. 6; Toril Moi, "Jealousy and Sexual Difference," *Feminist Review*, no. 11, Summer (1982), p. 55.

9. The external debt estimate of "more than $5 trillion today" projects from data from the World Bank, *International Debt Statistics 2013* (World Bank, 2013), p. 2, p. 8; World Bank, *International Debt Statistics 2014* (World Bank, 2014), p. 2. Scholars have long raised concerns about the social and ecological consequences of foreign debt. See, for example, Chris Jochnick and Fraser A. Preston, eds., *Sovereign Debt at the Crossroads: Challenges and Proposals for Resolving the Third World Debt Crisis* (Oxford University Press, 2006); Susan George, *The Debt Boomerang: How Third World Debt Harms Us All* (Pluto, 1992).

10. The World Bank estimates that 2.59 billion people were living on less than $2 a day in 1981. See World Bank, "Poverty Overview" (www.worldbank.org). The data on the world's millionaires are from the 2015 "Global Wealth Report" by the Credit Suisse Research Institute (www.credit-suisse.com), released October 13, 2015.

11. For data on urban slums, see United Nations Human Settlements Programme (UN-HABITAT), *State of the World's Cities 2012/13* (UN-HABITAT, 2012). For data on malnutrition, see Food and Agriculture Organization, World Food Programme, and International Fund for Agricultural Development, *The State of Food Insecurity in the World: Economic Growth Is Necessary But Not Sufficient to Accelerate Reduction of Hunger and Malnutrition* (Food and Agriculture Organization of the United Nations, 2012), p. 8. For a statistical analysis of health trends in emerging and developing economies, see Damien de Walque, ed., *Risking Your Health: Causes, Consequences, and Interventions to Prevent Risky Behaviors* (World Bank, 2014). For a detailed analysis of smoking, see Michael Eriksen, Judith Mackay, and Hana Ross, *The Tobacco Atlas*, fourth edition (American Cancer Society, 2012); and World Health Organization, *WHO Report on the Global Tobacco Epidemic, 2013* (WHO, 2013) (the estimate of 1 billion deaths over the twenty-first century is on p. 12).

12. For a sampling of more critical accounts of globalization, see Catherine Dauvergne, *The New Politics of Immigration and the End of Settler Societies* (Cambridge University Press, 2016); Paul Almeida, *Mobilizing Democracy: Globalization and Citizen Protest* (Johns Hopkins University Press, 2014); David Harvey, *Seventeen Contradictions and the End of Capitalism* (Oxford University Press, 2014); Geoffrey Pleyers, *Alter-Globalization: Becoming Actors in a Global Age* (Polity, 2010); Catherine Dauvergne, *Making People Illegal: What Globalization Means for Migration and Law* (Cambridge University Press, 2008); William I. Robinson, *Latin America and Global Capitalism: A Critical Globalization Perspective* (Johns Hopkins University Press, 2008); Andrew Herod, *Geographies of Globalization: A Critical Introduction* (Wiley-Blackwell, 2008); David Held and Anthony McGrew, *Globalization/Anti-Globalization: Beyond the Great Divide*, second edition (Polity, 2007); Jan Aart Scholte, *Globalization: A Critical Introduction*, second edition (Palgrave Macmillan, 2005); David Harvey, *A Brief History of Neoliberalism* (Oxford University Press, 2005); Michael Hardt and Antonio Negri, *Multitude: War and Democracy in the Age of Empire* (Penguin, 2004); Anthony Giddens, *Runaway World: How Globalisation Is Reshaping Our Lives*, second edition (Profile Books, 2002); Michael Hardt and Antonio Negri, *Empire* (Harvard University Press, 2000); Edward W. Said, *Orientalism: Western Conceptions of the Orient* (Knopf Doubleday, 1979).

13. I would like to thank Jie (T. J.) Tian for the privilege of acting in September 2013 as the university examiner for her doctoral dissertation in philosophy on the importance of collective responsibility for just and democratic decision making: a philosophy literature, as she demonstrates, with much value for those wanting to find ways to promote global sustainability. See Jie (T. J.) Tian, *Collective Responsibility and Democratic Practice* (University of British Columbia, 2014).

## Chapter 3

1. I would like to thank Rama Kiosh Iselin—whose master's thesis at the University of British Columbia I was fortunate to supervise in 2012—for reminding me of Nauru's history.

My telling of Nauru's history from 1798–1899 relies in particular on Nancy Viviani, *Nauru: Phosphate and Political Progress* (University of Hawaii Press, 1970), see especially pp. 3–28; and Carl N. McDaniel and John M. Gowdy, *Paradise for Sale: A Parable of Nature* (University of California Press, 2000), see especially pp. 29–41 (the British Navy quote is from p. 34, originally from Albert Fuller Ellis, *Ocean Island and Nauru: Their Story* [Angus and Robertson, 1935, p. 35]).

Captain Fearn's account (and the quote "a beautiful little island") is from *The Naval Chronicle*, Volume 2, Monthly Register, From July to December 1799, p. 536. For Fearn's account of his voyage past Nauru, see also Joseph Huddart, *The Oriental Navigator, Or, New Directions for Sailing to and from the East Indies, China, New Holland*, second edition (Robert Laurie and James Whittle, 1801), pp. 622–624.

2. This section draws on Rosamond Dobson Rhone, *The National Geographic Magazine* 40 (6) (December 1921), pp. 559–590 (the "worked-out phosphate field" quote is on p. 572); Nancy Viviani, "Nauru Phosphate Negotiations," *The Journal of Pacific History* 3 (1968), pp. 151–154; J. W. Davidson, "The Republic of Nauru," *The Journal of Pacific History* 3 (1968), pp. 145–150; Viviani, *Nauru*; Ron Crocombe, "Nauru: The Politics of Phosphate," in *Micronesian Politics* (Institute of Pacific Studies of the University of the South Pacific, 1988), pp. 38–66; McDaniel and Gowdy, *Paradise for Sale*; Christopher Weeramantry, *Nauru: Environmental Damage Under International Trusteeship* (Oxford University Press, 1992), see pp. 369–370, Table 16.2, for estimates of phosphate shipments from Nauru from 1921–1967; Nancy J. Pollock, "Impact of Mining on Nauruan Women," *Natural Resources Forum* 20 (2) (1996), pp. 123–134; and John M. Gowdy and Carl N. McDaniel, "The Physical Destruction of Nauru: An Example of Weak Sustainability," *Land Economics* 75 (2) (1999), pp. 333–338.

For more on the geology of Nauru, see P. J. Hill and G. Jacobsen, "Structure and Evolution of Nauru Island, Central Pacific Ocean," *Australian Journal of Earth Sciences* 36 (3) (1989), pp. 365–381. For the history of the Japanese occupation of Nauru, see Nancy J. Pollock, "Nauruans during World War II," in Geoffrey M. White, ed., *Remembering the Pacific War*, Occasional Paper Series 36 (Center for Pacific Islands Studies, School of Hawaiian, Asian, and Pacific Studies, University of Hawai'i at Mānoa, 1991), pp. 91–107.

The calculation of how far dump trucks filled with Nauruan phosphate (mined from 1906–1968) would stretch assumes a single dump-truck length of 9 meters (29.5 feet) and capacity of 35 metric tons (38 short tons), and a road distance from New York City to Los Angeles of 4,466 kilometers (2,775 miles).

3. The estimate of the area of Nauru mined during Australia's administration of the island is from Antony Anghie, "'The Heart of My Home': Colonialism, Environmental Damage, and the Nauru Case," *Harvard International Law Journal* 34 (2) (1993), p. 446. The estimates of Nauruan phosphate exports from 1968–1990 were compiled from the annual United States Bureau of Mines, *Minerals Yearbook*, with particular recognition to the staff scientist William F. Stowasser (archives are stored at http://minerals.usgs.gov/minerals/pubs/usbmmyb.html).

4. For an analysis of Nauru's economy (including the comparison with Saudi Arabia's GDP per capita in 1975), see Helen Hughes, *From Riches to Rags: What Are Nauru's Options and What Can Australia Do to Help?* Issue Analysis, No. 50, Centre for Independent Studies, August 18, 2004, (comparison on p. 3). The story of the Lamborghini is told in Nick Squires, "Nauru Seeks to Regain Lost Fortunes," *BBC News*, March 15, 2008, at http://news.bbc.co.uk. Manoa Tongamalo's comment is in Nick Squires, "Tough Times for Nauru as Money Runs Out," *Telegraph*, March 13, 2008, at http://www.telegraph.co.uk; note, the $50 Tongamalo refers to is the Australian dollar ($A), the currency of Nauru.

5. Australia's 1993 offer of Curtis Island did not include independence or sovereignty for Nauruans. A proud people with a strong identity, Nauruans rejected the

offer, worried about racism in Queensland and wanting more autonomy than the Australians were willing to grant (see Viviani, *Nauru*, pp. 144–147). For analysis of Nauru's case in international law see Anghie "'The Heart of My Home'," pp. 445–506, and Weeramantry, *Nauru*.

The estimate of 400 offshore banks in Nauru in the early 1990s is from the Organisation for Economic Co-operation and Development. See OECD, *Global Forum on Transparency and Exchange of Information for Tax Purposes, Peer Review Report, Phase 1, Legal and Regulatory Framework, NAURU* (OECD, 2013). Tony Audoa is quoted in Christopher Niesche, "Low Phosphate, but What a Laundering!" *The Australian*, August 11, 2001, p. 28. See also, "Paradise Well and Truly Lost—Nauru; A Little Island with Big Problems," *The Economist*, December 22, 2001, p. 73.

The estimates of Nauruan phosphate exports from 1990–2004 were compiled from the annual yearbooks of the US Bureau of Mines (until 1995) and the US Geological Survey (US Department of the Interior), annual *Minerals Yearbook*, "Phosphate Rock."

6. The Helen Hughes quote—"They have blown close to two billion"—is from Keller Easterling, *Enduring Innocence: Global Architecture and Its Political Masquerades* (MIT Press, 2005), p. 182. Hughes's estimate of the potential returns of Nauru's phosphate profits from 1968–2001 is in Helen Hughes, "Only Harsh Medicine Can Save Nauru," *The Courier Mail*, August 31, 2004. See also Hughes, *From Riches to Rags*. The Hughes's quote that "There's always sharks ..." is from "Resurgence in Sight But Nauru Remains 'a Sitting Duck,'" *The Australian*, October 25, 2010, at www.theaustralian .com.au.

7. For an analysis of Nauru's offshore banking, see OECD, *Global Forum on Transparency*, (the quote about "physical presence is from p. 7). Also see Glenn R. Simpson, "Tiny Island Selling Passports Is Big Worry for U.S. Officials," *Wall Street Journal*, May 16, 2003, at http://online.wsj.com.

For estimates of Nauru's phosphate production since 2006, see Stephen M. Jasinski, "Phosphate Rock," in US Geological Survey, *2011 Minerals Yearbook: Phosphate Rock* [Advance Release] (US Department of the Interior, January 2013), p. 10.

8. For Abbott's "15,000" figure for future Nauru camps, see Bianca Hall, "Hunger Strikers Slam 'Hell Hole' Camps on Nauru," *The Age*, November 6, 2012, p. 2. Also see Nic Maclellan, "What Has Australia Done to Nauru?" *Overland* 212 (Spring 2013), at http://overland.org.au. For statistics on Australia's detention of asylum seekers, see Australian Government, *Immigration Detention and Community Statistics Summary* (Australian Department of Immigration and Border Protection, October 2014), p. 3 for Nauru. For an overview of Nauru's water supplies, see United Nations Environment Programme (UNEP), *Freshwater under Threat: Pacific Islands—Vulnerability Assessment of Freshwater Resources to Environmental Change* (UNEP, 2011).

For Graham Thom's assessment of the Nauru camp, see Graham Thom, "Cruelty, in the Name of All of Us," *The Age*, November 26, 2012, p. 11; Nurse Evers is quoted in Karen Barlow, "O'Connor to Visit Nauru Amid Rape, Self-Harm Claims," Australian Broadcasting Corporation, February 6, 2013, www.abc.net.au.

9. Kathy McLeish, "Nauru: The World's Smallest Republic," *Australian Broadcasting Corporation*, October 23, 2013, at www.abc.net.au; for an insider's overview of Nauru's economy, see Jason Murphy, "Treasury Island: The Budget of the Smallest Republic," *Australian Financial Review*, September 7, 2013, p. 53.

No bank was operating in Nauru as of early 2016; however, in recent years a few banks have been looking into opening a branch in Nauru. See Robb M. Stewart and Lucy Craymer, "Nation of Nauru Rebuilds Bank System from Scratch," *Wall Street Journal*, November 3, 2013, at http://online.wsj.com.

10. For Nauru's worldwide obesity and smoking ranking, see Damien de Walque and Sébastien Piguet, "Overview of the Prevalence and Trends of Risky Behaviors in the Developing World," in Damien de Walque, ed., *Risking Your Health: Causes, Consequences, and Interventions to Prevent Risky Behaviors* (World Bank, 2014), p. 16, pp. 25–26.

11. James Aingimea is quoted in Philip Shenon, "A Pacific Island Nation Is Stripped of Everything," *New York Times*, December 10, 1995, p. 3.

## Chapter 4

1. Doug McMillon's remarks are quoted in *Walmart 2014 Global Sustainability Report* (Walmart, 2014), p. 2. For a highly optimistic account of the "greening" of Walmart, see Edward Humes, *Force of Nature: The Unlikely Story of Wal-Mart's Green Revolution* (HarperCollins, 2011); for a critical overview of Walmart, see Nicholas Copeland and Christine Labuski, *The World of Wal-Mart: Discounting the American Dream* (Routledge, 2013); for a critical case study of the consequences of Walmart's sourcing practices for farmers in developing countries, see Sara D. Elder and Peter Dauvergne, "Farming for Walmart: The Politics of Corporate Control and Responsibility in the Global South," *The Journal of Peasant Studies* 42 (5) (2015), pp. 1029–1046; for an analysis of the variability across big-box retailers in the uptake of CSR and sustainability programming, see Hamish van der Ven, "Socializing the C-Suite: Why Some Big-Box Retailers are 'Greener' than Others," *Business and Politics* 16 (1) (2014), pp. 31–63.

2. For quotes and background on Adbusters, see the Adbusters website at www .adbusters.org. Vancouver artist Ted Dave initiated the first Buy Nothing Day in September 1992. Also see Ecodefense.com, "Green Politics," at www.ecodefense.com (includes the quote "to topple existing …"); Jim Sutherland, "Kalle Lasn," *Vancouver Magazine*, April 9, 2012, at www.vanmag.com (includes the quote "… black-hole future"); Mark Leiren-Young, "His One Demand," *The Walrus* (December 2012), at www.thewalrus.ca; Mattathias Schwartz, "Pre-Occupied: The Origins and Future of Occupy Wall Street," *New Yorker*, November 28, 2011, at www.newyorker.com;

Simon Houpt, "After Adbusters and Occupy, Kalle Lasn Is Spoiling for Brand New Fights," *Globe and Mail*, February 9, 2013, at www.theglobeandmail.com (includes the quote "stolen our style ..."); Kalle Lasn, *Culture Jam: How to Reverse America's Suicidal Consumer Binge—and Why We Must* (HarperCollins, 1999).

3. See Patagonia, www.patagonia.com. Patagonia's 2008 and 2011 revenue estimates are from Hugo Martin, "Outdoor Retailer Patagonia Puts Environment Ahead of Sales Growth," *Los Angeles Times*, May 24, 2012, at http://articles.latimes.com. For background on Patagonia's "don't buy" campaign, see Kyle Stock, "Patagonia's 'Buy Less' Plea Spurs More Buying," *Bloomberg Businessweek*, August 28, 2013, at www .businessweek.com; Bradford Wieners, "Environmental Movement Has Lost, Says Patagonia Founder: 10Q," *Bloomberg Businessweek*, May 2, 2012, at www .businessweek.com.

4. For overviews of the sustainability pledges and programs of some of the world's leading brand retailers and manufacturers, see Walmart (http://corporate.walmart .com); Sustainability Apparel Coalition (www.apparelcoalition.org); McDonald's (www.aboutmcdonalds.com); Nike (www.nikeresponsibility.com); Coca-Cola (www .coca-colacompany.com). The New York Declaration on Forests (dated September 23, 2014) is available on the United Nations website, under the 2014 Climate Summit (www.un.org). Also see Further Readings, "Corporate Social Responsibility (business of)," in particular Peter Dauvergne and Jane Lister, *Eco-Business: A Big-Brand Takeover of Sustainability* (MIT Press, 2013), as well as Peter Dauvergne, "The Sustainability Story: Exposing Truths, Half-Truths, and Illusions," in Simon Nicholson and Sikina Jinnah, eds., *New Earth Politics: Essays from the Anthropocene* (MIT Press, 2016), pp. 387–404; Peter Dauvergne and Jane Lister, "Big Brand Sustainability: Governance Prospects and Environmental Limits," *Global Environmental Change* 22 (1) (2012), pp. 36–45; and Peter Dauvergne and Jane Lister, "The Power of Big Box Retail in Global Environmental Governance: Bringing Commodity Chains Back into IR," *Millennium: Journal of International Relations* 39 (1) (2010), pp. 145–160.

5. For a sampling of the literature on eco-efficiency, see William McDonough and Michael Braungart, *Cradle to Cradle: Remaking the Way We Make Things* (North Point, 2002); Livio DeSimone and Frank Popoff with the World Business Council for Sustainable Development, *Eco-Efficiency: The Business Link to Sustainable Development* (MIT Press, 1997).

6. For background on Procter & Gamble, see www.pg.com, including the *P&G 2013 Annual Report*. The advertising firm Porter Novelli designed and ran the Golden Sleep campaign: for details on Porter Novelli's marketing approach see, www .porternovelli.com. Data on diaper sales in China are from Euromonitor International, "Nappies/Diapers/Pants in China," April 2014, www.euromonitor.com; see also Takeshi Owada, "Japanese Diaper Makers Tap Into Growing China Market," *The Asahi Shimbun*, April 26, 2013; and Debra Bruno, "Disposable Diapers or Bare Bot-

toms? China Frets Over Potty Training," *The Christian Science Monitor*, November 29, 2012.

7. For P&G's campaign in India, see Mya Frazier, "How P&G Brought the Diaper Revolution to China," *MoneyWatch*, January 7, 2010 (www.cbsnews.com). For details and quotes on Bounty DuraTowels, see *P&G 2013 Annual Report*, p. 5 (available at www.pg.com).

8. Mattel's leading brand is Fisher-Price, with sales of $2.12 billion in 2012 and $2.25 billion in 2013 (see Mattel, *2013 Annual Report*, p. 29, including Barbie sales). Also see Lauren Sherman, "In Depth: Barbie by the Numbers," *Forbes*, March 5, 2009, p. 7 (www.forbes.com); Paul Burns, *Corporate Entrepreneurship: Building the Entrepreneurial Organization*, second edition (Palgrave Macmillan, 2008); Vince Calio, Thomas C. Frohlich, and Alexander E. M. Hess, "10 Best-Selling Products of All Time," *USA Today*, May 18, 2014 (www.usatoday.com); John Sousanis, "World Vehicle Population Tops 1 Billion Units," *WardsAuto*, August 15, 2011 (http://wardsauto.com); and Daniel Sperling and Deborah Gordon, *Two Billion Cars: Driving Toward Sustainability* (Oxford University Press, 2009), p. 4.

9. For a selection of readings critical of capitalism, see Further Readings, "Capitalism (critiques, for a general audience)." For statistics on GDP, see World Development Indicators database, World Bank, "GDP (current US$)," at http://data.worldbank .org. China's economy is leading an overall rise in the economies of Asia. The Asian Development Bank predicts that Asia will comprise more than half of the world economy by 2050. See Asian Development Bank (ADB), *Asia 2050: Realizing the Asian Century* (ADB, 2011), p. 1.

10. My calculations comparing the annual revenues of the world's largest brand retailers and manufacturers rely on data from the Global Fortune 500 (http://fortune.com/global500). For analysis of the history of Walmart and the globalization of the marketing and consumption of inexpensive, nondurable merchandise, see Further Readings, "Discount Retailing."

11. My comparisons of corporate sales and personal earnings rely on data from the 2015 Global Fortune 500 and data from the World Bank, "Poverty Overview," www.worldbank.org. I assume 1 billion people are living on $1.25 per day and 1 billion are living on $2 per day—best-case estimates of the income of the world's poorest 2 billion people.

12. For the latest ranking of the world's billionaires, see Forbes, www.forbes.com/billionaires/list. For estimates of gross domestic products, see World Development Indicators database, World Bank, "Gross Domestic Product 2013," December 16, 2014, at http://data.worldbank.org. For details on Bill Gates see Randall Lane, "Bill Gates Just Revealed His Goal for the Rest of His Life," *Forbes*, January 21, 2014, at www.forbes.com; Bill & Melinda Gates Foundation, at www.gatesfoundation.org;

"The Giving Pledge" at http://givingpledge.org (which includes the "Giving Pledge" quote).

For the estimate of the average pay of America's highest paid CEOs, see Scott DeCarlo, "America's Highest Paid CEOs," *Forbes*, April 4, 2012, at www.forbes.com. For a list of American CEO salaries in 2012, see GMI Ratings, "GMI Ratings' 2013 CEO Pay Survey Reveals CEO Pay Is Still on the Rise," October 22, 2013, at www .gmiratings.com.

13. See CNN, "Stop Shopping Kalle Lasn Interview by Carol Costello, on *Anderson Cooper 360 Degrees*," aired November 26, 2004, posted on www.youtube.com.

## Chapter 5

1. See "Just Tickled: The Man Behind Elmo, the Monster Who Nearly Ate Christmas, Couldn't Be Happier His Muppet's a Star," *People* 47 (1) January 13, 1997 (includes the quote by the Walmart clerk, "The crotch ..."); Roberto A. Ferdman, "From Tickle Me Elmo to Big Hugs Elmo: Nearly Two Decades of Christmas Toy Dominance," *Quartz*, November 22, 2013 (www.qz.com). The estimates of new vehicles sales are from IHS Automotive (www.ihs.com).

2. J. R. McNeill's quote "the screeching acceleration" is from *Something New Under the Sun: An Environmental History of the Twentieth-Century World* (W.W. Norton, 2001), p. 4.

3. Thorstein Veblen, *The Theory of the Leisure Class: An Economic Study of Institutions* (Macmillan, 1915, first published in 1899).

4. For the estimate of the number of cattle across the world, see the Food and Agriculture Organization (FAO) of the United Nations, Statistics Division of the FAO, FAOSTAT, at http://faostat3.fao.org. For estimates of cell phone use and trends, see the UN's International Telecommunication Union's *World Telecommunication/ICT Indicators Database 2013* (17th edition), December 2013, at www.itu.int. For trends and estimates of motor vehicle growth to 2050, see Organisation for Economic Cooperation and Development (OECD), International Transport Forum (ITF), *ITF Transport Outlook 2013: Funding Transport* (OECD/ITF, 2013).

5. For background on Walmart, see the websites http://corporate.walmart.com and www.wal-martchina.com.

6. Alejandro Fleming is quoted in Fabriola Sanchez and Karl Ritter, "High Demand Leads to Toilet Paper Shortage," *Globe and Mail*, May 17, 2013, p. A13.

7. For a sampling of the academic literature on the ecological consequences of consumption, see Richard H. Robbins, *Global Problems and the Culture of Capitalism*, sixth edition (Prentice Hall, 2013); Patrick Ophuls, *Plato's Revenge: Politics in the Age of Ecology* (MIT Press, 2011); JoAnn Carmin and Julian Agyeman, eds., *Environmental*

*Inequalities Beyond Borders: Local Perspectives on Global Injustices* (MIT Press, 2011); Thomas Princen, *Treading Softly: Paths to Ecological Order* (MIT Press, 2010); Karl Gerth, *As China Goes, So Goes the World: How Chinese Consumers Are Transforming Everything* (Hill and Wang/Farrar, Straus and Giroux, 2010); Annie Leonard, *The Story of Stuff: The Impact of Overconsumption on the Planet, Our Communities, and Our Health—And How We Can Make It Better* (Free Press, 2010); Hellmuth Lange and Lars Meier, *The New Middle Classes: Globalizing Lifestyles, Consumerism, and Environmental Concern* (Springer, 2009); Matthew Paterson, *Automobile Politics: Ecology and Cultural Political Economy* (Cambridge University Press, 2007); Ramachandra Guha, *How Much Should a Person Consume? Environmentalism in India and the United States* (University of California Press, 2006); Juliet B. Schor, *Born to Buy: The Commercialized Child and the New Consumer Culture* (Scribner, 2004); Thomas Princen, *The Logic of Sufficiency* (MIT Press, 2005); Julian Agyeman, Robert D. Bullard, and Bob Evans, eds., *Just Sustainabilities: Development in an Unequal World* (MIT Press, 2003); Thomas Princen, Michael Maniates, and Ken Conca, eds., *Confronting Consumption* (MIT Press, 2002), especially Jennifer Clapp, "Distancing of Waste: Overconsumption in a Global Economy," pp. 155–176, Jack P. Manno, "Commoditization: Consumption Efficiency and an Economy of Care and Connection," pp. 67–100, and Thomas Princen, "Distancing: Consumption and the Severing of Feedback," pp. 103–132; Juliet B. Schor, *The Overspent American: Upscaling, Downshifting, and the New Consumer* (Basic Books, 1998).

8. The estimates of average water consumption are from the Greater Vancouver Regional District, City of Surrey, "Typical Household Water Consumption," www .surrey.ca.

9. For estimates of national and individual ecological footprints, WWF (in collaboration with Global Footprint Network and ZSL Living Conservation), *Living Planet Report 2012: Biodiversity, Biocapacity and Better Choices* (WWF, 2012), pp. 138–145. See also, for background, Mathis Wackernagel and William E. Rees, *Our Ecological Footprint: Reducing Human Impact on the Earth* (New Society, 1996); and Robert Vale and Brenda Vale, eds., *Living within a Fair Share Ecological Footprint* (Routledge, 2013). For the estimate of the earth's productive biocapacity, see Global Footprint Network, *Global Footprint Accounts*, 2011 edition (Global Footprint Network, 2012), p. 5. For further discussion of the methodology of ecological footprint analysis, see Global Footprint Network Standards Committee, *Ecological Footprint Standards 2009* (Global Footprint Network, 2009). Also see Global Footprint Network (www .footprintnetwork.org; the quote "we would need 5 planets" is under the tab, "Footprint Basics—Information").

For an analysis of "the shadows of consumption," see Peter Dauvergne, *The Shadows of Consumption: Consequences for the Global Environment* (MIT Press, 2008).

10. For an estimate of ~8.7 million for the total number of species on earth, see Camilo Mora, Derek P. Tittensor, Sina Adl, Alastair G. B. Simpson, and Boris Worm, "How Many Species Are There on Earth and in the Ocean?" *PLOS|Biology* 9 (8)

(2011), DOI: 10.1371/journal.pbio.1001127. For estimates of species loss, see Richard Monastersky, "Biodiversity: Life—a Status Report," *Nature* 516, no. 7530, December 11, 2014, pp. 159–161; Gerardo Ceballos, Paul R. Ehrlich, Anthony D. Barnosky, Andrés García, Robert M. Pringle, and Todd M. Palmer, "Accelerated Modern Human–induced Species Losses: Entering the Sixth Mass Extinction," *Science Advances* 1, no. 5, June 19, 2015, DOI: 10.1126/sciadv.1400253; Center for Biological Diversity at www.biologicaldiversity.org; International Union for Conservation of Nature, the Red List of Threatened Species, at www.iucnredlist.org.

11. For estimates of average population declines (based on population sampling) for 4,000 species, see WWF and Zoological Society of London, *Living Blue Planet Report: Species, Habitats and Human Well-Being* (WWF, 2015); WWF, Zoological Society of London, Global Footprint Network, and Water Footprint Network, *Living Planet Report 2014* (WWF, 2014). For data on commercial fish populations since 1950, see "The Sea Around Us: Fisheries, Ecosystems and Biodiversity" at www.seaaroundus.org. For an estimate of the loss of seabirds (based on recorded species), see Michelle Paleczny, Edd Hammill, Vasiliki Karpouzi, and Daniel Pauly, "Population Trend of the World's Monitored Seabirds, 1950–2010," *PLOS|One*, June 9, 2015, DOI: 10.1371/journal.pone.0129342. The estimate of the coral reef damage is from the US National Ocean Service, National Oceanic and Atmospheric Administration, US Department of Commerce (www.oceanservice.noaa.gov/oceans/corals); see also Joshua S. Madin and Elizabeth M. P. Madin, "The Full Extent of the Global Coral Reef Crisis," *Conservation Biology*, July 28, 2015, DOI: 10.1111/cobi.12564.

12. The high-end estimate of tropical deforestation in 2014 is from satellite data analyzed by Global Forest Watch of the World Resources Institute, available at www.globalforestwatch.org (for an explanation of the methodology of Global Forest Watch, see note 10 in chapter 8 of this book). The estimate of the area of rainforest with full biological diversity is also from the World Resources Institute at www.wri.org. Data on the more than 600 species of primates are available from the International Union for Conservation of Nature (www.iucnredlist.org).

Among tropical countries Brazil has done the most over the past decade to rein in deforestation, with, according to Brazilian government satellite imaging, the rate from August 2013 to July 2014 about 75 percent lower than the yearly average from 1996 to 2005.

13. See A. Baccini et al., "Estimated Carbon Dioxide Emissions from Tropical Deforestation Improved by Carbon-Density Maps," *Nature Climate Change* 2 (2012), pp. 182–185 (due to high uncertainty in the carbon density of forests, these authors agree on a range of 6–17 percent as the contribution of deforestation to annual human-induced global carbon emissions). Surveying the many analyses of the consequences of deforestation for carbon emissions, and given the inevitable year-by-year shifts in the sources of carbon pollution (e.g., as the extent and locations of forest fires change), in my view 15 percent is a reasonable estimate of the contribution of deforestation to annual global carbon emissions.

14. For background on desertification, see the United Nations Convention to Combat Desertification (UNCCD), at www.unccd.int. For analysis and data on the global freshwater crisis, see UN-Water (the United Nations Inter-Agency Mechanism on all Freshwater Related Issues, Including Sanitation) at www.unwater.org. For analysis of the political economy of biofuels in the developing world, see Kate J. Neville and Peter Dauvergne, "Biofuels and the Politics of Mapmaking," *Political Geography* 31 (5) (2012), pp. 279–289; and Peter Dauvergne and Kate J. Neville, "The Changing North-South and South-South Political Economy of Biofuels," *Third World Quarterly* 30 (6) (2009), pp. 1087–1102. For analyses of the political economy of the overexploitation and overconsumption of natural resources, see Further Readings, "Consumption of Natural Resources" and "Consumption Politics."

15. See United Nations Environment Programme (UNEP), *GCO: Global Chemicals Outlook: Toward Sound Management of Chemicals* (UNEP, 2012), pp. 8–9; C. P. Baldé, F. Wang, R. Kuehr, and J. Huisman, *The Global E-waste Monitor—2014: Quantities, Flows and Resources* (United Nations University, 2015); Devin N. Perkins et al., "E-Waste: A Global Hazard," *Annals of Global Health* 80 (4) (2014), pp. 286–295.

16. For a balanced summary of the "Great Pacific Garbage Patch," see the encyclopedic entry in *National Geographic* (http://education.nationalgeographic.com). For data on persistent organic pollutants (POPs), hazardous waste, and pesticides, see the Stockholm Convention on Persistent Organic Pollutants (http://chm.pops.int), the Basel Convention on the Control of Transboundary Movements of Hazardous Wastes and Their Disposal (www.basel.int), and the Rotterdam Convention on the Prior Informed Consent Procedure for Certain Hazardous Chemicals and Pesticides in International Trade (http://www.pic.int).

17. J. Hansen et al., "Ice Melt, Sea Level Rise, and Superstorms: Evidence from Paleoclimate Data, Climate Modeling, and Modern Observations that 2°C Global Warming Is Highly Dangerous," *Atmospheric Chemistry and Physics* 15 (2015), pp. 20059–20179, DOI: 10.5194/acpd-15-20059-2015. For analyses of the global politics of climate change, see Further Readings, "Climate Change (politics of)."

## Chapter 6

1. Krause is quoted in Jamie Lincoln Kitman, "The Secret History of Lead," *Nation*, March 20, 2000, p. 31. For more on Midgley's research to find an "antiknock additive," see William Haynes, "Thomas Midgley, Jr.," in Eduard Farber, ed., *Great Chemists* (Interscience, 1961), pp. 1589–1597 (Midgley's comment about trying "melted butter" is at p. 1592). Also see R. R. Sayers, A. C. Fieldner, W. P. Yant, B. G. H. Thomas, and W. J. McConnell, *Exhaust Gases from Engines Using Ethyl Gasoline*, Reports of Investigations, Department of the Interior, Bureau of Mines, Serial No. 2661, December 1924, pp. 5, 21–22.

2. Howard is quoted in David Rosner and Gerald Markowitz, "A 'Gift of God'? The Public Health Controversy over Leaded Gasoline during the 1920s," *American Journal of Public Health* 75 (4) (1985), p. 348.

3. Hamilton is quoted in William Kovarik, "Ethyl-leaded Gasoline: How a Classic Occupational Disease Became an International Public Health Disaster," *International Journal of Occupational and Environmental Health* 11 (4) (2005), p. 388.

4. Parmalee is quoted in "Demands for Fair Play for Ethyl Gasoline," *New York Times*, May 7, 1925, p. 10.

5. The 1926 committee report is quoted in George B. Kauffman, "Midgley: Saint or Serpent?" *Chemtech* (December 1989), p. 721; also see, US Surgeon General, "The Use of Tetraethyl Lead and Its Relation in Public Health," *Public Health Bulletin*, no. 163, Washington, D.C., 1926. Edsall is quoted in Kitman, "The Secret History of Lead," p. 31. The estimate of the market share of "leaded" gasoline in the United States is from the abstract for Thomas Midgley, Jr., "From the Periodic Table to Production," *Industrial and Engineering Chemistry* 29 (2) (1937), p. 241.

6. See Clair C. Patterson, "Contaminated and Natural Lead Environments of Man," *Archives of Environmental Health* 11 (September 1965), pp. 344–360. The estimate of the market share of leaded gasoline in the United States in the early 1970s is from Jerome O. Nriagu, "The Rise and Fall of Leaded Gasoline," *The Science of the Total Environment* 92 (1990), pp. 16–17; and from Richard G. Newell and Kristian Rogers, *The U.S. Experience with the Phasedown of Lead in Gasoline* (Resources for the Future, June 2003), p. 24. Henderson's remarks are excerpted in "Sees Deadly Gas a Peril in Streets," *New York Times*, April 22, 1925, p. 25. For a more complete history of leaded gasoline, see Peter Dauvergne, *The Shadows of Consumption: Consequences for the Global Environment* (MIT Press, 2008), pp. 65–96.

7. J. R. McNeill, *Something New Under the Sun: An Environmental History of the Twentieth-Century World* (W.W. Norton, 2000), p. 111. For accounts of Midgley's life, see Charles F. Kettering, *Biographical Memoir of Thomas Midgley, Jr., 1889–1944* (National Academy of the Sciences of the United States of America, Biographical Memoirs, Volume XXIV, Eleventh Memoir, 1947); Thomas Midgley IV, *From the Periodic Table to Production: The Life of Thomas Midgley, Jr., the Inventor of Ethyl Gasoline and Freon Refrigerants* (Stargazer, 2001).

8. See Edward A. Parson, *Protecting the Ozone Layer: Science and Strategy* (Oxford University Press, 2003); Richard Elliot Benedick, *Ozone Diplomacy: New Directions in Safeguarding the Planet*, second edition (Harvard University Press, 1998); Karen T. Litfin, *Ozone Discourse: Science and Politics in Global Environmental Cooperation* (Columbia University Press, 1994); Seth Cagin and Philip Dray, *Between Earth and Sky: How CFCs Changed Our World and Endangered the Ozone Layer* (Pantheon Books, 1993).

9. See Henrik Selin, "Global Environmental Law and Treaty-Making on Hazardous Substances: The Minamata Convention and Mercury Abatement," *Global Environmental Politics* 14 (1) (2014), pp. 1–19; Henrik Selin, *Global Governance of Hazardous Chemicals: Challenges of Multilevel Management* (MIT Press, 2010); Jennifer Clapp, *Toxic Exports: The Transfer of Hazardous Wastes from Rich to Poor Countries* (Cornell University Press, 2001); Kate O'Neill, *Waste Trading among Rich Nations: Building a New Theory of Environmental Regulation* (MIT Press, 2000).

For an overview of different understandings of the precautionary principle, see Kerry H. Whiteside, *Precautionary Politics: Principle and Practice in Confronting Environmental Risk* (MIT Press, 2006).

10. See Mark F. Lunt et al., "Reconciling Reported and Unreported HFC Emissions with Atmospheric Observations," *Proceedings of the National Academy of Sciences of the United States of America* 112 (19) (2015), pp. 5927–5931, DOI: 10.1073/pnas.1420247112.

11. See Chemical Watch Research, "Perfluorinated Chemicals: A Persistent Problem," *Chemical Watch: Global Risk and Regulation News*, Global Business Briefing, May 2012, https://chemicalwatch.com.

12. See David Andrews and Bill Walker, *Poisoned Legacy: Ten Years Later, Chemical Safety and Justice for DuPont's Teflon Victims Remains Elusive* (Environmental Working Group, April 2015). The Environmental Working Group is now calling for strict regulations on all PFCs. For research questioning the safety of PFCs, or what these researchers call poly- and perfluoroalkyl substances (PFASs), see Arlene Blum et al., "The Madrid Statement on Poly- and Perfluoroalkyl Substances (PFASs)," Green Science Policy Institute, 2014, republished in *Environmental Health Perspectives* 123 (May 2015), pp. A107–A111.

13. The estimate of the world sugar substitute market is from MarketsandMarkets (M&M), *Sugar Substitutes Market*, summary "Sugar Substitutes Market Worth $14,355.0 Million by 2019," at www.marketsandmarkets.com. The source of the analysis of artificial sweeteners in Ontario waterways is John Spoelstra, Sherry L. Schiff, and Susan J. Brown, "Artificial Sweeteners in a Large Canadian River Reflect Human Consumption in the Watershed," *PLoS ONE* 8 (12) (2013), pp. 1–6: e82706. DOI: 10.1371/journal.pone.0082706 (the estimate of the number of soda cans floating downriver is on p. 4).

14. See Rachel Carson, *Silent Spring* (Houghton Mifflin, 1962); Bjørn Lomborg, *The Skeptical Environmentalist: Measuring the Real State of the World* (Cambridge University Press, 2001); Donella H. Meadows, Dennis L. Meadows, William W. Behrens, and Jørgen Randers, *The Limits to Growth* (Club of Rome, 1972); Paul R. Ehrlich, *The Population Bomb: Population Control or Race to Oblivion?* (Sierra Club–Ballantine, 1968). For an analysis of the marginalization of scholarship critiquing economic growth and arguing for "limits to growth," see Kerryn Higgs, *Collision Course: Endless Growth on a Finite Planet* (MIT Press, 2014). For yet another book-length attack on

this scholarship, see Leigh Phillips, *Austerity Ecology & the Collapse-Porn Addicts: A Defense of Growth, Progress, Industry and Stuff* (Zero Books, 2015).

15. For more on the history and power of anti-environmentalism, see Naomi Oreskes and Erik M. Conway, *Merchants of Doubt: How a Handful of Scientists Obscured the Truth on Issues from Tobacco Smoke to Global Warming* (Bloomsbury Press, 2010); William S. Laufer, "Social Accountability and Corporate Greenwashing," *Journal of Business Ethics* 43 (3) (2003), pp. 253–261; Sharon Beder, *Global Spin: The Corporate Assault on Environmentalism*, revised edition (Green Books, 2002); Naomi Klein, *No Logo: Taking Aim at the Brand Bullies* (Viking Canada, 2000); Andrew Rowell, *Green Backlash: Global Subversion of the Environmental Movement* (Routledge, 1996).

## Chapter 7

1. The quote "Can anyone believe ..." is from Rachel Carson, *Silent Spring*, 40th Anniversary Edition (First Mariner Books, 2002), pp. 7–8. Also see William Souder, *On a Farther Shore: The Life and Legacy of Rachel Carson, Author of Silent Spring* (Broadway Books, 2012). For bibliographies of other influential environmentalists, see Further Readings, "Environmentalists (biographies)."

2. The English word "environment" did not start to take on a political meaning linked to nature and ecosystems until the 1960s, before then referring mainly to home or work environments. See Gordon J. MacDonald, "Environment: Evolution of a Concept," *Journal of Environment & Development* 12 (2) (2003), pp. 151–176.

For a critical take on the history of global environmentalism, see Ramachandra Guha, *Environmentalism: A Global History* (Oxford University Press, 2000), and Ramachandra Guha, "Radical Environmentalism and Wilderness Preservation: A Third World Critique," *Environmental Ethics* 11 (Spring) (1989), pp. 71–83. For one of the more comprehensive histories of environmentalism, see Joachim Radkau, *The Age of Ecology: A Global History*, translated by Patrick Camiller (Polity Press, 2014); for a succinct overview of environmentalism, see the introduction to Peter Dauvergne, *Historical Dictionary of Environmentalism* (Scarecrow Press, 2009), released in paperback as *The A to Z of Environmentalism*.

Other valuable surveys of environmentalism include David Peterson del Mar, *Environmentalism*, third edition (Taylor & Francis, 2012); Paul Wapner, *Living Through the End of Nature: The Future of American Environmentalism* (MIT Press, 2010); Paul Hawken, *Blessed Unrest: How the Largest Movement in the World Came into Being and Why No One Saw It Coming* (Viking Penguin, 2007); Christof Mauch, Nathan Stoltzfus, and Douglas R. Weiner, eds., *Shades of Green: Environmental Activism around the Globe* (Rowman & Littlefield Publishers, 2006); Derek Wall, *Babylon and Beyond: The Economics of Anti-Capitalist, Anti-Globalist and Radical Green Movements* (Pluto Press, 2005); John Dryzek, *The Politics of the Earth: Environmental Discourses*, third edition (Oxford University Press, 2013); John Dryzek and David Schlosberg, eds., *Debating the Earth: The Environmental Politics Reader*, second edition (Oxford University Press, 2005); Terry L. Anderson and Donald R. Leal, *Free Market Environmentalism*, revised edition (Palgrave Macmillan, 2001); Sylvia Noble Tesh, *Environmental Activists and Scientific Proof* (Cornell University Press, 2000); Leslie Paul Thiele, *Environmentalism for a New Millennium: The Challenge of Coevolution* (Oxford University Press, 1999); Paul Wapner, *Environmental Activism and World Civic Politics* (SUNY Press, 1996); David Pepper, *Modern Environmentalism: An Introduction* (Routledge, 1996). For a succinct critique of the continuing focus of much of environmentalism on a "defense of nature," see Paul Wapner, "The Changing Nature of Nature: Environmental Politics in the Anthropocene," *Global Environmental Politics* 14 (4) (2014), pp. 36–54. For a recent optimistic account of the influence environmentalism, see David R. Boyd, *The Optimistic Environmentalist: Progressing Toward a Greener Future* (ECW Press, 2015).

For debates surrounding the concept of sustainability, see Margaret Robertson, *Sustainability: Principles and Practice* (Routledge, 2014), Neil E. Harrison, *Sustainable Capitalism and the Pursuit of Well-Being* (Routledge, 2014); Peter N. Nemetz, *Business and the Sustainability Challenge: An Integrated Perspective* (Routledge, 2013); Michael Blowfield, *Business and Sustainability* (Oxford University Press, 2013); Chris Gibson, Carol Farbotko, Nicholas Gill, Lesley Head, and Gordon Waitt, *Household Sustainability: Challenges and Dilemmas in Everyday Life* (Edward Elgar, 2013); Worldwatch Institute (Erik Assadourian), ed., *State of the World 2013: Is Sustainability Still Possible?* (Island Press, 2013); Andrés R. Edwards, *Thriving Beyond Sustainability: Pathways to a Resilient Society* (New Society Publishers, 2010); Melissa Leach, Ian Scoones, and Andy Stirling, *Dynamic Sustainabilities: Technology, Environment, Social Justice* (Earthscan, 2010); Simon Dresner, *The Principles of Sustainability*, second edition (Earthscan, 2008); Andrés R. Edwards, *The Sustainability Revolution: Portrait of a Paradigm Shift* (New Society Publishers, 2005); Julian Agyeman, Robert D. Bullard, and Bob Evans, eds., *Just Sustainabilities: Development in an Unequal World* (MIT Press, 2003).

For analyses of voluntary simplicity and eco-villages, see Karen T. Litfin, *Ecovillages: Lessons for Sustainable Community* (Polity, 2013); Duane Elgin, *Voluntary Simplicity: Toward a Way of Life That Is Outwardly Simple, Inwardly Rich*, second revised edition (HarperCollins, 2010); Deirdre Shaw and Terry Newholm, "Voluntary Simplicity and the Ethics of Consumption," *Psychology & Marketing* 19 (2) (2002), pp. 167–185; and Michael Maniates, "In Search of Consumptive Resistance: The Voluntary Simplicity Movement," in Tom Princen, Ken Conca, and Michael Maniates, eds., *Confronting Consumption* (MIT Press, 2002), pp. 199–235. For an overview of localization, see Raymond De Young and Thomas Princen, eds., *The Localization Reader: Adapting to the Downshift* (MIT Press, 2012).

3. See Paul Wapner, "Horizontal Politics: Transnational Environmental Activism and Global Cultural Change," *Global Environmental Politics* 2 (2) (2002), pp. 37–62; Paul Wapner, "Politics Beyond the State: Environmental Activism and World Civic Politics," *World Politics* 47 (3) (1995), pp. 311–340. Other scholars who have shown the power of environmental discourse and images to change cultural frames include Charlotte Epstein, *The Power of Words in International Relations: Birth of an*

*Anti-Whaling Discourse* (MIT Press, 2008) and Dryzek, *The Politics of the Earth*. The publication of Margaret E. Keck and Kathryn Sikkink, *Activists beyond Borders: Advocacy Networks in International Politics* (Cornell University Press, 1998) ignited research on transnational activist networks—widely known as TANs (see Further Readings, "Environmental NGOs and Transnational Networks"). Research on epistemic communities took off after the publications of Peter M. Haas, "Do Regimes Matter? Epistemic Communities and Mediterranean Pollution Control," *International Organization* 43 (3) (Summer) (1989), pp. 377–403, and Emanuel Adler and Peter M. Haas, "Conclusion: Epistemic Communities, World Order, and the Creation of a Reflective Research Program," *International Organization* 46 (1) (1992), pp. 367–390.

A large body of research demonstrates the influence of environmental activists on the framing of, and regulations for, particular issues. The following is a small sample. For mining in developing countries, see Robin Broad and John Cavanagh, "Poorer Countries and the Environment: Friends or Foes?" *World Development* 72 (August) (2015), pp. 419–431. For genetically modified organisms, see Peter Andrée, "Civil Society and the Political Economy of GMO Failures in Canada: A Neo-Gramscian Analysis," *Environmental Politics* 20 (2) (2011), pp. 173–191; Peter Andrée, *Genetically Modified Diplomacy: The Global Politics of Agricultural Biotechnology and the Environment* (UBC Press, 2007). For sealing, see Peter Dauvergne and Kate J. Neville, "Mindbombs of Right and Wrong: Cycles of Contention in the Activist Campaign to Stop Canada's Seal Hunt," *Environmental Politics* 20 (2) (2011), pp. 192–209. For whaling, see Epstein, *The Power of Words*; Charlotte Epstein, "Knowledge and Power in Global Environmental Activism," *International Journal of Peace Studies* 10 (1) (2005), pp. 47–67. For dams, see Patrick McCully, *Silenced Rivers: The Ecology and Politics of Large Dams* (Zed Books, 2001); John R. Wood, *The Politics of Water Resource Development in India: The Case of Narmada* (Sage, 2007). For cars and roads, see Matthew Paterson, *Automobile Politics: Ecology and Cultural Political Economy* (Cambridge University Press, 2007); Derek Wall, *Earth First! and the Anti-Roads Movement* (Routledge, 1999). For climate change, see Elisabeth Corell and Michele M. Betsill, "A Comparative Look at NGO Influence in International Environmental Negotiations: Desertification and Climate Change," *Global Environmental Politics* 1 (4) (2001), pp. 86–107; Lars H. Gulbrandsen and Steinar Andresen, "NGO Influence in the Implementation of the Kyoto Protocol: Compliance, Flexibility Mechanisms, and Sinks," *Global Environmental Politics* 4 (4) (2004), pp. 54–75; Harriet Bulkeley, Liliana B. Andonova, Michele M. Betsill, Daniel Compagnon, Thomas Hale, Matthew J. Hoffmann, Peter Newell, Matthew Paterson, Charles Roger, and Stacy D. VanDeveer, *Transnational Climate Change Governance* (Cambridge University Press, 2014).

Extensive research has also been done on the importance of environmental activism for the "greening" of national politics. Studies of the United States, the United Kingdom, and Germany are particularly common, although a vast literature exists, too, on Australia, Canada, Japan, New Zealand, and Western Europe (too extensive to illustrate fairly with examples). Research on developing countries is less common, although even here there is considerable scholarship documenting the influence of environmentalism on public policy, citizen attitudes, and development projects. A few examples are David McDermott Hughes, *From Enslavement to Environmentalism: Politics on a Southern African Frontier* (University of Washington Press, 2008); Kathryn Hochstetler and Margaret E. Keck, *Greening Brazil: Environmental Activism in State and Society* (Duke University Press, 2007); Yok-shiu F. Lee and Alvin Y. So, eds., *Asia's Environmental Movements: Comparative Perspectives* (M. E. Sharpe, 1999); Jane I. Dawson, *Eco-Nationalism: Anti-Nuclear Activism and National Identity in Russia, Lithuania, and Ukraine* (Duke University Press, 1996).

4. For background on Friends of the Earth International, see www.foei.org; for Greenpeace, see www.greenpeace.org/international; for WWF, see wwf.panda.org; for The Nature Conservancy, see www.nature.org; for the US Natural Resources Defense Council, see www.nrdc.org; for the US Sierra Club, see www.sierraclub.org.

The estimate of "one-fifth of consumer goods traded worldwide currently certified" is from Graeme Auld, Cristina Balboa, Steven Bernstein, and Benjamin Cashore, "The Emergence of Non-State Market-Driven (NSMD) Global Environmental Governance: A Cross-Sectoral Assessment," in Magali A. Delmas and Oran R. Young, eds., *Governance for the Environment: New Perspectives* (Cambridge University Press, 2009), p. 187. The reference to the US military using whales as target practice in the 1960s is from Paul Wapner, "Politics Beyond the State: Environmental Activism and World Civic Politics," *World Politics* 47 (3) (1995), p. 324.

For introductions to the subfield of "global environmental politics" see Further Readings, "Global Environmental Politics (overviews)" and "Global Environmental Politics," (collections of readings).

5. Evidence for this paragraph is from Michelle L. Bell, Devra L. Davis, and Tony Fletcher, "A Retrospective Assessment of Mortality from the London Smog Episode of 1952: The Role of Influenza and Pollution," *Environmental Health Perspectives* 112 (1) (2004), p. 8; Stuart Chape, Mark Spalding, and Martin Jenkins, eds., *The World's Protected Areas: Status, Values and Prospects in the 21st Century* (University of California, 2008); New South Wales Government, Metropolitan Water Directorate, "Planning for Sydney: Water Efficiency," at www.metrowater.nsw.gov.au/planning -sydney; World Meteorological Organization, at www.wmo.int.

6. See, for example, Paul F. Steinberg, *Environmental Leadership in Developing Countries: Transnational Relations and Biodiversity Policy in Costa Rica and Bolivia* (MIT Press, 2001); Sinan Koont, *Sustainable Urban Agriculture in Cuba* (University Press of Florida, 2011); for the estimate of the number of trees planted in Kenya, see the Green Belt Movement, www.greenbeltmovement.org.

7. President Obama's New York Climate Summit speech of September 23, 2014, is available at www.youtube.com. For details on the People's Climate March, see www .peoplesclimate.org. For details on the killings in Peru in June 2014, see David Hill, "Peru Now Has 'Licence to Kill' Environmental Protestors," *Guardian*, June 29, 2014 (www.theguardian.com). For an analysis of the interactions among anarchists,

environmentalists, and anti-globalization activists, see Giorel Curran, *21st Century Dissent: Anarchism, Anti-Globalization and Environmentalism* (Palgrave Macmillan, 2007).

8. Nearly 8,300 people attended the 2015 Paris climate negotiations as official observers; tens of thousands participated unofficially. UN statistics on accredited participants during meetings for the Framework Convention for Climate Change are available at the United Nations Framework Convention on Climate Change, Civil Society and the Climate Change Process, in the document "Participation Breakdown," at https://unfccc.int. For a discussion of state attendance, see Heike Schroeder, Maxwell T. Boykoff, and Laura Spiers, "Equity and State Representations in Climate Negotiations," *Nature Climate Change* 2 (2012), pp. 834–836.

For background analysis on the influence of civil society organizations on international environmental negotiations, see Michele M. Betsill and Elisabeth Corell, "NGO Influence in International Environmental Negotiations: A Framework for Analysis," *Global Environmental Politics* 1 (3) (2001), pp. 65–85; Michele M. Betsill and Elisabeth Corell, eds., *NGO Diplomacy: The Influence of Nongovernmental Organizations in International Environmental Negotiations* (MIT Press, 2007). For broader analyses of the role of nongovernmental forces in social change, see John Boli and George M. Thomas, *Constructing World Culture: International Nongovernmental Organizations since 1875* (Stanford University Press, 1999); Julie Fisher, *Nongovernments: NGOs and the Political Development of the Third World* (Kumarian Press, 1997). For a world society lens, see Ann Hironaka, *Greening the Globe: World Society and Environmental Change* (Cambridge University Press, 2014).

9. For an overview of the politics of the Minamata Convention, see Henrik Selin, "Global Environmental Law and Treaty-Making on Hazardous Substances: The Minamata Convention and Mercury Abatement," *Global Environmental* Politics 14 (1) (2014), pp. 1–19; Jessica Templeton and Pia Kohler, "Implementation and Compliance under the Minamata Convention on Mercury," *RECIEL: Review of European Community & International Environmental Law* 23 (2) (2014), pp. 211–220.

For the estimates of total protected areas, see Bastian Bertzky, Colleen Corrigan, James Kemsey, Siobhan Kenney, Corinna Ravilious, Charles Besançon, and Neil Burgess, *Protected Planet Report 2012: Tracking Progress toward Global Targets for Protected Areas* (International Union for Conservation of Nature, Gland, Switzerland and United Nations Environment Programme World Conservation Monitoring Centre, Cambridge, UK, 2012), p. 7; Biodiversity Indicators Partnership, "Coverage of Protected Areas," at www.bipindicators.net. For a sampling of the stories of conservationists, see Linda Tucker, *Saving the White Lions: One Woman's Battle for Africa's Most Sacred Animal* (North Atlantic Books, 2013); Tzeporah Berman, *This Crazy Time: Living Our Environmental Challenge* (Vintage Canada, 2012); and Edward Humes, *Eco Barons: The New Heroes of Environmental Activism* (Ecco/HarperCollins, 2010).

10. The claim by the Earth Day Network that Earth Day is "the largest secular holiday" is on the Earth Day Network website (www.earthday.org). Classic environmental bestsellers include Rachel Carson, *Silent Spring* (Houghton Mifflin, 1962); Paul R. Ehrlich, *The Population Bomb: Population Control or Race to Oblivion?* (Sierra Club/Ballantine, 1968); Donella H. Meadows, Dennis L. Meadows, William W. Behrens, and Jørgen Randers, *The Limits to Growth* (Club of Rome, 1972); E. F. Schumacher, *Small Is Beautiful: Economics as if People Mattered* (Harper & Row, 1973); and Herman E. Daly, *Steady-State Economics: The Economics of Biophysical Equilibrium and Moral Growth* (W.H. Freeman, 1977).

Environmental writers continue to influence public discourse and education, from academics to novelists to popular authors. Influential nonfiction writers include Jared M. Diamond, Edward O. Wilson, Bill McKibben, and Al Gore. For a sampling, see Jared M. Diamond, *The World Until Yesterday: What Can We Learn from Traditional Societies?* (Viking Penguin, 2012); Jared M. Diamond, *Collapse: How Societies Choose to Fail or Succeed*, revised edition (Penguin, 2011); Jared M. Diamond, *Guns, Germs, and Steel: The Fates of Human Societies* (W. W. Norton 1999); Bill McKibben, *Eaarth: Making a Life on a Tough New Planet* (Times Books, 2010); Bill McKibben, *The End of Nature* (Random House, 2006); Edward O. Wilson, *The Future of Life* (Knopf, 2002); Edward O. Wilson, *The Diversity of Life*, New Edition (Belknap Press, 2010); Al Gore, *The Future: Six Drivers of Global Change* (Random House, 2013); Al Gore, *An Inconvenient Truth: The Planetary Emergency of Global Warming and What We Can Do About It* (Rodale Books, 2006); Al Gore, *Earth in the Balance: Ecology and the Human Spirit*, Revised and Updated (Rodale Books, 2006).

The climate change skit on *The Daily Show* with Jon Stewart aired September 22, 2014, and is available on YouTube (www.youtube.com).

11. For analysis of the rising importance of private environmental governance, see Jessica F. Green, *Rethinking Private Authority: Agents and Entrepreneurs in Global Environmental Governance* (Princeton University Press, 2014); Frank Biermann and Philipp Pattberg, eds., *Global Environmental Governance Reconsidered* (MIT Press, 2012); Robert Falkner, *Business Power and Conflict in International Environmental Politics* (Palgrave Macmillan, 2008); Robert Falkner, "Private Environmental Governance and International Relations: Exploring the Links," in David Humphreys, Matthew Paterson and Lloyd Pettiford, eds., *Global Environmental Governance for the Twenty-First Century: Theoretical Approaches and Normative Considerations*. Special issue of *Global Environmental Politics* 3 (2) (2003), pp. 72–87; Benjamin Cashore, Graeme Auld, and Deanna Newsom, *Governing through Markets: Forest Certification and the Emergence of Non-State Authority* (Yale University Press, 2004); Jennifer Clapp and Doris Fuchs, eds., *Corporate Power in Global Agrifood Governance* (MIT Press, 2009); Jennifer Clapp, "The Privatization of Global Environmental Governance: ISO 14000 and the Developing World," *Global Governance* 4 (3) (1998), pp. 295–316.

12. See the stories of Goldman Environmental Prize Winners over the past twenty-five years at www.goldmanprize.org. For Silas Siakor's research on illegal logging and

corruption in Liberia under President Charles Taylor, see Samfu Foundation, *Plunder: The Silent Destruction of Liberia's Rainforest* (The Save My Future Foundation, September 2002).

13. In addition to the Goldman Prize website (www.goldmanprize.org), for more on Ruth Buendía's campaign, see Uri Friedman, "The Woman Who Breaks Mega-Dams," *The Atlantic*, April 30, 2014 (www.theatlantic.com). For background on the South Durban Community Environmental Alliance, see www.sdcea.co.za. (Desmond D'Sa's remark, "We've shown that ..." is from the video, "Desmond D'Sa, 2014 Goldman Environmental Prize, South Africa," available on YouTube (www.youtube .com). For background on the NGO Environmental Watch on North Caucasus, see www.ewnc.org. For more on the activism of Suren Gazaryan, see John Vidal, "Exiled Environmental Activist Speaks of 'Impossibility' of Protest in Russia," *Guardian*, April 28, 2014 (www.theguardian.com).

## Chapter 8

1. The quote "to live a life without money" is from Bruno Manser Fonds (www.bmf .ch), under the tab "About Us," "Bruno Manser." Also see Sulok Tawie, "Activist Bruno Manser Flies Into Arms of the Law," *New Straits Times* (Malaysia), March 30, 1999, p. 4; Wade Davis, "Dreams of a Jade Forest," in *Shadows in the Sun: Travels to Landscapes of Spirit and Desire* (Island Press/Shearwater Books, 1998), pp. 29–48 (the "jungle" quote is on p. 31); "Along Sega: Courageous Tribal Leader Who Laid Down His Blowpipe to Do Battle Against Loggers in His Native Borneo," *The Daily Telegraph*, February 9, 2011. For a documentary of Bruno Manser's life, translated into English by his cousin Mathias Manser, see Christoph Kühn, "Laki Penan," 2007, available on YouTube, www.youtube.com (this video includes the translation of Manser's diary entry, "My paradise turns into a prison").

2. The Prince of Wales, "The Rainforest Lecture for Friends of the Earth, the Royal Botanic Gardens, Kew, February 6, 1990, at www.princeofwales.gov.uk; Senator Albert Gore Jr., Resolution 280 (102nd), introduced April 2, 1992, not enacted.

3. Mahathir's letter to Manser is reprinted in Doug Tsuruoka, "The Pen and the Saw," *Far Eastern Economic Review*, August 27, 1992, pp. 8–9.

4. Simon Elegant (with Long Adang), "Without a Trace," *Time* (Asia), September 3, 2001, http://content.time.com (includes Manser's remark "less than zero" as well as Roger Graf's comments); Keith Harmon Snow, "Manser, Bruno (1954–2000) and the Penan of Sarawak," in *The Encyclopedia of Religion and Nature* (Continuum, 2005); Kühn's documentary "Laki Penan" is the source for the quote "Does this paradise really have to die?" See also William W. Bevis, "Bruno Manser and the Penan," in David Rothenberg and Marta Ulvaeus, eds., *The World and the Wild* (University of Arizona Press, 2001), pp. 109–126 (p. 125 contains the quote from Randy Hayes

beginning "Bruno Manser's story ..."); and J. Peter Brosius, "Voices for the Borneo Rain Forest: Writing the History of an Environmental Campaign," in Paul Greenough and Anna Lowenhaupt Tsing, eds., *Nature in the Global South: Environmental Projects in South and Southeast Asia* (Duke University Press, 2003), pp. 319–346.

5. Melai Nah's remarks are quoted in Rohan Sullivan, "No Sign of Borneo Forest Crusader," *The Associated Press*, August 5, 2001. The quote "failed utterly" is from Elegant (with Long Adang), "Without a Trace." For an example of Global Witness's campaign in Sarawak, see Global Witness, *Inside Malaysia's Shadow State: Backroom Deals Driving the Destruction of Sarawak* (Global Witness, 2013). For details on the Bruno Manser Fund, see Bruno Manser Fonds (www.bmf.ch). For an analysis of the politics of logging in Sarawak and Sabah, Malaysia, in the 1980s and 1990s, see Peter Dauvergne, *Shadows in the Forest: Japan and the Politics of Timber in Southeast Asia* (MIT Press, 1997), Peter Dauvergne, *Loggers and Degradation in the Asia-Pacific: Corporations and Environmental Management* (Cambridge University Press, 2001); and Michael L. Ross, *Timber Booms and Institutional Breakdown in Southeast Asia* (Cambridge University Press, 2001). For a more recent analysis, see Lukas Straumann, *Money Logging: On the Trail of the Asian Timber Mafia* (Bergli Books, 2014).

6. Global Witness, *Deadly Environment: The Dramatic Rise in the Killings of Environmental and Land Defenders (1.1.2002–31.12.2013)* (Global Witness, 2014); Global Witness, *How Many More?* (Global Witness, 2015).

7. Fuck for Forest was founded in Norway (in 2004), but later moved to Berlin. For background, see the 2012 documentary film *Fuck for Forest* (directed by Michal Marczak).

8. For a critical review of recent Japanese timber imports from Sarawak, see Global Witness, *An Industry Unchecked: Japan's Extensive Business with Companies Involved in Illegal and Destructive Logging in the Last Rainforests of Malaysia* (Global Witness, September 2013). For an estimate of China's timber imports, see William F. Laurance, Guangyu Wang, John L. Innes, Sara W. Wu, Shuanyou Dai, and Jiafu Lei, "The Need to Cut China's Illegal Timber Imports," *Science Magazine* 29 (February) (2008), pp. 1184–5. Also, see Peter Dauvergne and Jane Lister, *Timber* (Polity, 2011).

9. Organisation for Economic Co-operation and Development and the Food and Agriculture Organization, *OECD-FAO Agricultural Outlook 2012–2021* (OECD/FAO, 2012), p. 137, p. 142, p. 238; Sime Darby, "Palm Oil Facts and Figures," April 2014 (at www.simedarby.com); the estimate of packaged foods with palm oil is from WWF (www.wwf.panda.org).

10. The estimate of "13 million hectares a year" for average worldwide deforestation from 2000 to 2010 is from the Food and Agriculture Organization, *The Global Forest Resources Assessment 2010: Main Report*, FAO Forestry Paper 163, FAO 2010, p. xiii. Estimates by the Global Forest Watch (www.globalforestwatch.org) of the World Resources Institute are much higher, as Global Forest Watch uses satellite imaging

(rather than country reporting) and defines forests as 30 percent of crown cover (rather than 10 percent of crown cover, as the FAO does). Under this definition Global Forest Watch estimates total deforestation in 2014 at 17 million hectares (with, as mentioned in chapter 5, tropical deforestation accounting for 10 million hectares).

For details on forest degradation and deforestation in Sarawak, see Kamlisa Uni Kamlun, Mia How Goh, Stephen Teo, Satoshi Tsuyuki, and Mui-How Phua, "Monitoring of Deforestation and Fragmentation in Sarawak, Malaysia between 1990 and 2009 Using Landsat and Spot Images," *Journal of Forest Science* 28 (3) (2012), pp. 152–157.

11. Quoted in André Picard, "Youth Give Jane Goodall Reason to Hope," *Globe and Mail*, March 31, 2014, p. A4.

## Chapter 9

1. See The Jane Goodall Institute (www.janegoodall.org); Jane Goodall's Roots & Shoots (www.rootsandshoots.org); and Voiceless: The Animal Protection Institute (www.voiceless.org.au), with her quote on factory farming on the website under "Who We Are" and then "Dr Jane Goodall." Advocates for Animals is now called OneKind, with a mission to "end animal suffering"—see OneKind at www.onekind .org; Goodall's Edinburgh Zoo comment is in Mike Wade, "Zoos Are Best Hope, Says Jane Goodall," *Times* (London), May 21, 2008, p. 26.

2. The quotes and a summary of the San Francisco meeting of Greenpeace are in Frank Zelko, *Make It a Green Peace! The Rise of Counterculture Environmentalism* (Oxford University Press, 2013), p. 310. (Zelko's original source is the Minutes of the Extraordinary Meeting of the Board of Directors, Greenpeace Foundation of America, San Francisco, August 29, 1978). Zelko provides a comprehensive and objective history of Greenpeace.

3. Moore's remark that "really serious problems have been dealt with" is quoted in Anthony Browne, "Recovering Earth," *Observer*, June 10, 2001 (www.theguardian. com); his "antiscience" comment is in Patrick Moore, *Confessions of a Greenpeace Dropout: The Making of a Sensible Environmentalist* (Beatty Street Publishing, 2010), p. 1; Greenpeace's rebuke of Patrick Moore is posted at Greenpeace International, "Patrick Moore Background Information," December 7, 2010 (www.greenpeace.org/ international).

Rex Weyler was one of the Greenpeace activists who challenged Soviet whalers in 1975. For his history of Greenpeace, see Rex Weyler, *Greenpeace: How a Group of Journalists, Ecologists, and Visionaries Changed the World* (Raincoast Books, 2004). For a memoir on the emergence of Greenpeace, see Robert Hunter, *The Greenpeace to Amchitka: An Environmental Odyssey* (Arsenal Pulp Press, 2004). For memoirs of other notable environmentalists, see Further Readings, "Environmentalists (memoirs)."

4. The quote by Watson beginning "we're insane ..." is from the video "Greenpeace Confronts Russian Whalers in 1975," available on YouTube (www.youtube.com); the description of the Sierra as a "notorious prolific pirate whaler" and Watson's responses to the Grenada zoo raid and the Canadian Navy are both from Sea Shepherd Conservation Society (www.seashepherd.org). Celebrities have long lent their names to environmental causes. *Time* magazine's "Heroes of the Environment" include Al Gore (2007), Prince Charles (2007), Robert Redford (2007), Arnold Schwarzenegger (2008), and Cameron Diaz (2009). Leonardo DiCaprio is on the US board of WWF, the board of the International Fund for Animal Welfare, and the board of the Natural Resources Defense Council. Martin Sheen, sounding presidential from his days on the TV show *West Wing*, is a spokesperson for the International Fund for Animal Welfare. For a critique of celebrity activism, see Ilan Kapoor, *Celebrity Humanitarianism: The Ideology of Global Charity* (Routledge, 2013).

5. Watson's description of Greenpeace activists as "Avon ladies" is from Richard Grant, "Paul Watson: Sea Shepherd Eco-Warrior Fighting to Stop Whaling and Seal Hunts," *Telegraph*, April 17, 2009 (www.telegraph.co.uk); Watson's email to Moore, beginning "You're a corporate whore ..." is reprinted in Drake Bennett, "Eco-Traitor," *Wired*, March 1, 2004 (www.wired.com). Watson's profile on Interpol's "wanted persons" list is available at www.interpol.int.

For Watson's account of his environmental philosophy and campaign strategies, see Paul Watson, *Earthforce! An Earth Warrior's Guide to Strategy*, second edition (Sea Shepherd Conservation Society/Chaco Press, 2012); Paul Watson, *Seal Wars: Twenty-five Years on the Front Lines with the Harp Seals* (Firefly Books, 2003); and Paul Watson, *Ocean Warrior: My Battle to End the Illegal Slaughter on the High Seas* (Key Porter Books, 1995). Also see Lamya Essemlali (with Paul Watson), *Captain Paul Watson: Interview with a Pirate* (Firefly Books, 2013); and David B. Morris, *Earth Warrior: Overboard with Paul Watson and the Sea Shepherd Society* (Fulcrum Publishing, 1995).

6. See Jerome P. Bjelopera, *The Domestic Terrorist Threat: Background and Issues for Congress* (Congressional Research Services [CRS Report for Congress], 2013).

Following his arrest, Foreman moved on from Earth First! to cofound the Wildlands Project (in 1991) and The Rewilding Institute (2003) to promote wilderness conservation in North America (e.g., reintroducing wolves, bears, and cougars as ecosystem predators). See The Rewilding Institute (www.rewilding.org). Foreman's sentencing statement is quoted in "Man Gets 6 Years in Plot to Damage A-Plants," *New York Times*, September 8, 2001 (www.nytimes.com).

7. See The Animal Liberation Front (www.animalliberationfront.com); The Earth Liberation Front (www.earth-liberation-front.com). Also see Michael Loadenthal, "Deconstructing 'Eco-Terrorism': Rhetoric, Framing and Statecraft as Seen Through the Insight Approach," *Critical Studies on Terrorism* 6 (1) (2013), pp. 92–117; Paul Joosse, "Leaderless Resistance and Ideological Inclusion: The Case of the Earth Liberation Front," *Terrorism and Political Violence* 19 (3) (2007), pp. 351–368; Stefan H.

Leader and Peter Probst, "The Earth Liberation Front and Environmental Terrorism," *Terrorism and Political Violence* 15 (4) (2003), pp. 37–58. For an insider's account of the Earth Liberation Front in the United States, see Craig Rosebraugh, *Burning Rage of a Dying Planet: Speaking for the Earth Liberation Front* (Lantern Books, 2004).

8. See Peter Dauvergne and Genevieve LeBaron, *Protest Inc.: The Corporatization of Activism* (Polity Press, 2014); Amory Starr, Luis A. Fernandez, and Christian Scholl, *Shutting Down the Streets: Political Violence and Social Control in the Global Era* (New York University Press, 2011); Will Potter, *Green is the New Red: An Insider's Account of a Social Movement Under Siege* (City Lights Books, 2011); and Luis A. Fernandez, *Policing Dissent: Social Control and the Anti-Globalization Movement* (Rutgers University Press, 2008).

9. For the FBI's definition of eco-terrorism, see Federal Bureau of Investigation, "The Threat of Eco-Terrorism," Testimony of James F. Jarboe, Domestic Terrorism Section Chief, Counterterrorism Division, FBI, Before the House Resources Committee, Subcommittee on Forests and Forest Health, February 12, 2002 (www.fbi.gov). The FBI quote about the severity of eco-terrorism and the estimate of the total cost in the US are from Federal Bureau of Investigation, "Putting Intel to Work Against ELF and ALF Terrorists," June 30, 2008 (www.fbi.gov). For more on eco-terrorism in the United States, see, for example, Donald R. Liddick, *Eco-Terrorism: Radical Environmental and Animal Liberation Movements* (Praeger, 2006).

10. For Julia Butterfly Hill's story of her time living in a tree, see Julia Butterfly Hill, *The Legacy of Luna: The Story of a Tree, a Woman, and the Struggle to Save the Redwoods* (HarperCollins, 2000).

## Chapter 10

1. For the list of *Time* magazine's eco-heroes of the twentieth century, see Frederic Golden, "Century of Heroes," *Time* 155 (17), April 26, 2000, pp. 54–57. For more on the life and influence of the eco-hero Bob Hunter, see Robert Hunter, *Warriors of the Rainbow: A Chronicle of the Greenpeace Movement* (Holt, Rinehart and Winston, 1979); also see, Emily Hunter, ed., *The Next Eco-Warriors: 22 Young Women and Men Who Are Saving the Planet* (Conari Press, 2011). Hunter's final book was Robert Hunter, *Thermageddon: Countdown to 2030* (Arcade Publishing, 2003).

2. The Arctic 30 are citizens of the United States (the captain), Argentina (2), Australia (1), Brazil (1), Britain (6), Canada (2), Denmark (1), Finland (1), France (1), Italy (1), New Zealand (2), Poland (1), Russia (4), Sweden (1), Switzerland (1), the Netherlands (2), Turkey (1), and Ukraine (1).

Greenpeace documents its protests against Gazprom at Greenpeace, "Updates from the *Arctic Sunrise* Activists," December 29, 2013, www.greenpeace.org/international. Kumi Naidoo's first remarks in this section are quoted in Greenpeace

International, "Greenpeace International Ship Nears Murmansk Port as 30 Activists Await Possible Charges," September 24, 2013, Greenpeace Press Release; Naidoo's second remarks, the European Parliament's Press Release, the Nobel laureates' letter, and Captain Willcox's remarks are reproduced on the website of Greenpeace International, www.greenpeace.org/international.

For an example of the media coverage of the Arctic 30, see Andrew Darby, "I've Done Nothing Wrong," *The Age* (Melbourne, Australia), November 22, 2013, p. 18.

3. For a summary of the 2013–2014 Greenpeace financial scandal and budget details, see Adam Vaughan, "Greenpeace Losses: Leaked Documents Reveal Extent of Financial Disarray," *Guardian*, June 23, 2014, www.theguardian.com) (which includes Naidoo's comments on restructuring Greenpeace); Philip Oltermann, "Greenpeace Loses £3M in Currency Speculation," *Guardian*, June 16, 2014 , www.theguardian.com.

4. Laura Kenyon, "Success: Barbie and Mattel Drop Deforestation!" October 5, 2011, *Greenpeace International News* (blogpost), at www.greenpeace.org/international (includes the quote "continue to investigate" ...). See also Greenpeace International, "Stop MATTEL Destroying Rainforests," under Forests Campaigns at www.greenpeace.org/international; Greenpeace, *How Sinar Mas Is Pulping the Planet* (Greenpeace International, updated in September 2010); WWF–US, *Don't Flush Tiger Forests: Toilet Paper, U.S. Supermarkets and the Destruction of Indonesia's Last Tiger Habitats* (WWF–US, 2012); Mattel Inc., "Sustainability Sourcing Principles," at corporate.mattel.com.

Patrick Moore's consultancy report for APP is *Greenspirit Strategies Ltd., Plantation Forestry in Indonesia: The Greenspirit Strategies Perspective—An Assessment of Asia Pulp & Paper (APP) and Its Pulpwood Suppliers' Forestry Operations, November* (Greenspirit, 2010): the quote "world-class sustainable forest management" is on p. 4, although due to a typo this reads "word-class" in the original document.

5. See Greenpeace, "Major Breakthrough in Protection for Indonesia's Remaining Rainforests," Press Release, February 5, 2013; Fiona Harvey, "Leading Paper Firm Pledges to Halt Indonesian Deforestation," *Guardian*, February 5, 2013 (www.theguardian.com), which includes Greenbury's remark, "It is time to stop talking ..."; Damian Carrington, "Is APP's Zero Deforestation Pledge a Green Villain's Dramatic Turnaround?" *Guardian*, March 26, 2014 (www.theguardian.com), which includes Greenbury's remark, "We are the largest pulp ..." and, John Sauven's (UK executive director of Greenpeace) comment "seismic shift"; Urs Dieterich and Graeme Auld, "Moving Beyond Commitments: Creating Durable Change Through the Implementation of Asia Pulp and Paper's Forest Conservation Policy," *Journal of Cleaner Production* 107 (2015), pp. 54–63.

6. The Greenpeace Kit Kat video is posted on the website of Greenpeace International, at www.greenpeace.org. Also see Greenpeace International, "Sweet Success for Kit Kat Campaign: You Asked, Nestlé Has Answered," May 17, 2010 (www

.greenpeace.org); Nestlé, *The Nestlé Supplier Code* (Mandatory Policy) (Nestlé, December 2013) (www.nestle.com); Golden Agri-Resources, "Sustainable Palm Oil," (www .goldenagri.com.sg); Aileen Ionescu-Somers and Albecht Enders, *Financial Times*, December 3, 2012 (www.ft.com); The Forest Trust (www.tft-forests.org); Sam Lawson (with input from Art Blundell, Bruce Cabarle, Naomi Basik, Michael Jenkins, and Kerstin Canby), *Consumer Goods and Deforestation: An Analysis of the Extent and Nature of Illegality in Forest Conversion for Agriculture and Timber Plantations,* Forest Trends Report Series: Forest Trade and Finance (Forest Trends, September 2014).

For analysis of the political ecology of oil palm plantations in Indonesia and Malaysia, see John F. McCarthy, "Certifying in Contested Spaces: Private Regulation in Indonesian Forestry and Palm Oil," *Third World Quarterly* 33 (10) (2012), pp. 1871–1888; John F. McCarthy, Piers Gillespie, and Zahari Zen, "Swimming Upstream: Local Indonesian Production Networks in 'Globalized' Palm Oil Production," *World Development* 40 (3) (2012), pp. 555–569; John F. McCarthy and Zahari Zen, "Regulating the Oil Palm Boom: Assessing the Effectiveness of Environmental Governance Approaches to Agro-industrial Pollution in Indonesia," *Law and Policy* 32 (1) (2010), pp. 153–179; John F. McCarthy, "Processes of Inclusion and Adverse Incorporation: Oil Palm and Agrarian Change in Sumatra, Indonesia," *Journal of Peasant Studies* 37 (4) (2010), pp. 821–850; John F. McCarthy and R. A. Cramb, "Policy Narratives, Landholder Engagement, and Oil Palm Expansion on the Malaysian and Indonesian Frontiers," *Geographical Journal* 175 (2) (2009), pp. 112–123.

Hogg's comment on "eyes and ears on the ground" is in Erica Gies, "Greenpeace Report on P&G's Palm Oil Sources Could Spur Industry Change," *Guardian*, March 31, 2014, www.theguardian.com.

7. Maitar's remarks "If a well-known …" and "RSPO, from my perspective, …" is in Gies, "Greenpeace Report on P&G's Palm Oil Sources Could Spur Industry Change." Greenpeace has been quite critical of the Roundtable on Sustainable Palm Oil. See, for example, Greenpeace, *Certifying Destruction* (Greenpeace International, 2013).

8. The Greenpeace quote "take a moment to celebrate" is from Areeba Hamid, "Consumer Power! Procter & Gamble Decides to Wash Its Bad Palm Oil Away," Greenpeace International website, April 9, 2014, www.greenpeace.org. Also see Procter & Gamble, "P&G Is Committed to No Deforestation in Our Sourcing of Palm Oil, Palm Kernel Oil, and Derivatives," under "Sustainability: Policies and Practices," www.pg.com.

For the Greenpeace list of forest-friendly and non-friendly companies, see Greenpeace International, "The Tiger Challenge: How the Companies Line Up," at www.greenpeace.org/international (as of October 30, 2014). For background on POIG (and the mission and launch quotes), see "Palm Oil Companies Join NGOs to Find Palm Oil Solutions," Joint Statement of the Palm Oil Innovation Group, Jakarta, Tropical Forest Alliance Meeting, June 28, 2013, at wwf.panda.org. See also *Palm Oil Innovations Group Charter* at wwf.panda.org.

Other NGOs besides Greenpeace are also working to shame brands into reforming sourcing practices for palm oil. The Rainforest Action Network, for example, is campaigning against Pepsi to remove what it calls "conflict palm oil" from its supply chain. There are many other "shame campaigns" by activist organizations, too. For an analysis of campaigns against jewelry makers and retailers, see Michael John Bloomfield, "Shame Campaigns and Environmental Justice: Corporate Shaming as Activist Strategy," *Environmental Politics* 23 (2) (2014), pp. 263–281.

9. For the quote "Taken together ..." see the New York Declaration on Forests (dated September 23, 2014), p. 14.

Particularly contentious for rainforest activism has been the UN pilot program since 2008 for "reducing emissions from deforestation and forest degradation" (REDD) in developing countries. The program, as of 2015, has distributed around $200 million across 56 countries. Many NGOs support REDD, but some environmental and indigenous groups see it as a false solution for climate change and a way for states to sanction land grabs from forest peoples. For background on REDD, see UN-REDD Programme (www.un-redd.org). For analysis of REDD, see Rosemary Lyster, Catherine MacKenzie, and Constance McDermott, eds., *Law, Tropical Forests and Carbon: The Case of REDD+* (Cambridge University Press, 2013); Jen Iris Allan and Peter Dauvergne, "The Global South in Environmental Negotiations: The Politics of REDD+ Coalitions," *Third World Quarterly* 34 (8) (2013), pp. 1307–1322; Esteve Corbera and Heike Schroeder, "Governing and Implementing REDD+," *Environmental Science & Policy* 14 (2) (2011), pp. 89–99; Peter J. Kanowski, Constance L. McDermott, and Benjamin W. Cashore, "Implementing REDD+: Lessons From Analysis of Forest Governance," *Environmental Science & Policy* 14 (2) (2011), pp, 111–117.

10. See Julia Hailes's "yes" response in Julia Hailes and Clive Bates, "Can Green Consumers Save the World?" *Telegraph,* May 3, 2007, www.telegraph.co.uk; see also, Julia Hailes, *The New Green Consumer Guide* (Simon & Schuster, 2007).

11. For an estimate of the recycling trade, see Adam Minter, *Junkyard Planet: Travels in the Billion-Dollar Trash Trade* (Bloomsbury 2013). For a range of evaluations on the value and power of eco-consumerism, see Further Readings, "Eco-Consumerism." For critical analyses of the power of eco-consumerism to promote sustainable forestry, see Jane Lister and Peter Dauvergne, "Voluntary Zero Net Deforestation: The Implications of Demand-Side Retail Sustainability for Global Forests," in William Nikolakis and John Innes, eds., *Forests and Globalization: Challenges and Opportunities for Sustainable Development* (London: Earthscan, 2014), pp. 65–76, and Peter Dauvergne and Jane Lister, "The Prospects and Limits of Eco-Consumerism: Shopping Our Way to Less Deforestation?" *Organization & Environment* 23 (2) (2010), pp. 132–154.

12. For a summary of the results of China's plastic bag regulations, see Chris Peterson, "More Action Needed to Rid Us of the Plastic Plague," *China Daily European*

*Weekly*, November 6, 2015, p. 13. For an estimate of plastic production, see Gloria Galloway, "A 'Rescue Package' for the Fragile Ocean System," *Globe and Mail*, June 24, 2014, p. A6. For the estimate of the number of pieces of plastic in the world's oceans, see Marcus Eriksen, Laurent C. M. Lebreton, Henry S. Carson, Martin Thiel, Charles J. Moore, Jose C. Borerro, Francois Galgani, Peter G. Ryan, and Julia Reisser, "Plastic Pollution in the World's Oceans: More than 5 Trillion Plastic Pieces Weighing over 250,000 Tons Afloat at Sea," *PLoS ONE* 9 (12) (2014), DOI: 10.1371/journal. pone.0111913; Jenna R. Jambeck et al., "Plastic Waste Inputs from Land into the Ocean," *Science* 347 (6223), pp. 768–771, DOI: 10.1126/science.1260352. For an analysis of the influence of environmentalism on the consumption of plastic bags, see Jennifer Clapp and Linda Swanston, "Doing Away with Plastic Shopping Bags: International Patterns of Norm Emergence and Policy Implementation," *Environmental Politics* 18 (3) (2009), pp. 315–332.

13. The summary of electricity usage in British Columbia is in Justine Hunter, "Can Little Steps Have a Big Enough Impact?" *Globe and Mail*, May 3, 2014, p. S4. For global energy statistics see International Energy Agency, "Statistics" (www.iea.org); International Energy Agency, *Key World Energy Statistics* (IEA, 2013), especially pp. 28–29.

## Chapter 11

1. The "Morges Manifesto" was finalized in Morges, Switzerland, and is archived as J.G. Baer et al., "We Must Save the World's Wild Life: An International Declaration," signed April 29, 1961.

2. See International Union for Conservation of Nature and Natural Resources, *World Conservation Strategy: Living Resource Conservation for Sustainable Development* (with financial support and in cooperation with the UN Environment Programme and the World Wildlife Fund) (IUCN–UNEP–WWF, 1980); World Commission on Environment and Development (WCED), *Our Common Future* (Oxford University Press, 1987) (definition of sustainable development is on p. 43). For details on the NGO TRAFFIC, see www.traffic.org.

3. For analysis of early debt-for-nature swaps, see Stein Hansen, "Debt for Nature Swaps: Overview and Discussion of Key Issues," *Ecological Economics* 1 (1) (1989), pp. 77–93.

4. See the Stockholm Convention on Persistent Organic Pollutants (http://chm. pops.int); The World Conservation Union, United Nations Environment Programme, and the World Wide Fund for Nature, *Caring for the Earth: A Strategy for Sustainable Living* (IUCN, UNEP, and WWF, 1991); Convention on Biological Diversity (www.cbd.int).

5. See Forest Stewardship Council (https://ic.fsc.org); Marine Stewardship Council (www.msc.org); Roundtable on Sustainable Palm Oil (www.rspo.org); Round Table

on Responsible Soy (www.responsiblesoy.org); Global Roundtable for Sustainable Beef (www.grsbeef.org). For analyses of these institutions, see Further Readings, "Eco-Certification." The WWF quote "refusing to participate" is at WWF International, "WWF, the Round Table on Responsible Soy and Genetically Modified Soy," posted December 2010 (wwf.panda.org).

6. For an overview of the history of the early years of WWF, see Alexis Schwarzenbach, *Saving the World's Wildlife: The WWF's First Fifty Years* (Profile Books, 2011). Also see the documentation under various WWF websites, including WWF International (www.panda.org); WWF (US) (www.worldwildlife.org); WWF (Canada) (www.wwf.ca); WWF (Australia) (www.wwf.org.au); WWF (New Zealand) (www.wwf.org.nz); WWF (UK) (www.wwf.org.uk); WWF (Germany) (www.wwf.de); WWF (France) (www.wwf.fr); WWF (Japan) (www.wwf.or.jp); WWF (South Africa) (www.wwf.org.za); WWF (Brazil) (www.wwf.org.br); WWF (Indonesia) (www.wwf.or.id); and WWF (Malaysia) (www.wwf.org.my).

7. Carter Roberts and Muhtar Kent are quoted in Jay Moye, "Beyond Water: Coca-Cola Expands Partnerships with WWF, Announces Ambitious Environmental Goals," July 9, 2013, at www.coca-colacompany.com.

8. See WWF and Coca-Cola Company, *Partnering to Protect Our Freshwater Resources: Annual Review 2013* (WWF/Coca-Cola, 2013); WWF (US) website, under "Partnerships: Coca-Cola," at www.worldwildlife.org. The $66 million estimate for the amount raised for WWF water projects from 2007 to 2014 is from E. Richard Brownlee II and Allison Elias, "Coca-Cola, World Wildlife Fund Team Up for Water Conservation," *Washington Post*, October 17, 2014 (www.washingtonpost.com). The estimates of the world's top corporate brands are from the consulting firm Interbrand, available at www.bestglobalbrands.com. The estimate of the amount of water necessary to produce soda pop is from A. Ertug Ercin, Maite Martinez Aldaya, and Arjen Y. Hoekstra, "Corporate Water Footprint Accounting and Impact Assessment: The Case of the Water Footprint of a Sugar-Containing Carbonated Beverage," *Water Resources Management* 25 (2011), pp. 721–741, DOI: 10.1007/s11269-010-9723-8. The 2010 Coca-Cola purchasing estimates are by Gerald Butts, former WWF-Canada president, quoted in Simon Houpt, "Beyond the Bottle: Coke Trumpets Its Green Initiatives," *Globe and Mail*, January 13, 2011, p. B6.

For a critical history of Coca-Cola, see Bartow J. Elmore, *Citizen Coke: The Making of Coca-Cola Capitalism* (W.W. Norton, 2015). For a snapshot of Coca-Cola in China, see Coca-Cola, "Celebrating 35 Years of Coca-Cola in China," November 24, 2014, at www.coca-colacompany.com. See also Liza Lin and Stephen Engle, "Coca-Cola to Invest More Than $4 Billion in China from 2015–2017," *Bloomberg News*, November 2013 (www.bloomberg.com); Coca-Cola, *2013 Annual Review: Reasons to Believe* (The Coca-Cola Company, 2014), p. 2 (for Coke records set), p. 3 ($50 billion investment figure), p. 38 (2020 Vision).

9. See The Nature Conservancy, "Working with Companies: Making Better Business Decisions for Nature," Fact Sheet, available at www.nature.org/CorporateEngagement.

10. See Conservation International, "Join the 'Kung Fu' Panda Party at McDonald's," Media Release, June 4, 2008 (www.conservation.org) (this article includes Seligmann's remark; for details on the partnership, see the history of the partnership on this website, which includes the quote "empower kids ...").

11. EDF's and Murray's remarks are in Environmental Defense Fund, "Partnerships: The Key to Lasting Solutions," at www.edf.org. For a critique of the social costs of the global recycling industry, see Peter Dauvergne and Genevieve LeBaron, "The Social Cost of Environmental Solutions," *New Political Economy* 18 (3) (2013), pp. 410–430. For a fuller analysis of the consequences of corporate partnerships for the nature of environmental and social movements, see Peter Dauvergne and Genevieve LeBaron, *Protest Inc.: The Corporatization of Activism* (Polity, 2014); Adrian Parr, *Hijacking Sustainability* (MIT Press, 2012); and Lisa Ann Richey and Stefano Ponte, *Brand Aid: Shopping Well to Save the World* (University of Minnesota Press, 2011).

## Chapter 12

1. See Joachim Radkau, *The Age of Ecology: A Global History*, translated by Patrick Camiller (Polity Press, 2014). For analysis of the differing and shifting perspectives on biofuels within the environmental movement, see Kate J. Neville and Peter Dauvergne, "The Problematic of Biofuels for Development," Jean Grugel and Daniel Hammett, eds., *The Palgrave Handbook of International Development* (Palgrave Macmillan, 2016); Kate J. Neville, "The Contentious Political Economy of Biofuels," *Global Environmental Politics* 15 (1) (2015), pp. 21–40; and Peter Dauvergne and Kate J. Neville, "Forests, Food, and Fuel in the Tropics: The Uneven Social and Ecological Consequences of the Emerging Political Economy of Biofuels," *Journal of Peasant Studies* 37 (4) (2010), pp. 631–660.

2. See the World Social Forum (www.forumsocialmundial.org.br); Geoffrey Pleyers, *Alter-Globalization: Becoming Actors in a Global Age* (Polity, 2010); David McNally, *Another World Is Possible: Globalization & Anti-Capitalism*, revised edition (Arbeiter Ring, 2006); and Susan George, *Another World Is Possible, If ...* (Verso, 2004).

3. The estimate of the number of protected areas is from M. Deguignet, D. Juffe-Bignoli, J. Harrison, B. MacSharry, N. D. Burgess, and N. Kingston, *2014 United Nations List of Protected Areas* (United Nations Environment Programme, 2014), p. 1. For an analysis of the variable quality of the programs and practices of eco-labeling organizations, see Hamish van der Ven, "Correlates of Rigorous and Credible Transnational Governance: A Cross-Sectoral Analysis of Best Practice Compliance in Eco-Labeling," *Regulation & Governance* 9 (3) (2015), pp. 276–293.

4. For the figures on Walmart, see Walmart, Global Responsibility, Environmental Responsibility, Waste (http://corporate.walmart.com); Walmart, *2015 Global Responsibility Report* (Walmart, 2015), p. 67. For details on "dematerialization," see Jesse H. Ausubel and Paul E. Waggoner, "Dematerialization: Variety, Caution, and Persistence," *PNAS (Proceedings of the National Academy of Sciences of the United States of America)* 105 (no. 35) (2008), pp. 12774–12779.

5. For the figures on the palm oil trade and zero deforestation pledges, see Elizabeth Harball, "Green Groups Tell Agribusinesses that 'Zero-Deforestation' Pledges are Just the Beginning," *ClimateWire*, April 15, 2015, www.eenews.net; Elizabeth Harball, "How a Small Band of Activists Saved Tropical Forests by Turning Around 'Big Doughnut,'" *ClimateWire*, February 4, 2015, www.eenews.net.

6. The Breakthrough Institute's definition of eco-modernist is at www .thebreakthrough.org. See also, John Asafu-Adjaye, Linus Blomqvist, Stewart Brand, Barry Brook, Ruth Defries, Erle Ellis, Christopher Foreman, David Keith, Martin Lewis, Mark Lynas, Ted Nordhaus, Roger Pielke, Jr., Rachel Pritzker, Joyashree Roy, Mark Sagoff, Michael Shellenberger, Robert Stone, and Peter Teague, *The Ecomodernist Manifesto* (The Breakthrough Institute, April 2015).

7. See Ronald Bailey, *The End of Doom: Environmental Renewal in the Twenty-First Century* (Thomas Dunne Books, 2015); William McDonough and Michael Braungart, *The Upcycle: Beyond Sustainability—Designing for Abundance* (North Point, 2013), p. 11. See also Further Readings, "Eco-Efficiency, Eco-Technology, and Ecological Modernization."

8. See Rob Bailey, Antony Froggatt, and Laura Wellesley, *Livestock—Climate Change's Forgotten Sector: Global Public Opinion on Meat and Dairy Consumption* (Chatham House, December 2014), p. 4. For a discussion of the psychological difficulties of tackling climate change, see George Marshall, *Don't Even Think About It: Why Our Brains Are Wired to Ignore Climate Change* (Bloomsbury, 2014).

9. The quote "sustainable thinking is in everything we do" is from Procter & Gamble, "Sustainability," http://us.pg.com/sustainability.

10. For examples of "coercive conservation," see Nancy Lee Peluso, "Coercing Conservation? The Politics of State Resource Control," *Global Environmental Change* 3 (2) (1993), pp. 199–217.

11. For example, see Further Readings, "Degrowth, Sufficiency, and Steady-State Economics"; the academic association, Research and Degrowth (www.degrowth .org); and the Center for the Advancement of the Steady State Economy (www .steadystate.org).

12. Calculated in Bert Hölldobler and E. O. Wilson, *The Superorganism: The Beauty, Elegance, and Strangeness of Insect Societies* (W.W. Norton, 2009), p. 5.

13. For more on the "individualization of responsibility," see Michael F. Maniates, "Individualization: Plant a Tree, Buy a Bike, Save the World?" *Global Environmental Politics* 1 (3) (2001), pp. 31–52. For an analysis of the "paradoxes" of "sustainable consumption," see Michael Maniates, "Sustainable Consumption—Three Paradoxes," *Gaia: Ecological Perspectives for Science and Society* 23/S1 (2014), pp. 201–208. For an assessment of the value of campaigns to promote "ethical consumption," see Dara O'Rourke, *Shopping for Good* (MIT, 2012).

14. Paul F. Steinberg, *Who Rules the Earth? How Social Rules Shape Our Planet and Our Lives* (Oxford University Press, 2015). Also see Further Readings, "Global Environmental Governance."

# Further Readings

## Activism (corporatization of)

Dauvergne, Peter, and Genevieve LeBaron. *Protest Inc.: The Corporatization of Activism*. Polity, 2014.

Kapoor, Ilan. *Celebrity Humanitarianism: The Ideology of Global Charity*. Routledge, 2013.

Parr, Adrian. *Hijacking Sustainability*. MIT Press, 2012.

Richey, Lisa Ann, and Stefano Ponte. *Brand Aid: Shopping Well to Save the World*. University of Minnesota Press, 2011.

## Activism (crackdown on)

Fernandez, Luis A. *Policing Dissent: Social Control and the Anti-Globalization Movement*. Rutgers University Press, 2008.

Potter, Will. *Green Is the New Red: An Insider's Account of a Social Movement Under Siege*. City Lights Books, 2011.

Starr, Amory, Luis A. Fernandez, and Christian Scholl. *Shutting Down the Streets: Political Violence and Social Control in the Global Era*. New York University Press, 2011.

## Anti-Environmentalism (corporate)

Beder, Sharon. *Global Spin: The Corporate Assault on Environmentalism*, revised edition. Green Books, 2002.

Oreskes, Naomi, and Erik M. Conway. *Merchants of Doubt: How a Handful of Scientists Obscured the Truth on Issues from Tobacco Smoke to Global Warming*. Bloomsbury Press, 2010.

Rowell, Andrew. *Green Backlash: Global Subversion of the Environmental Movement*. Routledge, 1996.

## Capitalism (critiques, for a general audience)

Aschoff, Nicole. *The New Prophets of Capital*. Verso, 2015.

Elmore, Bartow J. *Citizen Coke: The Making of Coca-Cola Capitalism*. W. W. Norton, 2015.

Harvey, David. *Seventeen Contradictions and the End of Capitalism*. Oxford University Press, 2014.

Klein, Naomi. *The Shock Doctrine: The Rise of Disaster Capitalism*. Picador, 2008.

Klein, Naomi. *This Changes Everything: Capitalism vs. the Climate*. Simon & Schuster, 2014.

Korten, David C. *Agenda for a New Economy: From Phantom Wealth to Real Wealth*. Berrett-Koehler, 2009.

Korten, David C. *The Great Turning: From Empire to Earth Community*. Berrett-Koehler, 2006.

Piketty, Thomas. *Capital in the Twenty-First Century*. Belknap Press, 2014.

Robbins, Richard H. *Global Problems and the Culture of Capitalism*, sixth edition. Pearson, 2013.

## Climate Change (politics of)

Bulkeley, Harriet, Liliana B. Andonova, Michele M. Betsill, Daniel Compagnon, Thomas Hale, Matthew J. Hoffmann, Peter Newell, Matthew Paterson, Charles Roger, and Stacy D. VanDeveer. *Transnational Climate Change Governance*. Cambridge University Press, 2014.

Ciplet, David, J. Timmons Roberts, and Mizan R. Khan. *Power in a Warming World: The New Global Politics of Climate Change and the Remaking of Environmental Inequality*. MIT Press, 2015.

Giddens, Anthony. *The Politics of Climate Change*, second edition. Polity, 2011.

Harris, Paul G. *What's Wrong with Climate Politics and How to Fix It*. Polity,. 2013.

Held, D., C. Roger, and E.-M. Nag, eds. *Climate Governance in the Developing World*. Polity, 2013.

Hoffmann, Matthew J. *Climate Governance at the Crossroads: Experimenting with a Global Response after Kyoto*. Oxford University Press, 2011.

Newell, Peter, and Matthew Paterson. *Climate Capitalism: Global Warming and the Transformation of the Global Economy*. Cambridge University Press, 2010.

O'Lear, S., and S. Dalby, eds. *Reframing Climate Change: Constructing Ecological Geopolitics*. Routledge, 2015.

Parr, Adrian. *The Wrath of Capital: Neoliberalism and Climate Change Politics*. Columbia University Press, 2013.

Princen, T., J. P. Manno, and P. L. Martin, eds. *Ending the Fossil Fuel Era*. MIT Press, 2015.

Stern, Nicholas. *Why Are We Waiting? The Logic, Urgency, and Promise of Tackling Climate Change*. MIT Press, 2015.

Wright, Christopher, and Daniel Nyberg. *Climate Change, Capitalism, and Corporations: Processes of Creative Self-Destruction*. Cambridge University Press, 2015.

## Consumption of Natural Resources

Bridge, Gavin, and Philippe Le Billon. *Oil*. Polity, 2012.

Clapp, Jennifer. *Food*, second edition. Polity, 2016.

Dauvergne, Peter, and Jane Lister. *Timber*. Polity, 2011.

DeSombre, Elizabeth R., and J. Samuel Barkin. *Fish*. Polity, 2011.

Feldman, David Lewis. *Water*. Polity, 2012.

Fishman, Charles. *The Big Thirst: The Secret Life and Turbulent Future of Water*. Free Press, 2011.

Fridell, Gavin. *Coffee*. Polity, 2014.

Hall, Derek. *Land*. Polity, 2013.

Nest, Michael. *Coltan*. Polity, 2011.

Richardson, Ben. *Sugar*. Polity, 2015.

Smillie, Ian. *Diamonds*. Polity, 2014.

## Consumption Politics

Bakan, Joel. *Childhood Under Siege: How Big Business Targets Your Children*. Simon & Schuster, 2011.

Carmin, J., and J. Agyeman, eds. *Environmental Inequalities Beyond Borders: Local Perspectives on Global Injustices*. MIT Press, 2011.

Dauvergne, Peter. *The Shadows of Consumption: Consequences for the Global Environment*. MIT Press, 2008.

Gerth, Karl. *As China Goes, So Goes the World: How Chinese Consumers Are Transforming Everything*. Hill and Wang, 2010.

Guha, Ramachandra. *How Much Should a Person Consume? Environmentalism in India and the United States*. University of California Press, 2006.

Lange, H., and L. Meier, eds. *The New Middle Classes: Globalizing Lifestyles, Consumerism, and Environmental Concern*. Springer, 2009.

Leonard, Annie. *The Story of Stuff: The Impact of Overconsumption on the Planet, Our Communities, and Our Health—And How We Can Make It Better*. Free Press, 2010.

Lewis, Justin. *Beyond Consumer Capitalism: Media and the Limits of Imagination*. Polity. 2013.

Princen, T., M. Maniates, and K. Conca, eds. *Confronting Consumption*. MIT Press, 2002.

Schor, Juliet B. *Born to Buy: The Commercialized Child and the New Consumer Culture*. Scribner, 2004.

## Corporate Social Responsibility (business of)

Bhattacharya, C. B., Sankar Sen, and Daniel Korschun. *Leveraging Corporate Responsibility: The Stakeholder Route to Maximizing Business and Social Value*. Cambridge University Press, 2011.

Chandler, David, and William B. Werther, Jr. *Strategic Corporate Social Responsibility: Stakeholders in a Global Environment*. Sage, 2010.

Cramer, Aron, and Z. Karabell. *Sustainable Excellence: The Future of Business in a Fast-Changing World*. Rodale, 2010.

Dauvergne, Peter, and Jane Lister. *Eco-Business: A Big-Brand Takeover of Sustainability*. MIT Press, 2013.

Humes, Edward. *Force of Nature: The Unlikely Story of Wal-Mart's Green Revolution*. HarperCollins, 2011.

Laszlo, Chris, and Nadya Zhexembayeva. *Embedded Sustainability: The Next Big Competitive Advantage*. Greenleaf, 2011.

Lozano, Josep M., Laura Albareda, Tamyko Ysa, Heike Roscher, and Manila Marcuccio. *Governments and Corporate Social Responsibility: Public Policies Beyond Regulation and Voluntary Compliance*. Palgrave Macmillan, 2008.

Marcus, Alfred A. *Innovations in Sustainability: Fuel and Food*. Cambridge University Press, 2015.

McElhaney, Kellie. *Just Good Business: The Strategic Guide to Aligning Corporate Responsibility and Brand*. Berrett-Koehler, 2008.

Visser, Wayne. *The Age of Responsibility: CSR 2.0 and the New DNA of Business*. John Wiley & Sons, 2011.

## Degrowth, Sufficiency, and Steady-State Economics

Alexander, Samuel. *Prosperous Descent: Crisis as Opportunity in an Age of Limits, Collected Essays*. vol. I. Simplicity Institute, 2015.

Alexander, Samuel. *Sufficiency Economy: Enough, for Everyone, Forever, Collected Essays*. vol. II. Simplicity Institute, 2015.

D'Alisa, G., F. Demaria, and G. Kallis, eds. *Degrowth: A Vocabulary for a New Era*. Routledge, 2015.

Daly, Herman E. *Beyond Growth: The Economics of Sustainable Development*. Beacon Press, 1996.

Dietz, Robert, and Daniel W. O'Neill. *Enough Is Enough: Building a Sustainable Economy in a World of Finite Resources*. Berrett-Koehler Publishers, 2013.

Heinberg, Richard. *The End of Growth: Adapting to Our New Economic Reality*. New Society Publishers, 2011.

Jackson, Tim. *Prosperity without Growth: Economics for a Finite Planet*. Earthscan, 2009.

Latouche, Serge. *Farewell to Growth*. Polity, 2009.

Princen, Thomas. *The Logic of Sufficiency*. MIT Press, 2005.

Princen, Thomas. *Treading Softly: Paths to Ecological Order*. MIT Press, 2010.

Vale, R., and B. Vale, eds. *Living within a Fair Share Ecological Footprint*. Routledge, 2013.

## Discount Retailing

Andersen, Michael Moesgaard, and Flemming Poulfelt. *Discount Business Strategy: How the New Market Leaders Are Redefining Business Strategy*. John Wiley & Sons, 2006.

Brunn, S. D., ed. *Wal-Mart World: The World's Biggest Corporation in the Global Economy*. Routledge, 2006.

Cline, Elizabeth L. *Over-Dressed: The Shockingly High Cost of Cheap Fashion*. Portfolio/Penguin, 2012.

Fishman, Charles. *The Wal-Mart Effect: How the World's Most Powerful Company Really Works—and How It's Transforming the American Economy*. Penguin, 2006.

Laird, Gordon. *The Price of a Bargain*. McClelland & Stewart, 2009.

Lichtenstein, Nelson. *The Retail Revolution: How Wal-Mart Created a Brave New World of Business*. Henry Holt and Company, 2009.

Mitchell, Stacy. *Big-Box Swindle*. Beacon, 2006.

Shell, Ellen Ruppel. *Cheap: The High Cost of Discount Culture*. Penguin, 2009.

## Eco-Certification

Auld, Graeme. *Constructing Private Governance: The Rise and Evolution of Forest, Coffee, and Fisheries Certification*. Yale University Press, 2014.

Boström, Magnus, and Mikael Klintman. *Eco-Standards, Product Labelling and Green Consumerism*. Palgrave Macmillan, 2008.

Conroy, Michael. *Branded! How the Certification Revolution Is Transforming Global Corporations*. New Society, 2007.

Lister, Jane. *Corporate Social Responsibility and the State: International Approaches to Forest Co-Regulation*. UBC Press, 2011.

Gulbrandsen, Lars H. *Transnational Environmental Governance: The Emergence and Effects of the Certification of Forests and Fisheries*. Edward Elgar, 2010.

Honey, Martha. *Ecotourism and Certification Setting Standards in Practice*. Island Press, 2002.

## Eco-Consumerism

Bartley, Tim, Sebastian Koos, Hiram Samel, Gustavo Setrini, and Nik Summers. *Looking Behind the Label: Global Industries and the Conscientious Consumer*. Indiana University Press, 2015.

Divinney, Tim, Pat Auger, and Giana Eckhardt. *The Myth of the Ethical Consumer*. Cambridge University Press, 2010.

Harrison, R., T. Newholm, and D. Shaw, eds. *The Ethical Consumer*. Sage, 2005.

Henderson, Hazel, with Simran Sethi. *Ethical Markets: Growing the Green Economy*. Chelsea Green, 2006.

Micheletti, Michele. *Political Virtue and Shopping: Individuals, Consumerism, and Collective Action*. Palgrave Macmillan, 2003.

Stolle, Dietlind, and Michele Micheletti. *Political Consumerism: Global Responsibility in Action*. Cambridge University Press, 2015.

## Eco-Efficiency, Eco-Technology, and Ecological Modernization

Bailey, Ronald. *The End of Doom: Environmental Renewal in the Twenty-First Century.* Thomas Dunne Books, 2015.

Curran, Giorel. *Sustainability and Energy Politics: The Promises of Ecological Modernisation and Corporate Social Responsibility.* Palgrave Macmillan, 2015.

DeSimone, Livio, and Frank Popoff with the World Business Council for Sustainable Development. *Eco-Efficiency: The Business Link to Sustainable Development.* MIT Press, 1997.

McDonough, William, and Michael Braungart. *Cradle to Cradle: Remaking the Way We Make Things.* North Point, 2002.

McDonough, William, and Michael Braungart. *The Upcycle: Beyond Sustainability—Designing for Abundance.* North Point, 2013.

Mol, Arthur P. J. *Globalization and Environmental Reform: The Ecological Modernization of the Global Economy.* MIT Press, 2001.

Mol, A. P. J., D. A. Sonnenfeld, and G. Spaargaren, eds. *The Ecological Modernisation Reader: Environmental Reform in Theory and Practice.* Routledge, 2009.

World Business Council for Sustainable Development. *Eco-Efficiency: Creating More Value with Less Impact.* World Business Council for Sustainable Development, 2000.

## Ecological Imperialism

Crosby, Alfred W. *Ecological Imperialism: The Biological Expansion of Europe, 900–1900, new edition.* Cambridge University Press, 2004.

Grove, Richard. *Green Imperialism: Colonial Expansion, Tropical Island Edens and the Origins of Environmentalism, 1600–1860.* Cambridge University Press, 1995.

Hornborg, A., J. R. McNeill, and J. Martinez-Alier, eds. *Rethinking Environmental History: World-System History and Global Environmental Change.* AltaMira Press, 2007.

Kirch, P. V., and J.-L. Rallu, eds. *The Growth and Collapse of Pacific Island Societies: Archaeological and Demographic Perspectives.* University of Hawai'i Press, 2007.

Petras, James, and Henry Veltmeyer. *Globalization Unmasked: Imperialism in the 21st Century.* Zed Books, 2001.

Petras, James, and Henry Veltmeyer. *Extractive Imperialism in the Americas: Capitalism's New Frontier.* Brill Academic Publishers, 2015.

Trigger, Bruce G. *The Children of Aataentsic: A History of the Huron People to 1660.* McGill–Queen's University Press, 1987, first printing 1976.

## Environmental Activism ("insider" critiques of)

Lomborg, Bjørn. *The Skeptical Environmentalist: Measuring the Real State of the World.* Cambridge University Press, 2001.

MacDonald, Christine Catherine. *Green, Inc.: An Environmental Insider Reveals How a Good Cause Has Gone Bad.* Lyons Press, 2008.

Moore, Patrick. *Confessions of a Greenpeace Dropout: The Making of a Sensible Environmentalist.* Beatty Street Publishing, 2010.

Nordhaus, Ted, and Michael Shellenberger. *Break Through: From the Death of Environmentalism to the Politics of Possibility.* Houghton Mifflin, 2007.

## Environmental Discourses and Movements (varieties of)

Amster, Randall. *Peace Ecology.* Routledge, 2015.

Cianchi, John. *Radical Environmentalism: Nature, Identity and More-Than-Human Agency.* Palgrave Macmillan, 2015.

Dryzek, John. *The Politics of the Earth: Environmental Discourses*, third edition. Oxford University Press, 2013.

Epstein, Charlotte. *The Power of Words in International Relations: Birth of an Anti-Whaling Discourse.* MIT Press, 2008.

Guha, Ramachandra, and Joan Martinez-Alier. *Varieties of Environmentalism: Essays North and South.* Earthscan, 1997.

Liddick, Donald R. *Eco-Terrorism: Radical Environmental and Animal Liberation Movements.* Praeger, 2006.

Martinez-Alier, Joan. *The Environmentalism of the Poor: A Study of Ecological Conflicts and Valuation.* Edward Elgar, 2003.

Merchant, Carolyn. *Radical Ecology: The Search for a Livable World.* Routledge, 2005.

Nixon, Rob. *Slow Violence and the Environmentalism of the Poor.* Harvard University Press, 2011.

Rudel, Thomas K. *Defensive Environmentalists and the Dynamics of Global Reform.* Cambridge University Press, 2014.

## Environmental History (general)

Guha, Ramachandra. *Environmentalism: A Global History.* Oxford University Press, 2000.

Macekura, Stephen J. *Of Limits and Growth: The Rise of Global Sustainable Development in the Twentieth Century.* Cambridge University Press, 2015.

McNeill, J. R. *Something New Under the Sun: An Environmental History of the Twentieth-Century World.* W. W. Norton, 2000.

McNeill, J. R., and E. S. Mauldin, eds. *A Companion to Global Environmental History.* Wiley-Blackwell, 2015.

Radkau, Joachim. *The Age of Ecology: A Global History.* Trans. P. Camiller. Polity, 2014.

Simmons, I. G. *Global Environmental History: 10,000 BC to AD 2000.* Edinburgh University Press, 2008.

## Environmental Justice Movements

Carruthers, D. V., ed. *Environmental Justice in Latin America: Problems, Promise, and Practice.* MIT Press, 2008.

Faber, D., ed. *The Struggle for Ecological Democracy: Environmental Justice Movements in the United States.* The Guilford Press, 1998.

Ottinger, G., and B. R. Cohen, eds. *Technoscience and Environmental Justice: Expert Cultures in a Grassroots Movement.* MIT Press, 2011.

Pellow, David Naguib. *Garbage Wars: The Struggle for Environmental Justice in Chicago.* MIT Press, 2002.

Pellow, David Naguib. *Resisting Global Toxics: Transnational Movements for Global Justice.* MIT Press, 2007.

Pellow, D. N., and R. J. Brulle, eds. *Power, Justice, and the Environment: A Critical Appraisal of the Environmental Justice Movement.* MIT Press, 2005.

Sandler, R., and P. C. Pezzullo, eds. *Environmental Justice and Environmentalism: The Social Justice Challenge to the Environmental Movement.* MIT Press, 2007.

## Environmental NGOs and Transnational Networks

Betsill, M. M., and E. Corell, eds. *NGO Diplomacy: The Influence of Nongovernmental Organizations in International Environmental Negotiations.* MIT Press, 2007.

Bryner, Gary C. *Gaia's Wager: Environmental Movements and the Challenge of Sustainability.* Rowman & Littlefield, 2001.

Doherty, Brian, and Timothy Doyle. *Environmentalism, Resistance and Solidarity: The Politics of Friends of the Earth International.* Palgrave Macmillan, 2013.

Hironaka, Ann. *Greening the Globe: World Society and Environmental Change*. Cambridge University Press, 2014.

Keck, Margaret E., and Kathryn Sikkink. *Activists beyond Borders: Advocacy Networks in International Politics*. Cornell University Press, 1998.

Saunders, Clare. *Environmental Networks and Social Movement Theory*. Bloomsbury, 2013.

Zelko, Frank. *Make It a Green Peace! The Rise of Counterculture Environmentalism*. Oxford University Press, 2013.

## Environmentalism (developing countries)

Dawson, Jane I. *Eco-Nationalism: Anti-Nuclear Activism and National Identity in Russia, Lithuania, and Ukraine*. Duke University Press, 1996.

Hochstetler, Kathryn, and Margaret E. Keck. *Greening Brazil: Environmental Activism in State and Society*. Duke University Press, 2007.

Hughes, David McDermott. *From Enslavement to Environmentalism: Politics on a Southern African Frontier*. University of Washington Press, 2008.

Koont, Sinan. *Sustainable Urban Agriculture in Cuba*. University Press of Florida, 2011.

Mathews, Andrew S. *Instituting Nature: Authority, Expertise, and Power in Mexican Forests*. MIT Press, 2011.

Nustad, Knut G. *Creating Africas: Struggles Over Nature, Conservation and Land*. Hurst Company, 2015.

Shapiro, Judith. *China's Environmental Challenges*, second edition. Polity, 2016.

Slovic, S., S. Rangarajan, and V. Sarveswaran, eds. *Ecocriticism of the Global South*. Lexington Books, 2015.

Sowers, Jeannie L. *Environmental Politics in Egypt: Activists, Experts, and the State*. Routledge, 2014.

Steinberg, Paul F. *Environmental Leadership in Developing Countries: Transnational Relations and Biodiversity Policy in Costa Rica and Bolivia*. MIT Press, 2001.

Yok-shiu, F. L., and A. Y. So, eds. *Asia's Environmental Movements: Comparative Perspectives*. M.E. Sharpe, 1999.

## Environmentalism (overviews)

Anderson, Terry L., and Donald R. Leal. *Free Market Environmentalism*, revised edition. Palgrave Macmillan, 2001.

Boyd, David R. *The Optimistic Environmentalist: Progressing Towards a Greener Future.* ECW Press, 2015.

Hawken, Paul. *Blessed Unrest: How the Largest Movement in the World Came into Being and Why No One Saw It Coming.* Viking Penguin, 2007.

Haq, Gary, and Alistair Paul. *Environmentalism Since 1945.* Routledge, 2012.

Mauch, C., N. Stoltzfus, and D. R. Weiner, eds. *Shades of **Green:** Environmental Activism around the Globe.* Rowman & Littlefield Publishers, 2006.

Peterson del Mar, David. *Environmentalism,* second edition. Routledge, 2011.

Thiele, Leslie Paul. *Environmentalism for a New Millennium: The Challenge of Coevolution.* Oxford University Press, 1999.

Wall, Derek. *Babylon and Beyond: The Economics of Anti-Capitalist, Anti-Globalist and Radical Green Movements.* Pluto Press, 2005.

Wapner, Paul. *Environmental Activism and World Civic Politics.* SUNY Press, 1996.

Wapner, Paul. *Living Through the End of Nature: The Future of American Environmentalism.* MIT Press, 2010.

## Environmentalists (biographies)

Essemlali, Lamya (with Paul Watson). *Captain Paul Watson: Interview with a Pirate.* Firefly Books, 2013.

Humes, Edward. *Eco Barons: The New Heroes of Environmental Activism.* Ecco/HarperCollins, 2010.

Parkin, Sara. *The Life and Death of Petra Kelly.* HarperCollins, 1995.

Peterson, Dale. *Jane Goodall: The Woman Who Redefined Man.* Houghton Mifflin, 2006.

Souder, William. *On a Farther Shore: The Life and Legacy of Rachel Carson, Author of Silent Spring.* Broadway Books, 2012.

## Environmentalists (memoirs)

Berman, Tzeporah. *This Crazy Time: Living Our Environmental Challenge.* Vintage Canada, 2012.

Hill, Julia Butterfly. *The Legacy of Luna: The Story of a Tree, a Woman and the Struggle to Save the Redwoods.* HarperCollins, 2000.

Hunter, Robert. *The Greenpeace to Amchitka: An Environmental Odyssey.* Arsenal Pulp Press, 2004.

Maathai, Wangari Muta. *Unbowed: A Memoir*. Knopf, 2006.

McKibben, Bill. *Oil and Honey: The Education of an Unlikely Activist*. Henry Holt and Company, 2013.

Rosebraugh, Craig. *Burning Rage of a Dying Planet: Speaking for the Earth Liberation Front*. Lantern Books, 2004.

Tucker, Linda. *Saving the White Lions: One Woman's Battle for Africa's Most Sacred Animal*. North Atlantic Books, 2013.

Watson, Paul. *Seal Wars: Twenty-five Years on the Front Lines with the Harp Seals*. Firefly Books, 2003.

Weyler, Rex. *Greenpeace: How a Group of Journalists, Ecologists, and Visionaries Changed the World*. Raincoast Books, 2004.

## The Global Ecological Crisis

Barnosky, Anthony D. *Dodging Extinction: Power, Food, Money, and the Future of Life on Earth*. University of California Press, 2014.

Diamond, Jared M. *Collapse: How Societies Choose to Fail or Succeed*, revised edition. Penguin, 2011.

Diamond, Jared M. *Guns, Germs, and Steel: The Fates of Human Societies*. W. W. Norton, 1999.

Gore, Al. *An Inconvenient Truth: The Planetary Emergency of Global Warming and What We Can Do About It*. Rodale Books, 2006.

Higgs, Kerryn. *Collision Course: Endless Growth on a Finite Planet*. MIT Press, 2014.

Kolbert, Elizabeth. *The Sixth Extinction: An Unnatural History*. Henry Holt and Company, 2014.

McDaniel, Carl N., and John M. Gowdy. *Paradise for Sale: A Parable of Nature*. University of California Press, 2000.

McKibben, Bill. *Eaarth: Making a Life on a Tough New Planet*. Times Books, 2010.

McKibben, Bill. *The End of Nature*. Random House, 2006.

Ophuls, Patrick. *Plato's Revenge: Politics in the Age of Ecology*. MIT Press, 2011.

Piper, Karen. *The Price of Thirst: Global Water Inequality and the Coming Chaos*. University of Minnesota Press, 2014.

Wilson, Edward O. *The Diversity of Life, new edition*. Belknap Press, 2010.

Wilson, Edward O. *The Future of Life*. Knopf, 2002.

Wright, Ronald. *A Short History of Progress*. House of Anansi Press, 2004.

## Global Environmental Governance

Baber, Walter F., and Robert V. Bartlett. *Consensus and Global Environmental Governance: Deliberative Democracy in Nature's Regime.* MIT Press, 2015.

Bernstein, Steven. *The Compromise of Liberal Environmentalism.* Columbia University Press, 2001.

Biermann, Frank. *Earth System Governance: World Politics in the Anthropocene.* MIT Press, 2014.

Biermann, F., and P. Pattberg, eds. *Global Environmental Governance Reconsidered.* MIT Press, 2012.

Conca, Ken. *An Unfinished Foundation: The United Nations and Global Environmental Governance.* Oxford University Press, 2015.

Galaz, Victor. *Global Environmental Governance, Technology and Politics: The Anthropocene Gap.* Edward Elgar, 2014.

Hale, Thomas, David Held, and Kevin Young. *Gridlock: Why Global Cooperation Is Failing Just When We Need It Most.* Polity, 2013.

Jinnah, Sikina. *Post-Treaty Politics: Secretariat Influence in Global Environmental Governance.* MIT Press, 2014.

Newell, Peter. *Globalization and the Environment: Capitalism, Ecology and Power.* Polity, 2012.

Steinberg, Paul F. *Who Rules the Earth? How Social Rules Shape Our Planet and Our Lives.* Oxford University Press, 2015.

Whiteside, Kerry H. *Precautionary Politics: Principle and Practice in Confronting Environmental Risk.* MIT Press, 2006.

## Global Environmental Politics (overviews)

Axelrod, R. S., and S. D. VanDeveer, eds. *The Global Environment: Institutions, Law, and Policy*, third edition. CQ Press, 2014.

Chasek, Pamela S., David L. Downie, and Janet Welsh Brown. *Global Environmental Politics*, seventh edition. Westview Press, 2016.

Clapp, Jennifer, and Peter Dauvergne. *Paths to a Green World: The Political Economy of the Global Environment*, second edition. MIT Press, 2011.

Death, C., ed. *Critical Environmental Politics.* Routledge, 2013.

Jinnah, S., and S. Nicholson, eds. *New Earth Politics: Essays from the Anthropocene.* MIT Press, 2016.

Kütting, G., ed. *Global Environmental Politics: Concepts, Theories and Case Studies.* Routledge, 2010.

Mitchell, Ronald B. *International Politics and the Environment.* Sage Publications, 2009.

O'Neill, Kate. *The Environment and International Relations.* Cambridge University Press, 2009.

Vig, N. J., and M. E. Kraft, eds. *Environmental Policy: New Directions for the Twenty-First Century*, ninth edition. CQ Press, 2016.

## Global Environmental Politics (collections of readings)

Conca, K., and G. D. Dabelko, eds. *Green Planet Blues: Critical Perspectives on Global Environmental Politics*, fifth edition. Westview Press, 2014.

Dauvergne, P., ed. *Environmental Politics.* Edward Elgar, 2013.

Dauvergne, P., ed. *Handbook of Global Environmental Politics*, second edition. Edward Elgar, 2012.

Falkner, R., ed. *The Handbook of Global Climate and Environment Policy.* Wiley-Blackwell, 2013.

Harris, P. G., ed. *Routledge Handbook of Global Environmental Politics.* Routledge, 2013.

Nicholson, S., and P. Wapner, eds. *Global Environmental Politics: From Person to Planet.* Routledge, 2014.

## Global Environmental Problems (politics of)

Andrée, Peter. *Genetically Modified Diplomacy: The Global Politics of Agricultural Biotechnology and the Environment.* UBC Press, 2007.

Andrews-Speed, Philip, Raimund Bleischwitz, Tim Boersma, Corey Johnson, Geoffrey Kemp, and Stacy D. VanDeveer. *Want, Waste, Or War? The Global Resource Nexus and the Struggle for Land, Energy, Food, Water and Minerals.* Routledge, 2015.

Clapp, Jennifer. *Toxic Exports: The Transfer of Hazardous Wastes from Rich to Poor Countries.* Cornell University Press, 2001.

Geiser, Ken. *Chemicals Without Harm: Policies for a Sustainable World.* MIT Press, 2015.

Hannigan, John. *The Geopolitics of Deep Oceans.* Polity, 2016.

McCully, Patrick. *Silenced Rivers: The Ecology and Politics of Large Dams.* Zed Books, 2001.

Minter, Adam. *Junkyard Planet: Travels in the Billion-Dollar Trash Trade.* Bloomsbury, 2013.

Parson, Edward A. *Protecting the Ozone Layer: Science and Strategy.* Oxford University Press, 2003.

Paterson, Matthew. *Automobile Politics: Ecology and Cultural Political Economy.* Cambridge University Press, 2007.

Selin, Henrik. *Global Governance of Hazardous Chemicals: Challenges of Multilevel Management.* MIT Press, 2010.

## Global Environmentalism (seminal books)

Carson, Rachel. *Silent Spring.* Houghton Mifflin, 1962.

Daly, Herman E. *Steady-State Economics: The Economics of Biophysical Equilibrium and Moral Growth.* W. H. Freeman, 1977.

Ehrlich, Paul R. *The Population Bomb: Population Control or Race to Oblivion?* Sierra Club–Ballantine, 1968.

Meadows, Donella H., Dennis L. Meadows, William W. Behrens, and Jørgen Randers. *The Limits to Growth.* Club of Rome, 1972.

Schumacher, E. F. *Small Is Beautiful: Economics as if People Mattered.* Harper and Row, 1973.

## Globalization (critical accounts)

Almeida, Paul. *Mobilizing Democracy: Globalization and Citizen Protest.* Johns Hopkins University Press, 2014.

Dauvergne, Catherine. *Making People Illegal: What Globalization Means for Migration and Law.* Cambridge University Press, 2008.

Dauvergne, Catherine. *The New Politics of Immigration and the End of Settler Societies.* Cambridge University Press, 2016.

Hardt, Michael, and Antonio Negri. *Multitude: War and Democracy in the Age of Empire.* Penguin, 2004.

Harvey, David. *Seventeen Contradictions and the End of Capitalism.* Oxford University Press, 2014.

Held, David, and Anthony McGrew. *Globalization/Anti-Globalization: Beyond the Great Divide,* second edition. Polity, 2007.

Herod, Andrew. *Geographies of Globalization: A Critical Introduction.* Wiley-Blackwell, 2008.

McNally, David. *Another World Is Possible: Globalization & Anti-Capitalism,* revised edition. Arbeiter Ring, 2006.

Pleyers, Geoffrey. *Alter-Globalization: Becoming Actors in a Global Age*. Polity, 2010.

## Private Environmental Governance

Cashore, Benjamin, Graeme Auld, and Deanna Newsom. *Governing through Markets: Forest Certification and the Emergence of Non-State Authority*. Yale University Press, 2004.

Clapp, J., and D. Fuchs, eds. *Corporate Power in Global Agrifood Governance*. MIT Press, 2009.

Falkner, Robert. *Business Power and Conflict in International Environmental Politics*. Palgrave Macmillan, 2008.

Fuchs, Doris. *Understanding Business Power in Global Governance*. Nomos, 2005.

Glasbergen, P., F. Biermann, and A. P. J. Mol, eds. *Partnerships, Governance and Sustainable Development*. Edward Elgar, 2007.

Green, Jessica F. *Rethinking Private Authority: Agents and Entrepreneurs in Global Environmental Governance*. Princeton University Press, 2014.

Levy, D., and P. Newell, eds. *The Business of Global Environmental Governance*. MIT Press, 2005.

Prakash, Aseem, and Matthew Potoski. *The Voluntary Environmentalists: Green Clubs, ISO 14001, and Voluntary Environmental Regulations*. Cambridge University Press, 2006.

Utting, P., and J. Clapp, eds. *Corporate Accountability and Sustainable Development*. Oxford University Press, 2008.

## Sustainability

Agyeman, J., R. D. Bullard, and B. Evans, eds. *Just Sustainabilities: Development in an Unequal World*. MIT Press, 2003.

Caradonna, Jeremy L. *Sustainability: A History*. Oxford University Press, 2014.

Dresner, Simon. *The Principles of Sustainability*, second edition. Earthscan, 2008.

Edwards, Andrés R. *The Sustainability Revolution: Portrait of a Paradigm Shift*. New Society Publishers, 2005.

Edwards, Andrés R. *Thriving Beyond Sustainability: Pathways to a Resilient Society*. New Society Publishers, 2010.

Harrison, Neil E. *Sustainable Capitalism and the Pursuit of Well-Being*. Routledge, 2014.

Leach, Melissa, Ian Scoones, and Andy Stirling. *Dynamic Sustainabilities: Technology, Environment, Social Justice.* Earthscan, 2010.

Meadows, Donella H. *Thinking in Systems: A Primer,* edited by Diana Wright of the Sustainability Institute. Chelsea Green, 2008.

Nemetz, Peter N. *Business and the Sustainability Challenge: An Integrated Perspective.* Routledge, 2013.

Robbins, Paul. *Political Ecology,* second edition. Wiley-Blackwell, 2011.

Robertson, Margaret. *Sustainability: Principles and Practice.* Routledge, 2014.

Thiele, Leslie. *Sustainability.* Polity, 2013.

## Tropical Rainforests (global politics of)

Dauvergne, Peter. *Shadows in the Forest: Japan and the Politics of Timber in Southeast Asia.* MIT Press, 1997.

Dauvergne, Peter. *Loggers and Degradation in the Asia-Pacific: Corporations and Environmental Management.* Cambridge University Press, 2001.

Humphreys, David. *Logjam: Deforestation and the Crisis of Global Governance.* Earthscan, 2006.

Owusu, J. Henry. *Africa, Tropical Timber, Turfs, and Trade: Geographic Perspectives on Ghana's Timber Industry and Development.* Lexington Books, 2012.

Ross, Michael L. *Timber Booms and Institutional Breakdown in Southeast Asia.* Cambridge University Press, 2001.

Straumann, Lukas. *Money Logging: On the Trail of the Asian Timber Mafia.* Bergli Books, 2014.

## Voluntary Simplicity, Localization, and Eco-Villages

Dawson, Jonathan. *Ecovillages: New Frontiers for Sustainability.* Green Books, 2006.

Elgin, Duane. *Voluntary Simplicity: Toward a Way of Life That Is Outwardly Simple, Inwardly Rich,* revised edition. HarperCollins, 2010.

De Young, R., and T. Princen, eds. *The Localization Reader: Adapting to the Downshift.* MIT Press, 2012.

Grisby, Mary. *Buying Time and Getting By: The Voluntary Simplicity Movement.* State University of New York Press, 2004.

Litfin, Karen T. *Ecovillages: Lessons for Sustainable Community.* Polity, 2013.

# Index